The Cruise Experience

Global and regional issues in cruising

PEARSON

Hospitality
Press

Norman Douglas
and Ngaire Douglas

Pearson Education Australia
Unit 4, Level 2
14 Aquatic Drive
Frenchs Forest NSW 2086

www.pearsoned.com.au

Acquisitions Editor: David Cunningham
Senior Project Editor: Julian Gray
Cover design: Antart

Printed in Malaysia

1 2 3 4 5 08 07 06 05 04

National Library of Australia
Cataloguing-in-Publication Data

Douglas, Norman.
    The cruise experience: global and regional issues.

    ISBN 1 86250 512 8.

    1. Cruise ships. 2. Cruise lines. 3. Ocean travel.
    4. Tourism. I. Douglas, Ngaire. II. Title. (Series :
    Australian studies in tourism).

387.542

PEARSON
Hospitality
Press   An imprint of Pearson Education Australia
         (a divisionof Pearson Australia Group Pty Ltd)

Contents

List of illustrations   vii

Preface   ix

Acknowledgements   xiv

PART 1

1   International cruising: the state of the art   3

2   Inside a cruise ship   18

3   Rank and status   25

4   Rank and file   34

5   A day in the life of a passenger   45

6   Safety, health and supply   51

PART 2

7   The historical growth of cruising   61

8   Destination development in the cruise business   85

PART 3

9   Star Cruises   109

10   Small ship cruises   116

11   Adventure cruises   127

12   Freighter cruises   133

13   River cruises   142

PART 4

14   Romancing the sea: the imagery of cruising   151

PART 5

15   Cruise passenger behaviour   177

PART 6

16   A framework for assessing the economic
     impacts of cruise tourism   197
     (by Larry Dwyer & Peter Forsyth)

17   Cruise ship passenger spending: a South Pacific
     case study   211

Conclusion   221

Abbreviations used   226

References   227

Glossary   233

Index   237

List of Illustrations

2.1	A side section of P&O's *Pacific Sky*	21
3.1	Cruise ship hierarchies	26
5.1	The entrance to Caesar's Palace casino on *Crystal Symphony*	49
7.1	An early (1895) Orient Line cruise poster	65
7.2	*Viceroy of India*'s swimming pool attracted participants and spectators	69
7.3	P&O's *Stratheden*	73
7.4	Matson's *Mariposa* in Pago Pago, American Samoa	76
8.1	Princess Cruises' *Regal Princess* in Seward, Alaska	88
8.2	P&O's new *Oriana* in Venice, a perennially favoured destination	93
8.3	The Caribbean: the most popular cruise region	96
8.4	*Fairstar*'s leaping dolphins were a metaphor for the activity on board	104
9.1	Star Cruises' *SuperStar Virgo*	112
10.1	Blue Lagoon's *Mystique Princess* in Fiji's Yasawa Islands	121
10.2	Captain Cook's *Reef Escape* passengers take a coral-viewing trip	125
11.1	A Lindblad team prepares the huskies for an Antarctic adventure	130
13.1	Sepik villagers perform a crocodile dance for visitors on *Melanesian Discoverer*	145
14.1	'The boat deck is a great centre of romance'	155
14.2	The reception area of Star Cruises' *SuperStar Virgo*	160
14.3	Matson's menu covers helped define the tourism imagery of the Pacific	163
14.4	Newsome's poster of caparisoned elephants	167
14.5	Greig's famous poster evoked the exotic for P&O travellers	168
14.6	'Best of British' cruising	169
14.7	A young boy's ambition (1958)	170
14.8	P&O revives a 1958 slogan, with artwork for the 21st century	171

14.9   *Normandie* posters were much influenced by the
       Art Deco style   172
14.10 Cunard's recent promotion for *QE2*   173
15.1   An elephant greets *QE2* passengers at Cochin   184
15.2   Day in the life of a cruise passenger   187
15.3   'There aren't enough men on board ...   192
17.1   *Pacific Sky*'s itinerary, Cruise P221   213
17.2   Small traders in Port Vila do regular business with
       Pacific Sky passengers   218

Preface

Behold — *The World*

On 18 September 2000 the keel of a new cruise ship was laid at Bruce's shipyard in Landskrona, Sweden. The ceremony—which included a gesture to Viking traditions—was attended by the usual assortment of people present at such occasions. Although it is generally an impressive sight to see such a vast amount of steel being manoeuvred into place, there is nothing particularly remarkable about the laying of a ship's keel or the subsequent launching of the vessel. Ships of all sizes and types are built and launched all over the world every year.

This, however, was not a normal ship, except perhaps in its general appearance and its ocean-going capabilities. In many other respects, it represented a complete departure from normal standards. In an industry known for habitual exaggeration and the use of excessive promotional language, the limit seems to have been reached in descriptions of this vessel. It offered 'the ultimate lifestyle on earth: [and] the ultimate address—*The World*'. 'What better way is there to travel round the globe', it continued, 'than from the comfort of your own home?' (<www.residensea.com>). The company responsible for the ship was not talking about sitting in one's living room watching travel programs on TV, but about actually staying permanently on its vessel, by owning and living in one of the accommodation spaces, described as 'residences' and varying in size from 103.5 square metres to 289 square metres. There are 110 of these residences, and also 88 guest suites 'of ultra luxury standard' for the 'family, friends, business associates or personal staff' of the occupants of the residences.

Clearly it would be inappropriate to refer to the occupants of the larger spaces by the conventional cruise ship terms of 'passengers' or even 'clients'. They are, of course, **'the Residents'** and represent a 'unique international community', 40 per cent of whom were expected to come from North America and the remainder from Europe, Asia (a very large catchment area) and Latin America. The unique privilege of occupying one of 'the Apartments' cost between US$2 million and US$6.8 million; it was expected that sales, according to the company's business plan, would cover the cost of the ship. In addition, there would be an annual charge to cover the ship's operating expenses, rather in the manner of the body corporate fees paid by residents of condominiums.

Compared with many other ships of recent construction, *The World* is no more than medium-sized—43 000 gross registered tonnes (GRT)—but it contains only 198 passenger accommodation spaces. The usual number of accommodation spaces on a ship of that tonnage would be between 500 and 600, capable of housing from 1100 to 1500 passengers.

What should one make of this? The idea of living for long periods on a ship is far from new: many seafarers spend most of their lives on a vessel. Early explorers and traders and their crews were absent from home for years, spending their time mostly aboard their ships. Many of them, indeed, had no land-based home to return to and no possessions other than those they travelled with. Many preferred not to have other encumbrances; many still feel the same way. But, generally speaking, most of these people—excepting perhaps the ship's captain and senior officers—came from economically disadvantaged communities or, as is increasingly the case today, economically disadvantaged countries. It is no accident that the nationalities most strongly represented in the crews of cruise ships in the early 21st century are Filipinos, Indonesians and, increasingly, Eastern Europeans, whose home countries are in perpetual economic and political turmoil, making the prospect of any kind of steady employment ashore very uncertain.

But the passengers expected to live aboard *The World of Residensea* (the name under which the vessel was first promoted) represent a totally different economic order. They are—necessarily—millionaires, and for those of them still engaged in making money a wide range of information technology services will also be provided on board the ship. They need never go ashore to check on the stock market or their other investments. The majority of them will almost certainly be aged, and some may be infirm. Special services will be provided for those residents also.

If all this appears a trifle far-fetched to the average holiday maker who regards cruise ships as just another vacation option on which to spend a week or two at the most, it should be pointed out that the trend to permanent living on board luxury vessels has been evident for some time. On several occasions we have met passengers on cruise ships who had been there for over a year: one elderly woman on *Queen Elizabeth 2* (*QE2*) was said to live on the ship. On another ship a woman was making her 65th consecutive voyage. She saw no reason to leave the vessel, certainly not to go ashore at any of those 'funny' places the ship called into. If she were to become extremely ill or die on the vessel, as she joked she might, her body would, if necessary, be airlifted by helicopter. We have been witnesses to a similar such event. In the meantime she spent most of her waking hours sitting in the ship's lobby, needleworking appropriate homilies ('God bless our ship', and so on) and encouraging the reception staff to hang them in their offices. For these women, and an increasing number of others, the ship functioned as a kind of retirement home. McCauley notes that one elderly lady 'holds the all-time record [for living on a ship] of fourteen years!' (1997, p. 133). Perhaps anticipating a growing demand among passengers to spend extended periods aboard ship, in 1993 Seabourn Cruises initiated a time-share program, in which prospective cruisers could buy, in advance, up to 120 days of cruising at a time, to be used in quantities of 45, 60, 90 or 120 days over three years. Many wealthy American—and an increasing number of other—cruisers routinely take a round-the-world voyage every year, a practice that occupies up to four months of their time.

The concept of travelling the world 'without leaving home' was evidently developed by Knut U. Kloster, member of a Norwegian shipping family which is considered to be among the pioneers of the modern cruise industry, having been responsible for the luxury-conscious Royal Caribbean Line, Royal Viking Line and a number of other innovations. As novel as all this may seem, however, it had long ago been anticipated. In the mid-1930s a British writer (Oliver P. Bernard, quoted in Prior 1993, p. 94) who was invited to travel on the French vessel *Normandie*, the supership of its day, wrote:

> Cabins and staterooms far better and much cheaper than so-called 'luxury flats' in [London's] Park Lane; liners of this calibre will establish the habit of living at sea, away from petrol fumes, hoardings, murderous traffic, hideous shopfronts, and noise, noise, noise; even children happy in wonderful nurseries. As for servant problems, where in this muddled world can there be greater courtesy and finer cuisine than aboard this floating province of France?

'Where, indeed', the many cruise enthusiasts of the early 21st century might reply, 'could one find greater service, courtesy or finer cuisine?'.

In at least one other way, *The World* has broken with precedent. It is an age-old convention not to use the definite article 'the' when referring to ships of any kind, a form of address which is related to the formality of personifying vessels, generally by applying feminine gender terms to them. Thus *Titanic*, *QE2*, *Oriana* and so on represent the correct usage or form of address when referring to vessels, not 'the' *Titanic*, 'the' *QE2* and so on. To do otherwise is to display one's ignorance of the subject, since this is no trivial matter with people who understand the formalities of ships. That *The World* has chosen to do so may be the owners' way of showing a certain indifference to maritime tradition. This in no way excuses the number of writers, including some whose work is cited in this book, who continue to use the definite article before the name of a ship.

When *The World* began its inaugural voyage, from Oslo on 29 March 2002, between 75 and 80 per cent (sources differ slightly) of its apartments had been sold. This may have been fewer than the owners had wished, but was probably many more than the cynics had predicted. Whether *The World* proves ultimately to be an aberration in the development of cruise vessels or the forerunner of future trends within the industry remains to be seen. In its way, however, it represents a peak of development in cruising—not for its size, which is relatively modest, but for its purpose. But the cruise industry has seen a considerable number of peaks and troughs in the past century or so; at least enough to suggest to observers and commentators that none could be regarded as an 'ultimate achievement'.

Structure of the book

Oddly, cruising seems to have had an uncertain relationship to tourism generally. The term 'cruise tourism' has begun to appear, although its use seems to be exclusive to academics and perhaps illustrates the academic fondness for category splitting as much as anything else: compare 'special-interest tourism', 'eco-tourism', 'events tourism', 'soft adventure tourism', 'sport tourism', 'sex tourism' and 'wild-life tourism'. (So far there is no 'domestic-life tourism' but, with the prevalence and popularity of 'reality' television, it may not be far away.)

The literature on passenger and cruise ships is vast, but the literature on cruising as a sector of tourism or as a sociocultural phenomenon is remarkably small. In this general context only two other books have appeared, both of which should be mentioned here. They are Dickinson and Vladimir (1997) *Selling the sea; an inside look at the cruise industry* and Cartwright and Baird *The development and growth of the cruise industry* (1999), both very valuable contributions to an understanding of the cruise phenomenon. However, the first is firmly grounded in the United States of America in its approach and its examples; the second is equally firmly grounded in the United Kingdom and Europe. The present book takes a different approach but may be seen as complementary to these, rather than in competition with them. It offers another perspective by choosing many of its examples and case studies from the Asia–Pacific, a region almost completely overlooked by the others. It also deals in detail with a number of vital and sometimes controversial aspects of the cruise experience that are given fairly superficial treatment in the previous books: these include labour relations, destination development and cruise imagery. The latter, indeed, appears to have been almost totally ignored by most writers on the subject of cruising and yet, as with other forms of travel and tourism, it forms an inescapable part of the appeal.

This book is divided into a number of parts, rather than chapters, each part containing related sections. Part 1 provides a detailed examination of the contemporary nature of cruising, including such facets as the internal structure (physical and human) of a cruise ship, gambling, and health and safety. Part 2 deals with the history of cruising as a leisure activity and the development of cruise regions or destinations. Rather than risk deadening the reader's interest with endless lists of names of ships (and their tonnages), many of which are of marginal relevance to a historical survey of the subject, we have chosen to concentrate on trends and on major developments. One of the most significant developments of the past three decades concludes this section. Destination development should preferably be read in conjunction with the previous section as it provides historical reasons for some cruise itineraries as well as present trends. Part 3 offers a number of case studies from the Asia–Pacific region, illustrating varieties of cruise experience, from limited-range ocean cruising to river cruising. Parts 4 and 5 each deal in considerable detail with a single topic: the imagery of cruising and passenger behaviour respectively. Part 6 provides a framework for, and a regional case study of, the economic impacts of cruise ship visits, while a conclusion considers the impact of international crises and makes a number of cautious predictions concerning the future of cruising. Appendixes are devoted to a glossary of terms necessary to an understanding of cruising generally and a list of abbreviations used in the text. In general, amounts of money are given in US dollars as the cruise industry is largely dominated by the US market. However, where relevant, Australian and other currencies are given. Other currencies have not been connected to the Australian dollar as the exchange rate is so volatile at present.

Acknowledgements

The title of this book was chosen not only to illustrate the range of issues and interests involved in cruising, but also to suggest the personal acquaintance of the authors with the subject. As special-interest lecturers we have made more than 40 cruises since 1986 with a number of different companies, giving us a familiarity with many aspects of the phenomenon not always covered in the existing literature, and enabling us from first-hand experience to verify, supplement or contradict, where necessary, many of the assertions made about the business by writers with far less experience of it. While undeniably having enjoyed our cruise experiences, we have never become addicted to the pastime as have many travellers, and are thus able to maintain a dispassionate, at times critical, attitude to many aspects of cruising, as may be seen in this book. Because of our association with it we have chosen most of the time not to refer to ourselves in the third person but to use the personal pronouns 'we' or 'us' when our own experiences of cruising are used in this book as evidence or example.

The tourism industry has sometimes seemed unsure about whether cruising belongs to tourism or not. Regional and national statistics on tourism often omit reference to cruising completely, and representatives of tourism bodies occasionally seem remarkably indifferent to it. 'Nothing to do with us', the marketing manager of the Fiji Visitors Bureau once told us, although Fiji has been receiving cruise visitors for well over a century. 'What cruise industry?' we were asked when we sought information on Australian aspects of the subject from a spokesman for the organisation Tourism Australia. A spokesman for Tourism New South Wales had made much the same comment the previous day.

Fortunately, a great number of other people and organisations responded generously with their time and assistance. We would particularly like to thank the cruise companies, among them Royal Viking,

Princess Cruises, P&O Australia, Crystal Cruises, Cunard, the Swire Corporation of Hong Kong, Star Cruises, Blue Lagoon Cruises (Fiji), Captain Cook Cruises (Sydney) and Melanesian Tourist Services (Papua New Guinea) for inviting us to travel with them as lecturers, writers or both, and for providing us with much of the raw material for this book. Many of them did not realise they were doing this at the time, but nor, in the early stages, did we.

Individuals who deserve special thanks include Esther Corley of El Cahon, California, who provided us with much of her own collection of cruise memorabilia; veteran cruisers Peggy and Cy Nathan of various parts of the United States; Stephen Rabson of P&O, London; Robert Peutherer, Suzie Drinkwater, Phil Young, Luigi Nappa and Gavin Smith of P&O Australia; Sarina Bratton, then of Norwegian Capricorn Line; Jackie Foggitt of World's Leading Cruise Lines, Australia; Diane Patrick of Wiltrans, Sydney; Braydon Holland of Star Cruises, Australia; Jeff S. Hull of Matson Navigation, San Francisco; Steve Hunt of Seacruise Services, Sydney; John Maxtone-Graham of New York, an inspiration to anyone writing on this subject; and a considerable number of captains, cruise directors, entertainers, waiters, bar staff, cabin attendants and cruise passengers, the majority of whom gave freely of their observations, comments and occasional complaints.

Portions of this book have appeared in somewhat different form in the following publications and are used here with permission of the publishers: *Special Interest Tourism: Context and Cases* (John Wiley & Sons 2001 Milton (Qld)); *Consumer Behaviour in Travel and Tourism* (Haworth Hospitality Press 1999 Binghampton (NY)); and the *Journal of Tourism Studies* (James Cook University 1996).

We would like to thank Maris Freighter Cruises of Westport, Connecticut, United States, for permission to reproduce a selection of letters from their clients describing their freighter cruise experiences. Picture credits are given in the captions. Thanks are due also to Larry Dwyer and Peter Forsyth for their contribution, 'A framework for assessing the economic impacts of cruise tourism', which appears in Part 6.

Part 1

1

International cruising: the state of the art

The cruise business, although its origins can be traced back to the mid-1800s, is a major phenomenon of the 20th century and promises to display even more remarkable characteristics in the 21st century. Just as the growth in size, scope and technology of passenger shipping revolutionised transport by sea, so the growth of cruising (originally an incidental offspring of passenger shipping, but one that eventually outgrew and overcame its parent) has revolutionised much of the leisure industry. Viewed retrospectively, the passenger/cruise ship business appears as a series of remarkable leaps forward in technology and design, punctuated by a number of disasters, many of which helped to encourage and stimulate further advances in safety also. A history of the major trends and developments in cruising may be found in Part 2 of this book.

But in addition to representing the largest method ever devised for transporting humans, passenger liners and their cruise ship manifestations represented a social and cultural experience with which no other form of transport could compete. For all the glamour that nostalgia bestows on early rail and air travel, neither could ever offer the same level of comfort, service and variety of diversions as that offered by cruise ships, even those of relatively minor rank: neither rail nor air travel can to this day. One does not have to spend a great deal of time in a passenger train or in the economy section of an aircraft to confirm the validity of this claim.

We have chosen to begin by offering the reader a synoptic view of the contemporary cruise business, bearing in mind that the business has been changing rapidly over the past three decades, and will doubtless continue to do so as a consequence of both internal dynamics and external factors.

The growth

The international cruise business has grown at a remarkable rate since 1980, with reports from the Cruise Lines International Association (CLIA) confirming an average annual growth rate of 8.4 per cent. This success is attributed particularly to the practices of four companies that dominated the sector throughout the 1990s: Carnival Cruise Lines, Royal Caribbean Cruises, P&O/Princess Cruises and Star Cruises. These major players exhibit characteristics in common including the building of mega-ships, company takeovers or mergers, skilful target marketing and the development of niche products, and they continue to shape the cruise world in the early 21st century. Minor players in the great game are still numerous and many have their own devoted clientele, although the majority of small companies have little impact on the international scene.

The appeal of a cruise package compared with other holiday choices is likely to continue. Products targeting the whole spectrum of the travelling life cycle—from energetic young singles to gracefully aging seniors and all categories in between—ensure that tourists can choose a cruise to suit their needs, budgets and expectations. Since 1980 some 82 million people have chosen to take a deepwater cruise lasting longer than two days. Annual figures are difficult to ascertain, and various statistical sources differ in their predictions. One source claims that there will be 12 million people cruising annually by 2010. Another claims that figure was reached in 2001. Whichever is correct, it is undeniable that the consistent growth of the cruise holiday market is likely to be the envy of most other tourism and hospitality sectors.

The markets

The North American market accounts for some two-thirds of global demand. In 2001 6.9 million Americans took a cruise. This was a growth of nearly 75 per cent over the decade from 1991, a significant achievement. The European cruise market grew from 0.7 million passengers in 1991 to 2.3 million in 2001, a considerable growth rate, although from a small base. The United Kingdom has led European demand with a cumulative annual growth of 15 per cent, compared with 8.4 per cent in the United States. Europe is identified as the region with the most growth potential, with the Germans and the French, in particular, showing a proclivity to cruise. In the Asia–Pacific region Star Cruises claims that over 500 000 people cruise annually with its ships, home-ported in various East Asian nations and specifically targeting the local populations. The specialist nature of Malaysia-based Star Cruises is discussed in Part 3 of this book. The Japanese market grew at a spectacular 146 per cent annually, albeit from a very low base of only 20 000 in the early 1990s (Peisley 2000). In Australia and New Zealand, the monopoly of the market for many years by a single ship operated by P&O meant that fewer than 100 000 people cruise annually within this region. This could well change as P&O brings new ships into the region for longer cruise seasons and as other cruise lines seek out new destinations to deploy their growing fleets. Research by CLIA finds that a cruise holiday is the dream of 50 per cent of all adults, and although the United States accounts for such a large market segment, only 13 per cent of its population has actually cruised. If this research result can even cautiously be extrapolated to other national markets, there is enormous potential for growth.

The profile of cruise passengers

Data produced regularly by CLIA (a US-based organisation that is the largest and most influential of its kind, representing 95 per cent of all US-marketed berths) provide comprehensive statistics on the cruise business. Its longitudinal market profile studies conclude that cruising is increasingly appealing to a younger market. In the early 1970s, the average age of the cruise passenger was 65 years. By 2001 it was between 43 and 45 years. This is attributed primarily to the availability of shorter cruises of three or four days. Table 1.1 shows the characteristics of the cruise market.

Recent cruise market segments

CLIA research identifies six categories in the cruise market, each with differing expectations. The terminology is, understandably, American, but the attitudes and preferences displayed by each category are almost universal. The only significant exception appears to be the Asian market dominated by Star Cruises, for which few of these categories would have any relevance. CLIA's categories are:

- **Restless baby boomers**, who constitute 33 per cent of the market. The majority are first-time cruisers who claim they will do it again but need convincing that the cruise experience provides value for money over other potentially new travel experiences.

Table 1.1   A cruise passenger profile (from 1996–2001 data)

Characteristics	%
Status	
• Married	78
• Single	22
Age	
• 25–39 years	28
• 40–59 years	42
• 60 years or older	30
Average age 50 years	
Have children under 18 years	35
• Holiday with children	59
• Do not holiday with children	41
Gender	
• Male	51
• Female	48
Education	
• Some college or less	36
• College graduate or more	64
Household income	
• US$20 000 – $39 900	15
• US$40 000 – $59 900	31
• US$60 000 – $99 900	30
• US$100 000 plus	25
Average income $79 100	

Source: Adapted from CLIA, 2002.

- **Enthusiastic baby boomers** are enthusiastic cruisers, accounting for 20 per cent of the market. They lead stressful lives and look for escape and relaxation for their holiday experiences. For them cruising is seen as the ideal way of 'getting away from it all' either on their own or with their families. Together these segments make up 53 per cent of total market potential. They are big business for every cruise company.

- **Consummate shoppers**, so categorised by CLIA, contribute 16 per cent of the market. This label refers not to their souvenir buying but to their skills and persistence in looking for the best value for their holiday money. They are very committed cruisers and look for different experiences and levels of cruising according to their holiday needs.

- **Luxury seekers**, on the other hand, willingly pay for the best experience in terms of accommodation, inclusions and service quality. For this 14 per cent of the market, a 'topdrawer' cruise holiday confirms their sophistication and status, and the cruise companies have recognised the need to provide an exclusive product for these people.

- **Explorers** and **ship buffs** account for 11 per cent and six per cent respectively of the cruise market. The former are well-educated, well-travelled people who seek an educational cruise experience. They are much more interested in the ports of call than are many other cruise passengers, who focus on the shipboard experience as the primary motivation for choosing to cruise. Cruise companies recognise the needs of this segment by providing specialist lecturers on many cruise itineraries and by designing products centred on visits to more remote and less accessible destinations in smaller, well-equipped vessels. Ship buffs, who constitute the most senior group, cruise simply because they love the comfort, service and sheer pleasure of a cruise. This market needs no special encouragement. Their commitment to particular lines and even particular ships within the fleet is well known, and companies will have so much data on the preferences of these passengers that for many the ship is a home away from home.

The average cruise passenger is willing to spend up to US$300 per day. Only two per cent will spend more than US$500 per day. Cruise lines have products to cater to all categories; and while the top level might be very small, it is a very profitable niche to provide for. For all passengers, a cruise holiday is popular because of its all-inclusive nature, the opportunity to visit several different destinations, the experience of being constantly waited on (a high priority in service provision for companies and of expectation for passengers) and the chance, however brief, to live in luxurious surroundings. Ship designers are obliged to show more and more ingenuity in providing diversions once considered impossible for a ship; ice skating, rock walls for climbing and multistoried atriums with cascading waterfalls are just some of the features which surprise and delight passengers unprepared for such novelties.

Cruise clients have identified friends, family and magazines as the most influential sources of information assisting in their decision making. These provide far more detail about the cruise experience than any of the other most frequently identified sources. Cruise prospects—as potential new cruisers are known—are more inclined to use the Internet than a travel agent for information, which indicates opportunities for skilled marketing in this medium. The idea of taking a cruise, whether for new cruisers or experienced cruisers, is usually initiated by women. This is evidently encouraged by cruise advertising, which almost always shows a woman being graciously served in a variety of shipboard environments—breakfast in her cabin, a cool drink by the pool or a fine meal in an elegant dining room. The cruise experience rates most highly in the satisfaction stakes when compared with resort holidays and package tours, while cruises are rated highest over other types of holidays when it comes to pampering, dining and value for money. Table 1.2 shows the factor ratings found by CLIA (2002a) among experienced cruisers and potential cruisers.

Taking a cruise is seen as a good way to sample a variety of destinations with a view to returning for a longer stay. More than half of all cruise passengers say they will return in a different holiday mode after they have had a short stay in a port of call. This is a factor often ignored by tourism operators in many destinations. They have a limited opportunity to promote their products to several hundred—perhaps even several thousand—passengers and crew during the few hours of a ship's visit. Both of these groups spend some time wandering along the wharves and waterfront areas as they wait for tours to depart or return from tours, browse the souvenir stalls, take a stroll on land between work shifts or simply wait for the ship to sail. It is a time when people pick up bits of information to read later in their cabins, often with a view to returning.

Table 1.2   Perceptions of cruising versus other holidays

Feature	Experienced better %	Experienced same or better %	Potential better %	Potential same or better %
Being pampered	75	93	65	85
Fine dining	74	92	62	87
Being hassle-free	71	93	44	83
Relaxing	69	91	57	82
Chance to visit several destinations	68	88	61	83
Easy to plan and arrange	65	92	45	82
Good value for money	65	91	31	65
High-quality entertainment	64	88	50	84
Variety of activities	64	86	35	69
Luxury	62	89	58	84
Chance to explore destination for potential return	62	85	41	71
Exciting and adventurous	60	85	42	74
Romantic getaway	59	86	56	82
Reliable	58	89	33	78
Fun holiday	58	87	39	78
Being safe	53	90	24	71
Comfortable accommodations	51	78	29	70
Cultural learning experience	47	79	41	74
Participation in enjoyable sports	36	67	19	54
Good activities for children	28	45	25	53

Source: Adapted from CLIA, 2002.

Capacity

A glance at the order books of the major ship builders confirms the spectacular growth of the cruise business. At the beginning of the 21st century 61 new ships totalling US$22 billion were in the advanced planning or construction stages: these were being delivered to their owners at a rate of 16 ships a year. By 2006 the major companies are expected to increase their capacity (number of passenger lower berths) by 75 per cent. Although some market analysts caution against the effects of oversupply, the cruise business has repeatedly seen cycles of supply stimulating demand.

Table 1.3 indicates that new ships are getting progressively larger. P&O Princess Cruises' *Grand Princess* launched in 1998 was, at the time, the largest liner ever built, accommodating 2600 passengers. Its luxurious design and fittings heralded a new era in the grand liners of the sea. The new ships, however, also dictate where world cruising will continue to grow; they are simply too big to pass through the Panama Canal, thus restricting their movements to the Caribbean and Mediterranean 'ponds'. Their size is a deliberate move on the part of major cruise lines, where economies of scale and the need to replace the aging small ships drive the design. 'After all', one cruise director told us, 'the captain is the highest paid person on board and you only need one whether you have 200 or 2000 passengers!'. In the new ship area, Silversea Cruises, in particular, acknowledges the niche market of passengers who seek a small, stylish and very expensive cruise experience. While the mega-ships are certainly magnificent in their fittings and design, a common complaint by frequent cruisers is that they are far too impersonal because of their sheer size and the multitudes of people on board. The big ships are also much more restricted as to where they can go, while the small ships can include a far greater variety of ports in their itineraries. Small-ship enthusiasts are increasingly prepared to pay for their exclusive, soft-adventure holidays.

Tonnage, however, does not necessarily reflect passenger numbers. For example, a Star Cruises ship of 112 000 gross registered tonnes (GRT) will be configured to take 4000 passengers while a 137 000 GRT Royal Caribbean ship will accommodate 3838 passengers. Variables determining configuration include target market, cabin size, berths per cabin and a range of other facilities such as casinos, restaurants and theatres. Building a new ship is, as Table 1.3 shows, a very expensive business. It also requires a long time frame, as illustrated in the following example presented by Crystal Cruises for its new vessel *Serenity*:

8 March 2000	Commitment to build announcement
7 November 2000	Letter of intent signed
12 December 2000	Contract signed

Table 1.3   Ships on order, 2003–06

Line	Ship	Tonnage	Passengers	US$ millions	Area of operation *
2003					
Aida Cruises	*AidaAura*	42 000	1270	200	Eur/Carib
Carnival	*Carnival Glory*	110 000	2974	500	Carib
Costa	*C Mediterranea*	86 000	2100	350	Carib/Med
Costa	*C Fortuna*	105 000	2720	400	Eur/Carib
Crystal	*Serenity*	68 000	1080	300	World
Cunard	*Queen Mary 2*	150 000	2800	780	Atl/Carib
Holland America	*Oosterdam*	84 000	1800	400	Med/Carib
Mediterranean	*MSC Lirica*	60 000	1600	250	Med/Carib
Princess	*Island Princess*	88 000	1950	330	Ak/Canal
Princess	*Diamond Princess*	113 000	2600	500	Ak/Mexico
Royal Caribbean	*Serenade/Seas*	88 000	2000	400	tba
Royal Caribbean	*Mariner/Seas*	142 000	3100	550	Carib
2004					
Carnival	*Carnival Miracle*	86 000	2100	375	Carib
Carnival	*Carnival Valour*	110 000	2974	500	Carib
Costa	*Costa Magica*	105 000	2720	400	Med/Carib
Holland America	*Westerdam*	84 000	1800	400	tba
Mediterranean	*MSC Opera*	60 000	1600	250	Med/Carib
Norwegian	tba	70 000	2000	250	Carib
Princess	*Sapphire Princess*	113 000	2600	500	Carib
Princess	*Crown Princess*	116 000	3100	500	tba
Royal Caribbean	*Jewel/Seas*	88 000	2000	400	tba
2005					
Carnival	tba	110 000	2974	450	Carib
Carnival	tba	84 000	1968	400	tba
Holland America	*Vista 4*	84 000	1800	400	tba
Princess	tba (option)	88 000	1950	330	tba
Royal Caribbean	tba (option)	88 000	2500	400	tba
2006					
Holland America	*Vista 5*	84 000	1800	400	tba
Princess	tba (option)	88 000	1950	330	tba
Royal Caribbean	tba (option)	88 000	2000	400	tba
	29 ships		63 330 lower berths	US$11.6 billion	

* Eur/Europe, Med/Mediterranean, Carib/Caribbean, Ak/Alaska, Atl/Atlantic, Canal/Panama Canal
Source: *Cruise Industry News Quarterly*: Fall 2002.

October 2001	Steel cutting begins
7 November 2001	Name announcement
2 July 2002	Keel-laying ceremony
8 November 2002	Float out
May 2003	Sea trials
June 2003	Delivery
7 July 2003	Inaugural cruise

Building *Serenity* required 14 000 tonnes of steel, more than 1000 kilo-metres of electric cable, 100 kilometres of pipes, more than 500 tonnes of air-conditioning ducts, 120 469 litres of paint, 13 020 square metres of internal public space, 6008 square metres of teak for outside decks, 3003 square metres of teak for private verandas, 2000 workers and 2 500 000 construction hours (<crystalcruises.com>).

Some leading cruise companies

Carnival Cruise Lines

This is by far the world's largest cruise company. It was launched in 1972 with one ship, *Mardi Gras*, which promptly ran aground. According to Slater and Basch (1996, p. 158), 'There was nowhere to go but up'. The company was listed on the New York Stock Exchange in 1987 and, as the largest cruise company and still growing, continues to introduce 'firsts' in cruise ship developments and achievements. These include the first dedicated performance stage in 1975; first cruise line to use TV commercials on a saturation schedule during the network news time in 1984; first to make a casino payout of over US$1 million to two players in 1994; first to launch the smoke-free ships in 1988; and first to coin the term 'fun ship' as a marketing ploy (Slater & Basch 1996, p. 150). Carnival ships are instantly recognised by their winged red, white and blue funnels. In 2002 Carnival Cruise Lines had 30 742 berths and 15 ships.

Carnival Corporation

This is now the parent company of Carnival Cruise Lines. Its aggressive expansion policy has two thrusts: new ship orders totalling US$7.0 billion to come into service by 2006 and brand takeovers. These include Holland America Line, Windstar Cruises, Cunard, Seabourn and Costa Crociere. Carnival also holds a 26 per cent share of the British group Airtours. In April 2003 it announced a successful 'merger' with P&O Princess, giving it another six brand names—P&O, Princess, P&O Australia, Swan Hellenic, Aida and Ocean Village. Details of the largest of these are given separately below. The company has its headquarters in Miami, Florida.

Costa Cruise Lines

Of Italian origin, Costa Cruises is now part of the Carnival group. The family moved from freight into passenger services just after World War II and into pleasure cruises in 1959. The distinctive big blue C on a yellow stack has historical connections with the company's first ship—*Anna C*—and also is a confirmation of the family's continuing control of the company. The ambience on all Costa ships reinforces their Italian style and heritage. Costa Cruises has 10 183 berths on eight ships and is part of Carnival Corporation. Its headquarters are in Miami, Florida.

Cunard Line

Founded in 1840 as a transport service between Britain and America, Cunard has long been famous in the shipping business with such great liners as *Mauretania* and *Queen Mary*, the latter now a popular tourist attraction and hotel in Long Beach, California. *Queen Elizabeth 2* (*QE2*) has been its flagship since 1968 and continues to hold a special place in the cruise world because of its style, its history and its classical ship lines. *Queen Mary 2*, launched in 2003 and being promoted as the grandest ship yet, will no doubt take *QE2*'s place eventually. Cunard, with 2459 berths and two ships (pre *Queen Mary*), is one of Carnival's many brands and has its headquarters in Miami, Florida.

Holland America Line

Originating as Netherlands–America Steamship Company in 1873, the name soon changed to Holland America because of its role as a leading shipper of migrants to the New World. In the post World War II period, Holland America shifted its operations to cruises as a response to the increased demand from middle-class Americans for moderately priced tourist cruises. It was the first line to introduce the casual buffet style dining option. With 13 348 berths on ten ships, Holland America is part of Carnival Corporation and has headquarters in Seattle, Washington.

P&O Princess Cruises

In effect these are two companies, often linked for convenience but with separate strategies. P&O claims to have started the concept of cruising in 1844 when it advertised round trips on its mail ships to the Mediterranean. The company became one of the world's great shipping companies, with activity particularly in India, Asia and the Pacific. Its most famous cruise ship was *Canberra*, which was finally scrapped in 1997. In 2002 P&O had 3500 berths and three ships. It retains its British ambience on all the ships and is popular for this reason with travellers from United Kingdom in particular. Its headquarters are in Southampton, United Kingdom.

The Princess company started in 1965 when an American entrepreneur charted *Princess Patricia*—giving the company its name—for cruises to the Mexican Riviera. In 1974 P&O took over Princess Cruises, its established way of dealing with competition. In 1977 the TV series *The Love Boat* was filmed partly on *Pacific Princess* and was seen in 93 countries and heard in at least 29 languages. Almost 30 years later the musical theme from the series is still played on every Princess cruise and episodes are played on cabin television. Princess was the first cruise line to introduce, in 1984, a ship that featured all outside cabins, a high proportion of which had private balconies. These have become almost mandatory on every new ship.

The combined company includes the brands P&O, Princess, P&O Australia, Swan Hellenic, Ocean Village and, in the German market, Aida. In 2002 a corporate face-off took place when Carnival challenged a prospective merger between P&O Princess and Royal Caribbean, seeing this as a threat to its own predominance. Carnival had previously made 'playful' overtures for the acquisition of Princess Cruises from P&O. In 2003 the playfulness became quite serious with the merger described above. Princess Cruises has headquarters in Los Angeles, California.

Royal Caribbean Cruises

The fact that the Hyatt hotel group holds 41 per cent of shares is an indication of the way cruise ships have come to be acknowledged as floating resorts. The company was founded in 1969 by three Norwegian shipping companies with the sole purpose of introducing year-round seven- and 14-day cruises into the Caribbean. Other firsts include the 1990 commissioning of the first ship specially designed for short three- and four-day cruises, first 18-hole miniature golf course at sea in 1995, and in the same year the first cruise company to open hospitality centres on shore for their passengers while in port. Royal Caribbean International in 2002 had 33 042 berths on 15 ships and holds 20 per cent of the British tour operator First Choice in a marketing and European sales alliance. Headquarters are in Miami, Florida.

Celebrity Cruises

The company evolved from the Chandris Group, a Greek company which played a significant role in bringing European migrants to Australia in the post World War II era and returning with young Australians travelling to the United Kingdom. Chandris also pioneered the fly/cruise product in both the Mediterranean and the Caribbean in the 1960s. The Celebrity brand was launched in 1989 and now has 14 068 berths on eight ships. It is known for 'luxury without ostentation' (Slater & Basch 1996, p. 180) and its excellent cuisine. Now a part of the Royal Caribbean stable, Celebrity's headquarters are in Miami, Florida.

Star Cruises

This company is the rising star of the cruise industry, having been established only in 1993. Star operates cruises in the East and South-East Asian regions and in 2003, following an urgent need to reposition its ships during the Severe Acute Respiratory Syndrome (SARS) crisis, it introduced two ships to Australian ports for a trial three-month period with short cruises in Australian coastal waters and into the South Pacific. The original rationale for establishment was the operation of gaming facilities in international waters off Singapore. From the initial 'cruises' lasting just a few hours on converted Scandinavian ferries, the company quickly developed two-, three- and four-day packages and acquired or built new superships to accommodate them. An acknowledged first for the multiple-award-winning company is the introduction of freestyle dining on its ships. Initially, a ploy to appeal to its clientele who like to graze frequently and who do not want to conform to traditional meal times, particularly if they are enjoying good fortune in the casino, this has been increasingly adopted by other cruise lines whose passengers are demanding more choices in dining styles.

Following a period of rapid expansion in 2001, Star Cruises (with 8222 berths on the eight ships under its own brand in 2002) incorporates Norwegian Cruise Line and Orient Line, giving the company a global reach. Star Cruises is owned by the Malaysian resort and property development group Genting Bhd. The company is based in Singapore and at Port Klang, a purpose-built wharf, passenger terminal and office facility in Malaysia.

Norwegian Cruise Line

NCL was founded in 1966 by Norwegian Knut Kloster and Ted Arison, who later established Carnival when the partnership disintegrated. Its original aim was to introduce one-class, casual Caribbean cruises for the mass tourism market. Its most prominent 'first' was the introduction of short cruises to the Bahamas where passengers spent the day on a private island. The company has undergone many changes in both direction and in the mix of companies incorporated at various times. It is now under the auspices of Star Cruises. In 2002 NCL had 14 682 berths on 11 ships, including the two Orient Line vessels. Headquarters are in Coral Gables, Florida.

Crystal Cruises

This company was founded in 1988 by Japanese company Nippon Yusen Kaisha (NYK) although the first ship did not appear until 1990. NYK, the massive, veteran Tokyo-based shipping company, continues to own the line outright. In 2003 Crystal, which had 1884 berths on two ships in 2002, introduced a third ship designed to satisfy cruise passengers seeking the most luxurious experience. Many staff were trained by the now defunct Royal Viking Line which set the standards for quality in service. Crystal ships were the first to claim six-star status. The cruise company is located in Los Angeles, California.

Disney Cruise Line

Launched in the mid-1990s, Disney Cruise Line has 3508 berths on two ships. As its name indicates, it is part of the great Disney empire and its ships take Mickey Mouse and all his companions to sea for short cruises out of Miami. The product is specifically targeted at families but all the expected services and facilities to entertain parents at sea are available. Disney's cruise operation is based in Fort Lauderdale, Florida.

Radisson Seven Seas Cruises

As the name might show, this is a partnership. In this case the partnership is between three companies—the Radisson Hotel Group, Seven Seas Cruises and Hanseatic Cruises. Launched in 1995, the company specialises in small, very luxurious ships directed at adventurous people who want to travel on innovative programs to exotic locations. In 2002 Radisson had 2224 berths on six ships. The company is based in Fort Lauderdale, Florida.

Royal Olympia Cruises

Royal Olympia further illustrates the fact that not all cruise lines are US-based. The Greek-flagged fleet is based in Piraeus, the port of Athens, and the name 'Olympia' (previously 'Olympic') is said to represent the tradition (albeit an uneven one) of giving ships female names. The company proclaims intense pride in its national heritage, as the names of its vessels suggest. In 2002 Royal Olympia's seven ships comprised 4600 berths.

Beneath the towering superstructure of the major companies exists a multitude of smaller organisations worldwide. These range from companies with a few vessels but almost no international scope, to companies with no permanent vessels at all—an apparent anomaly accounted for by the practice of chartering ships as required from other organisations.

Length of the cruise

The average length of a cruise varies according to the market. In the United States and Europe six- to nine-day cruises are most popular, while in Japan and East Asia generally three- to six-day cruises dominate because of the lower availability of leisure time. The trend towards shorter cruises is likely to continue because of the preference for more frequent holidays spread throughout the year. The Asia–Pacific market has two distinct categories. The first is the Star Cruises market that specialises in products designed by Asians for Asians, who have much shorter holidays than the majority of travellers elsewhere. The major motivation for the majority of passengers is to access on Star's vessels the gaming facilities that are illegal in most Asian countries. Normal policy for Asian clientele is the 'add-on' price formula, in which they pay extra for a number of activities on board, compared to the 'all-inclusive' policy preferred by Westerners. Two- and three-day cruises are the most popular in this market, with weekend 'Cruises to Nowhere' strongly promoted domestically. The Australian/New Zealand market is another area with growth potential, and has been effectively dominated for many years by P&O Australia. Abbreviating the cruise package time is decidedly more challenging for P&O Australia, because of much greater distances between possible ports of call in the Pacific, but the international trend can be seen there as well with the introduction of seven-day cruises in 2001 (P&O 2000).

Distribution channels

Cruise companies have traditionally sold their product through travel agencies or direct to small niche markets. The big cruise companies still rely on travel agents because of their huge product range but the small, specialised cruise companies prefer direct contact with their real and potential markets. CLIA reports that only one in five people use a travel agent most of the time when they make holiday reservations. Cruise passengers, however, show a stronger inclination to use agents. Some 34 per cent mostly use a travel agent. The strong growth of cruise sales particularly over the past decade has required a more complex reservations structure, with the use of CRSs (Computer Reservation Systems) and call centres. A revolution in communication technology such as the Internet has opened up new distribution channels. According to CLIA, one in three holiday makers uses the Internet to make reservations, while more than half of the total has used the web as a source of information. Their analysts expect that first-time cruisers will continue to use agents while experienced cruisers will consult the Internet for their middle/low price category cruise reservations. By 2010 it is estimated that 20–40 per cent of reservations will be made on the web, making up a third of direct sales. The use of CRSs has been slower in the cruise sector than in other tourism sectors because of low penetration in outbound markets and their relative complexity. Royal Caribbean International has led the field in this development with the introduction in 1991 of its own system called 'CruiseMatch 2000'. Some 7000 of the 27 000 US agencies that sell cruises use this new system. Its acceptability and growth potential is confirmed by the fact that by the end of the 20th century 27 per cent of reservations from the North American outbound market were made through this system.

The cruise business is meeting the many challenges of the early 21st century in a variety of innovative ways. Big companies continue to swallow up smaller ones. Many traditional ports are being bypassed and alternatives sought as terrorism, wars, political unrest and global epidemics impose their own threats over itinerary planning. Increased sophistication in the market means that companies must develop even better facilities and strategies to attract the fickle public. New destinations are opening as companies design products for special niche markets. It is, in effect, a business where rapid action and reaction are the drivers of the most successful companies.

2

Inside a cruise ship

The context

The 21st century realities of the cruise business mean that few vessels now match the traditional image of a passenger ship. The shift to 'big is better' and economies of scale in cruise ship design and operation mean that only the older ships fit long-held perceptions. *QE2* is probably the best surviving example of an earlier style. Now more than 40 years old, the ship is much loved because of her classic lines. Newer large ships, it is often said, more closely resemble floating hotels or apartment blocks. The driving economies of 'big is better' have been noted by both industry insiders and critics (e.g. Dickinson & Vladimir 1997; Wood 2000).

An increase in accommodation capacity by two per cent can mean an increase in revenue of up to US$1.5 million. The apparent need for every cabin to have its own open balcony, and the race to provide more entertainment and recreational facilities than competitors' ships offer mean that the superstructure grows higher while the hull has begun to resemble a barge to support the facilities rather than a ship to sail through deep seas. Indeed, the very large vessels are now referred to as 'post-Panama' vessels, since their size makes it impossible for them to pass through the Panama Canal. The basic principles of ship weight distributions and the causes and controls for pitching and rolling are discussed by Cartwright and Baird (1999). It is sufficient here, however, to state that the high superstructure/flatter hull combination means that repositioning these vessels from one major cruise area to another presents some challenges. Sailing on them through the roaring forties of the southern hemisphere is not a particularly comfortable experience. The massive superstructure acts like a sail and even the most modern engineering techniques to overcome unwanted and excessive movement are tested in these environments. Therefore, to anticipate a point made elsewhere in this book, as the ships get bigger for company purposes, the places to which they can go become fewer.

A counter to this trend is the concept of the ship itself as the ultimate destination, so that where it sails may become incidental. By satisfying every passenger expectation and demand on board the company retains total control of the experience, the product and, consequently, the profits. Corporations might argue, in addition, that this total control is a very effective form of risk management. Why expose their valued passengers to potential hazards in a foreign location? If they can provide an experience of 'staged authenticity' on board the vessel, this may be quite enough for many people. Thus, when the brochure offers people the opportunity to meet 'friendly, smiling locals', if the meeting is confined to trained employees of the company who are, or at least appear to be, indigenous to the location, passengers will be guaranteed a positive experience. They need not be exposed unnecessarily to the unscrupulous taxi drivers, avaricious shopkeepers, petty criminals, urban poverty, congestion and pollution of many ports of call, to say nothing of the contaminated drinking water and dubious hygiene in food practices that they might encounter. This prospect is not nearly as unlikely as it may first appear. It is already well established in resort areas in the Pacific, South-East Asia and the Caribbean, where the indigenous daytime room attendant or roustabout may double as a night-time dancer or musician.

Carbonara (1997), an Italian architect whose company has designed some of the post-Panama ships, suggests that cruise ships will become in essence floating theme parks and artificial islands, replacing real-life destinations. Ritzer (1998) and Wood (2000) use the terms 'McDisneyization' and 'fantasyscapes' respectively when referring to trends in cruise ship design and activity. The former relates to the visual theming of ships in which the holiday experience is packaged around a single entertaining concept in every aspect of the ship's design. And while some new ships certainly present elements of fantasy, Wood, in this instance, is referring to the port experience being offered by companies such as Carnival and the Disney Corporation. Of eight major companies operating in the Caribbean, Wood notes that six actually own their own islands or have created enclaves on peninsulas of larger islands which they market as the true Caribbean experience—only better (Wood 2000, p. 361). Orenstein

(1997) claims that when most cruise passengers visit Labadee, Royal Caribbean's private piece of Haiti surrounded by three-metre-high walls and patrolled by armed guards, they fail to realise that they are in the country of Haiti at all.

Again, this situation is not entirely peculiar to cruising, but is a fairly common misconception in countries where an enclave style of tourism development is encouraged, either on off-shore islands or on land isolated from local development. In Fiji, for example, tourists usually arrive at Nadi International Airport at night and are then whisked off immediately to resorts well away from the main towns or, after a short night in an airport hotel, board boats to farther-flung islands where the resort is an enclave well removed from local villages. At some island resorts, employees live on yet another island and commute every day by small boat. Tourists have very little contact with the indigenous people—save the workers at the resort—and little or no concept of the country they are visiting in such locations. They perceive their destination to be the resort—Plantation Island, Castaway, Turtle and so on—rather than the country.

The order of things

A ship's layout reflects a hierarchical structure of society. At the top live the captain and his most senior members of staff. They need instant access to the ship's control centre (the bridge) that, for obvious reasons, is at the highest front point of the vessel's superstructure—or very nearly so. Gone are romantic notions of salty sailors wrestling with great wooden wheels to steer the ship through stormy seas. The modern bridge is a sleek, highly computerised creation. While there is still a wheel 'to steer her by', it seems to most traditionalists a small, insignificant thing of stainless steel that might be easily missed on the standard bridge tour unless pointed out. At the bottom of the ship live the crew members in their own hierarchical living arrangements. On any cruise ship there are two parallel worlds in operation. The public areas and accommodations between these two extremes are for passengers, senior crew from both hotel and ship operations and for other crew strictly while on duty. So carefully concealed are the crew living quarters, and the passageways and stairwells through which they move to get from their quarters to their work stations, that jokes about this have become standard in the repertoire of many entertainers. 'Do the crew all sleep ashore at night?' asks the little old lady, puzzled about where the crew live!

The sundeck or sports deck is the highest level on a cruise ship. Jogging tracks, sun chairs, golf driving ranges and half tennis courts are

Figure 2.1 A side section of P&O's *Pacific Sky* (Crew quarters are below Gala Deck.)

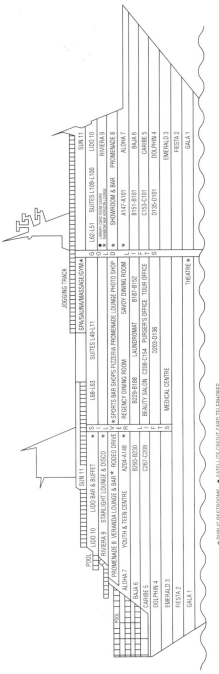

Source: Passenger Information, *Pacific Sky*.

outside. Inside at the highest levels is where the nightclub or disco is usually located. (See Figure 2.1.) The logic is to keep this late-night, noisy venue as far away as possible from the cabins of paying passengers, although there is something of a paradox here in that the most expensive suites are usually near this same deck. What the captain and his senior officers think of this proximity is not generally known, although they too have their quarters nearby. They can also frequently be seen enjoying these same facilities!

Food, as any brochure on the subject of cruising will confirm, is of the utmost importance. The main dining rooms and other restaurants are found on levels above or immediately below the main promenade deck. Tables by the windows are highly sought after, and while the daylight and views are evident at breakfast and lunch time, drapes and innovative window coverings transform the atmosphere into a more formal dining experience in the evening. Throughout modern ships, passengers find a whole range of eating experiences. The traditional cruise experience meant that the passenger was consigned to a particular table, dining time (e.g. first sitting lunch 12 noon, dinner 6:30 pm, second sitting lunch 1:30 pm, dinner 8:30 pm) was set and the same waiter served for the entire voyage. Shifts in consumer preferences now mean that freestyle dining options are being demanded. This means that passengers do not want to be restricted in when and where they eat. They want to choose the location, culinary style, the time and, perhaps most importantly, how they can dress for the occasion. Dress codes are becoming increasingly flexible as the market profile changes as well. For the majority of passengers the requirement to dress formally for dinner has limited appeal. 'After all', many complain, 'I'm on a relaxing holiday. Why would I want to get into a dinner suit every night?'. Cruise lines are responding by introducing a variety of dining options. While the central dining room and allocation system still operates and is normally the place passengers have their first meal on board, the choice is growing every time a new ship is launched or an older one undergoes a makeover. Norwegian Cruise Line has claimed credit for this innovation, but others have rapidly responded. Casual cafés, culinary and culturally themed restaurants, smorgasbords, intimate and exclusive fine dining rooms, 24-hour room service, hamburger bars and pizza shops are all supplemented by 11 am bouillon on deck, traditional English afternoon tea and the midnight buffet. Special diets have become more readily available. Kosher, halal, vegetarian, low fat, wheat free and salt free are just the beginning. Nothing, apparently, is too much trouble.

To provide a regional example, Table 2.1 indicates the formal meal times on *Pacific Sky*, P&O's ship in the South Pacific, a moderately priced, year-round vessel. For constant grazers other eating options on board included a 24-hour Pizzeria, Harry's Café de Waves serving traditional Australian pies, the New Zealand Ice Cream bar, and Sky Dogs serving hotdogs, as well as continuous room service.

Scattered through the superstructure are the entertainment lounges and venues. These range from professional show lounges with stages, to lounges for orchestras and dancing, to themed cocktail bars or pubs. There is almost always a very comfortable cinema screening the latest releases. The casino, sometimes small and discreet and sometimes huge and splendid in the Las Vegas tradition, depends on the policy of the shipping line and the known preference of its clientele. For quieter pastimes there are libraries, writing rooms and dedicated card rooms or corners where people can be found just sitting and gazing out to sea. At different times of the day any of the public areas can be dedicated to special activities—dance classes, origami lessons, language lessons, guest lectures or chef's demonstrations. While all this activity is taking place inside, outside on the decks other passengers are using swimming pools and spa pools, playing deck games, reading or dozing in deck chairs, strolling, jogging, eating and drinking.

Central to the hotel operations of the ship and usually also centrally located is the purser's desk. As this is normally the area that passengers see first, the first impressions are paramount. Modern pursers' desks rival anything in design that land-based hotels can present, and are increasingly referred to as reception areas, since the 'desk' may be in a space also containing soaring atriums, cascading waterfalls, grand pianos, and sweeping fixtures of marble and gilt and glass to greet the newly arrived passenger. The reception space on a Star Cruises supership is one example of this

Table 2.1 Today's meal hours (*Pacific Sky*)

6:45 am	Early bird coffee	Promenade deck aft
7:00 am to 9:00 am	Buffet breakfast on deck	Promenade deck aft
7:30 am to 9:30 am	Open sitting breakfast	Both restaurants
7:15 am to 10:00 am	Continental breakfast in cabin	(room service)
12 noon to 1:30 pm	Fiesta Mexicana buffet	Promenade deck aft
12 noon	Luncheon for 1st sitting passengers only—open sitting arrangement	Both restaurants
1:15 pm	Luncheon for 2nd sitting passengers only—open sitting arrangement	Both restaurants
3:30 pm to 4:00 pm	Tea and pastries	Savoy restaurant
5:00 pm	Children's dinner	Regency restaurant
6:15 pm	Welcome gala dinner—1st sitting	Both restaurants
8:30 pm	Welcome gala dinner—2nd sitting	Both restaurants
11:45 pm to 12:45 am	Late night delicatessen buffet	Regency restaurant

Source: *Sky Daily, Pacific Sky,* Monday 13 August 2001

trend. On the other hand, the very conservative, functional nature of *QE2*'s reception area typifies the deliberately traditional quality of the vessel. As with any good hotel lobby, there are always people asking questions, sometimes complaining, collecting daily sheets of information, paying accounts, querying bills, buying stamps, posting cards, sending messages or just milling about meeting new friends. It is the 'community centre' of any cruise ship. Or, on recent ships, it might be thought of as the central square of the shopping boulevard, for nearby one finds the boutiques, galleries and specialty shops in ever increasing numbers as ships' shopping arcades get bigger and more diverse. Because the central area of a ship is the most stable, this is where designers try to locate the facilities that require the most stable environment. Thus, as one moves below decks and into the heart of the ship, one finds the medical centre and the kitchens (accessible to passengers only on organised tours during a non-busy period).

Accommodations are ranked from suites at the very top levels to the more fundamental cabins on the lower levels. In between there are numerous variations in size, layout, facilities and inclusions. The most luxurious accommodation is usually designated the 'owner's suite'. Spacious, and often incorporating at least two rooms, it is near the bridge and the captain's accommodation to enhance the sense of ownership. But owners rarely seem to cruise and the suite is generally available for the highest price on the vessel. In earlier days of cruising suites were relatively few, but in many 21st-century cruise ships nearly all cabins are referred to as suites because of their more spacious layout, with beds replacing bunks, full bathrooms often with bath and separate shower and, at the more expensive levels, twin handbasins. Complimentary toiletries are common with the range and brand increasing in amount and status from lower-level bathrooms to those at higher levels. Televisions, videos, bar refrigerators and lounge seating are also inclusions that are ranked in quality, quantity and size according to level of accommodation. In the 1990s the first cruise ships appeared with private open verandas, which only a few of the top-level suites could boast. By the end of the century new ships had this facility built into at least half of the accommodations and their popularity and subsequent demand are strongly influencing ship design. There are fewer opportunities to observe the sea passing by one's porthole—or even over it in rough weather—except in crew accommodations. So intent are ships on being resorts that most seating configurations face inward and curtains often cover windows even during the day, so the presence of the sea becomes quite incidental to the overall experience.

3

Rank and status

Cruise ships have two distinct areas of operation. The technical operations and navigation of the ship, under the management of the captain, are managed by a relatively small team of highly trained maritime experts assisted by other experienced mariners (see Figure 3.1). They are not often seen around the public areas unless specific maintenance jobs are under way or during berthing and departure procedures. Officers are generally European (British, Scandinavian or Italian) although in more recent times, and on certain lines such as Star Cruises, Asian officers are moving through the ranks of their chosen areas. Third World and developing countries are widely represented among the able seamen, particularly the Philippines and Indonesia, India and Pakistan.

While the ship operations team might be relatively small because of enormous innovations in the technology that assists in the control of a cruise ship, the hotel operations side is very large. An average ratio of passengers to staff is 2:1; thus as ships take more passengers, they require more hotel staff to take care of them, and in the 21st century the national and ethnic mix of the staff is becoming more diverse as political climates and employment opportunities ebb and flow. Table 3.1 gives a good indication of the functions and numerical distribution of staff on a large cruise ship.

It is instructive to look at the size of the main departments on one of the large ships of Star Cruises. The figures clearly reflect the importance

Figure 3.1 Cruise ship hierarchies

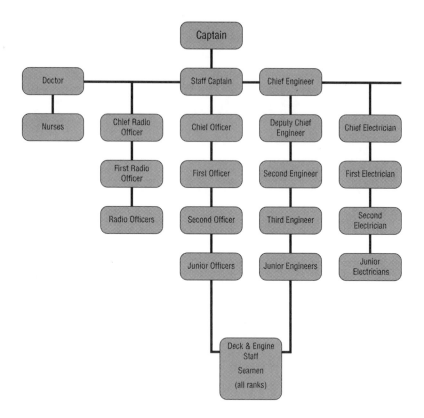

Adapted from Ward 1994 (not all positions may be present on all ships).

of gambling to this company when compared to the statistics for *QE2*. *SuperStar Virgo* maintains 850 in the hotel section, 120 in ship operations (decks and engineering) and 300 in the 'club' sector. At the time of data collection (2001) the ship had a higher than usual staff-to-passenger ratio because of training programs that the company was operating on board in preparation for forthcoming expansion. The balance of the departments, however, is fairly constant.

Ship operations

The staff structure on a cruise ship resembles a mini United Nations. At the top is the captain—usually British, Scandinavian, Italian or, occa-

Figure 3.1 *continued*

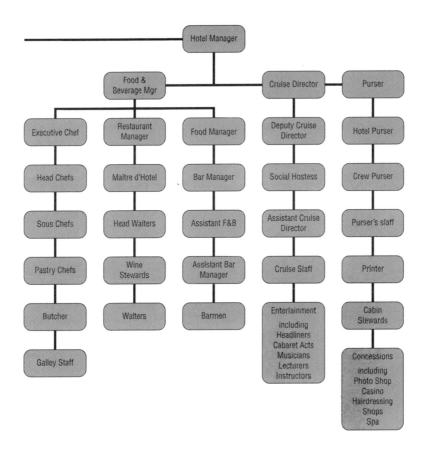

sionally, Greek. These countries have a long-standing and high reputation for their rigorous nautical training and licensing, and their nationals are to be found at the helm of most cruise ships. The captain has ultimate responsibility for the ship and all who sail therein. 'P&O Captains', observed one early traveller, 'derived their authority from God and the P&O Board, especially the Former' (quoted in Rabson & O'Donoghue 1988, p. 173). The captain implements company policies and procedures and ensures compliance with all international and national maritime laws and regulations. His principal duty of care concerns the safety of everyone on board. He is assisted particularly by the staff captain, chief engineer and the hotel manager/chief purser. Also present at daily meetings of this team is the cruise director, a senior ranking officer on most

Table 3.1   Typical crew profile of a large ship

Baggage Master	1	Deck Stewards	3	Night Stewards	6
Barkeepers	17	Deck Supervisors	5	Nursery Attendants	2
Bedroom Stewards	69	Disc Jockey	1	Nursing Sisters	3
Bell Boy	2	Dispenser	1	Personnel Manager	1
Bosun	1	Doctors	2	Photographers	4
Bosun's Mate	1	Engineering/Electrical		Physiotherapist	1
Captain	1	Officers	26	Priest, Rabbi, Reverend	3
Casino Staff	16	Engineering/Electrical		Printers	3
Chefs de Cuisine	5	Ratings	51	Public Room Staff	36
Chefs	101	Entertainers	5	Purser	1
Chief Engineer	1	Executive Chef	1	Receptionists	13
Chief Maintenance		Florists	1	Safety/Security Officer	1
Mechanic	1	Furnishing Manager	1	Shop Staff	18
Cocktail Pianist	2	Furnishing Team	6	Staff Bedroom Stewards	2
Commis Waiters	13	Gentlemen Hosts	6	Staff Captain	1
Crew Administrative		Hospital Attendants	2	Staff Chief Engineer	1
Assistant	1	Hotel Manager	1	Steiners Salon/Spa Staff	20
Crew Supervisor	1	Hotel/Kitchen Officers	48	Storekeepers	5
Crew Purser	1	Hotel Utility Staff	151	Tech. Stores Data Clerk	1
Cruise Sales	2	Laundrymen	17	Telephonist	1
Cruise Director	1	Librarians	2	Travel & Tour Staff	4
Cruise Staff	9	Lido Supervisor	1	Television Station	
Dancers	10	Linen-keeper	1	Manager	1
Data Input Clerks	1	MAN Engine Technicians	3	Waiters	170
Deck Officers	10	Master at Arms	8	Wine Stewards	21
Deck Ratings	30	Musicians	23		

Source: Daily Program *QE2*, 8 March 2002.

cruise ships, who brings up any issues directly concerning the smooth operations of passenger care on board. Items on a long list of essential skills that one cruise line lists in the job description for a captain (cited Dickinson & Vladimir 1997, pp. 72–3) read as follows:

> The Captain shall have a thorough knowledge of the ship, including the construction, safety equipment, stability characteristics, ship handling procedures, and emergency procedures. He shall ensure that his officers have the same knowledge in their area of responsibility. He shall ensure that the ship's maintenance program meets or exceeds that required by the Company and the authorities.

The buck stops at the captain. Dickinson and Vladimir state that 'a ship is a paramilitary organisation, in which officers wear uniforms, and regulations, laws, rank, and discipline play a prominent role in the way things get done' (1997, p. 73). Strict adherence to rules and discipline, they claim, can have both advantages and disadvantages in the service industry where customer satisfaction is everything. But ultimately, unless the safety and smooth operations of something as complex as a cruise ship can be assured by staff maintaining strong codes of practice, conformity and consistency in every aspect of their work and life on board, a quality customer experience cannot be guaranteed. While the association with a paramilitary organisation may be regarded as unfortunate, it helps to remind one not only of the necessary link between cruise ships and maritime traditions generally but also of the degree of efficiency and security required for even a recreational operation on such a scale.

A good captain takes the time to walk about his ship under the principle of 'management by walking around' (or 'management by being visible'). Passengers enjoy recognising the captain and saying 'Hello' (or something like: 'If you're here, who's steering this thing?') to a captain and if possible to shake his hand. A photograph with the captain is a valued souvenir. In the earlier days of passenger shipping the captain's table was always the central focus of the dining room, and an invitation to dine at his table was highly prized. On a modern cruise ship the captain may enter the main dining room and sit at his designated table only occasionally. But every passenger gets the opportunity to meet the captain at the traditional welcome and farewell cocktail parties which he hosts on every ship. These are formal occasions where the officers appear resplendent in their uniforms—white for summer, black or navy for winter; female guests shimmer and shine in their best evening clothes; and male guests resemble waiters in their dinner suits—except for the occasional Scot in full clan regalia or the well-to-do Indian or Chinese wearing a custom-tailored version of traditional garb. The captain's handshake is well orchestrated by members of the entertainment staff, who introduce each guest for a 10-second chat and the obligatory photograph. We have noticed, after shaking the hands of many captains, that they are trained in a skill which enables them to shake a hand, say something friendly and move the guest on in one single, unbroken movement. Politicians and royal families, to both of whom ships' captains affect some resemblance, evidently learn the same technique.

At the welcome cocktail party the captain introduces his senior staff from both ship and hotel operations. The staff captain, chief engineer, doctor, chief purser, hotel manager, entertainment director, and food and beverage manager are key figures on board. The staff captain is second in command to the captain and his principal responsibilities include safety, security, communication and normal discipline. The first two areas are of extreme importance. All crew members—from both hotel and ship operations—are trained in fire fighting and basic first aid. A fire at sea is to be avoided at all costs, and both regular and 'surprise' emergency drills—the latter mainly for crew—are held on all ships throughout any cruise. While some passengers occasionally express annoyance at the very minor inconvenience caused by safety drills, they should be comforted by the fact that the ship's company is taking every possible precaution to avoid any real hazardous incident. Security is paramount. Where once the prospect of piracy or hijacking of a cruise liner was fairly remote, the hijacking of *Achille Lauro* off the coast of Egypt in October 1985, the events of 11 September 2001, and the threats and fears that followed have changed that. Constant situation appraisal and vigilance at all levels is of the highest priority. Unauthorised visitors have not been permitted for many years, and electronically scanned identification is carried by both passengers and crew.

In the earlier days of cruising, before the introduction of a specific position for cruise or entertainment director in the 1970s, the staff captain was assigned this responsibility. A P&O regulations guide of 1952 (P&O 1952, p. 12) specifically states that this person is expected to devote himself primarily to the entertainment of passengers and to ensure that all departments on board fully cooperate to this end:

> The entertainment of passengers is no light or easy duty, but if it is tackled energetically and with system, it can make a very great difference to the enjoyment of a voyage ... Enthusiasm is a necessary ingredient for successful entertainment of passengers. Like boredom, it is catching.

The manual goes on to endorse the value of deck games, cinema, dancing, (indoor) racing games, light orchestral music, tours of the ship, and talks or performances given by other passengers with some expertise. A glance at the ship's daily program in Table 3.2 confirms that the basic ingredients of cruise entertainment have remained much the same; only the level of sophistication has changed.

Another important area of safety and care lies with the medical staff. One study (*Conde Nast Traveller* 1994, cited in Dickinson & Vladimir 1997) found that the two most important determinants of the level of health services offered on board were the distance that the vessel was likely to be from ports where passengers could be evacuated and the age profile of the passengers. According to the first criterion, ships running short trips out of Miami to the Caribbean would not feel the same obligation to provide extensive facilities as those on longer voyages into the South Pacific or through the scattered archipelagos of South-East Asia. For the latter, a ship that is popular with older passengers, who usually take longer cruises, will provide a more comprehensive range of possible medical services for the clientele. Medical staffs, however, are responsible for crew health issues as well as those of passengers. They must deal with the burns, bruises, cuts and broken bones caused by work accidents as well as the inevitable seasickness and coughs and colds that passengers

Table 3.2   Today at a Glance (on *Pacific Sky*)

8:30am	Walk a mile	Jogging track
9:00 am	Yoga	Show lounge
9:00 am	Tour desk open	Caribe deck foyer
9:15 am	Hi-lo aerobics	Riviera deck aft
9:30 am	Jigsaw enthusiasts	Library
10:am	Fun trivia quiz	Show lounge
	The card area is set up each day to play	Card room
	T-shirt painting	Lido deck port side
11:00 am	Funky jazz class	Show lounge
	Library open	Library, Deck 9
	Table tennis	Lido deck starboard side
	Cards, cards, cards	Card room
	ABT & stretch	Riviera deck aft
	Earring making	Rainbow bar
11:30 am	Beer quoits	Promenade deck aft
12 noon	Show lounge	Closed for rehearsals
2:00 pm	Aqua hut open	Lido deck aft
	Informative port talk	Show lounge
	Scrabble fun time	Card room Deck 9
2:30 pm	Golf classic Part 1	Prom. deck aft, pool
	T-shirt painting	Lido deck port side
	Two-up	Horizon lounge
2:45 pm	Registration for marriage match	Show lounge bar area
3:00 pm	Kids' fancy dress parade	Legends sports bar
	Marriage match	Show lounge
	Shuffleboard	Promenade deck fwd
3:30 pm	Library open	Riviera deck
4:00 pm	Snowball jackpot bingo	Show lounge
	Tummy, hips & thighs	Riviera deck aft
4:45 pm	Show lounge and legends sports bar	
	Closed in preparation for tonight's cocktails	
5:00 pm	Sunset stroll	Jogging track
5:30 pm	1st sitting welcome cocktail party	Show lounge and Legends
	Bliss (pop group)	sports bar
	Jesse Banez (pianist)	Veranda lounge
8:45 pm	1st sitting show	Show lounge
9:15 pm	Bliss (pop group)	Veranda lounge
	Favourite video hits	Legends sports bar
	Jesse Banez (pianist)	Horizon lounge
9:30 pm	Dancing under the mirrored ball	Show lounge
10:15 pm	2nd sitting show	Show lounge
11:00 pm	Late night karaoke	Promenade deck aft
	Disco	Starlight lounge

Source: *Sky Daily*, Monday 13 August 2001.

acquire. Too-frequent visits to the ship's doctor by passengers are kept in check by the formidable fees normally applied.

The chief engineer is responsible for the extremely complex machinery and technologies which run a modern cruise ship. Diesel engines, electrical generators, heating, cooling and desalinisation plants, sewage disposal, plumbing and electrical systems, and the computers to control a complex web of operations all come under his command. The isolation from supplies and services means that the engineer and his team have to be prepared for any situation with backup services and replacement parts for any possible contingency. A failure of the electrical system—hence, the air-conditioning and other essential requirements—is a very serious problem indeed, but by no means unknown. The chief engineer reports directly to the captain.

Hotel operations

Of the department managers, the hotel manager has the largest number of staff under his/her command. On some ships this person is still called the chief purser, but as the demands and complexities of ensuring a quality experience for the paying passenger have increased with the new 'floating resort' style of vessel, this role has been separated into two areas of responsibility. Thus a chief purser is 'banker, information officer and complaint handler, and is responsible for clearing the ship through foreign ports' (Dickinson & Vladimir 1997, p. 83), while the hotel manager's job incorporates food and beverage management, hotel operations, entertainment, passenger services such as shops and salons, and the casino. There are also managers who lead each of these specialty departments. Increasingly, ship hotel managers are expected to have extensive experience, training and formal qualifications in land-based hotel operations.

The first contact most passengers have with the hotel operations side is at the purser's office (see above). Positions within this sector are often held by Americans, Australians, British and various European nationalities. Passenger requirements usually mean that the staff here need to be able to communicate in several languages and, as with hotel reception desks everywhere, they need to know how to deal with myriad complaints. The position which has evolved most specifically for the cruise market is that of cruise director. So important are cruise directors in ensuring an enjoyable experience for all on board that they are part of the ship's senior management team together with the captain and his most senior officers in both hotel and ship operations. The skills and personalities of these individuals can make or break the cruise experience for many. They have a permanent dedicated entertainment staff, which can include musicians, youth activity officers, sports managers, shore excursion planners, television station operators and social hosts and hostesses, all of whom are answerable to the cruise director. On the post-Panama ships this can number up to 75 people. They may also have a variable number of people who join the ship on shorter, casual contracts, such as guest performers and enrichment lecturers. They even oversee the staging requirements for the many big-name performers who are engaged as headliners for many short cruises—people who can be very demanding in their expectations. Film and stage actors, opera singers and cabaret artists regularly appear at sea, filling a variety of roles. Considerable status may be achieved by passengers being able to tell their friends that on their last cruise they played bridge with film star and internationally renowned bridge player Omar Sharif, for example. Thus, human resource management skills are a high priority. Some possess the ability to make every passenger feel as though the cruise director knows them personally. This is no mean achievement, and is by no means achieved by a majority. In a four-month contract they may greet some 32 000 new faces (2000 passengers per seven-day cruise multiplied by 16 weeks). The cruise director may work an 18-hour day and is always the last person in the department to retire after a late-night turn through all the entertainment venues on the ship to make sure that programs have run smoothly. Many have extensive entertainment backgrounds as performers and/or entrepreneurs. Others come into the position after working as a ship's purser or in land-based resorts. Some eventually move into senior management positions in the head office.

4

Rank and file

Waters (1995, p. 3) defines globalisation as 'a social process in which the constraints of geography on social and cultural arrangements recede and in which people become increasingly aware that they are receding'. Cruise ship operations, according to Wood (2000 p. 350), present an excellent opportunity to study the concept of globalisation:

> Its distinctive characteristics of sea-based mobility has enabled it to participate fully in the processes of globalization, however, and because of this one can see in cruise sector tourism both potential future trends in tourism generally and some of the complex ways globalization plays itself out. This development offers a particularly clear and extreme manifestation of/or [sic] how global economic restructuring both reflects and promotes new forms of the 'deterritorialization' of capital, labour, and touristic place itself.

One of the most distinctive characteristics defining globalisation of cruise ship employment is the use of flags of convenience (FOCs) to bypass the labour laws and taxes of the countries where ships are home-ported. They also assist ship owners to avoid stringent safety regulations which many countries demand. The increasing number of environmental disasters caused by unsafe ships, particularly oil carriers, is bringing this sorry situation increasingly to world attention. Studies cited by the US Department of Transportation (c.2000, pp. 4–29) have found that ships bearing a flag of convenience are more likely to suffer from poor material condition, lack of maintenance, inadequately trained crews and more frequent casualties. The European Union and other countries such as the United States and Australia have launched initiatives such as the Port State Control (PSC) to force substandard ships out of trade, and in 1999 the United Kingdom revised its tax laws affecting shipping in order to encourage British ship owners and others to transfer their registrations. In the main these comments refer to the state of merchant ships.

Although the majority of the world's cruise ships are based in the United States, none of the large liners fly the American flag, for example, although this may be changing. Crews on ships flying flags of convenience are subject to the labour laws of that country and not those of the country in which the actual employer is located or those of their own country of origin. It is acknowledged that companies register in countries where laws protecting the rights and working conditions of workers are practically non-existent and, as Wood (2000) points out, if the laws that do exist do not suit company operations, companies have the influence to cause change. Wood's example of this power is when cruise companies realised that the labour laws of Panama, a popular flag of convenience, guaranteed workers one day off a week, they successfully lobbied for an exemption.

A 2002 study entitled *What it's really like to work on board cruise ships* by the International Transport Workers Federation (ITWU) and the organisation War on Want (cited in Wazir & Mathiason 2002) claims that many of the 150 000 global cruise ship workers suffer sweatshop working practices, poor living conditions and intimidation from their superiors if they complain. 'If you look at the inequality of the world, then it is mirrored through the decks of a cruise ship', said Celia Mather, the author of the report (cited in Wazir & Mathiason 2002). Many workers, particularly from developing countries, are sold a vision of a luxurious and glamorous career that would allow them to see the world in style. Staffs are often tied to contracts of six to eight months. They sleep in cramped, noisy cabins. In comparison to that of the passengers, their food is poor—usually eaten in a crew canteen. An authoritarian management code often ensures an abrupt dismissal for breaching regulations concerning dress codes and contact with passengers.

The report indicates that, technically, cruise ship workers have even more explicit international protection than do workers in many other sectors of the global economy. As well as rights enshrined in international law, such as freedom of association and collective bargaining, seafarers are specifically covered by International Labour Organisation and International Maritime Organisation conventions on minimum standards on board ships, including regulations on hours of work and crewing levels needed to maintain safety standards (<www.waronwant.org/?lid=2860>). Port authorities, the authors say, are given unprecedented powers to detain substandard vessels. However, the problem is one of enforcement. The bodies issuing international regulations all too often seem powerless in the face of the companies they are supposed to regulate—rather, one might observe, like the apparent powerlessness of the United Nations in dealing with rogue states. The report criticises the flags of convenience system, adding that since World War II it can be seen as a forerunner of the 'runaway' subcontracting practices of globalisation so eagerly taken up by manufacturing industries in more recent decades. The International Transport Workers Federation has been campaigning for over 50 years against flags of convenience and the substandard shipping that the FOC system encourages.

There is certainly evidence to support claims of inequality in cruise ship employment, and the ITWF claims that cruise employees, whether in the hotel/catering or deck/engine departments, experience some, if not all of the following conditions.

1. insecure, short-term contracts;

2. low wages and high costs, including illegal agents' fees to get the job;

3. extremely long working hours and high work intensity, leading to fatigue;

4. poor management practices, including bullying and favouritism, plus racial and gender discrimination;

5. high labour turnover, fatigue and inadequate training, giving cause for concern about safety;

6. employers who are hostile or resistant to trade union organisation and collective bargaining.

(cited in <www.waronwant.org/?lid=2860>)

We would not dispute most of these claims but would offer some additional information, derived from long familiarity with cruise ships and personal communication with staff at all levels, which might help give an added perspective.

Item 1

Item 1 refers to insecure, short-term contracts. These contracts vary generally from four to ten months, depending on a whole range of factors including classification of the position, responsibilities and cultural background of the employee. Workers from highly industrialised Western nations have many decades of strong unionisation and of individualism as opposed to collectivism influencing their expectations in a workplace. They secure the shorter contracts. Many young Westerners who eagerly sign up to 'see the world' find themselves unable to adapt to four or six months of seven-day working weeks in broken and long shifts. They are happy to get off when their first contract ends. Conversely, many sign up for as many repeat contracts as they can obtain. They get, even if briefly, glimpses of many parts of the world. They make sure they exploit their 'living expense free' environment and save for a particular goal.

For the majority of workers from less developed and emerging nations where unemployment is very high and living conditions often substandard, a ten-month contract for steady work is highly desirable. These workers often react in the same way as Westerners: they either hate it or accept it and try to turn it to their advantage. There are many workers on ships who have successful small business ventures funded by their earnings or who are getting better education opportunities for their families. Their numbers include not only unskilled or blue-collar workers but also educated and trained professionals such as teachers who can earn better money at sea as stewards. They certainly find the long contracts hard to bear but they are able to balance the absences from home with the financial outcomes.

Wood (2000, p. 353) uses the terms 'clear ethnic caste', 'horizontal and vertical lines of ethnic stratification', 'ethnoscape' and 'institutional racism' in his discussion of a cruise ship labour force. There is a certain naiveté in all this, obscured to some extent by the jargon, and an apparent ignorance of the history of both merchant shipping and hotel/resort operations. Certain nationalities are favoured by different companies as suitable employees in specific areas, and Landon (1997, cited by Wood 2000, p. 353) claims that a common mistake made by many Europeans is to apply for a job that is traditionally held by someone from a Third World country. It should be pointed out, however, that Landon has a cruise employment site on the Internet, and is offering his observation not as criticism, as is implied in the context of Wood's article, but as advice to prospective applicants.

This ethnic division is not a recent phenomenon but rather a practice of long standing in the cruise world. Since 1842 P&O has employed Asians in a variety of areas on its ships. On deck were Lascars from the Malabar Coast, mainly Hindu; Indian Moslems (later from Pakistan) were in the engine room; and Roman Catholic Goans worked in the purser's department and dining rooms (French 1995). While this may be regarded simply as another example of the 'divide and rule' policy of the Raj, the fact remains that this preferential employment provided an income for thousands of Indian workers through the years. The British India Steam Navigation Company—later in its history a subsidiary of P&O—made a policy of training Anglo-Indians for its junior officer ranks. P&O issued guides to its officers detailing how to deal with Asian crews—specifically Indians, Pakistanis, Goans and Chinese (e.g. P&O c.1967). The publications outlined religious acknowledgements and dietary requirements for each group as well as employment and pay specifications. They stressed the need to ensure that the proper respect was given to status and hierarchies within each culture, particularly as it applied to team leaders in work groups, and that every effort should be made to ensure that the Asian custom of 'saving face' was facilitated.

As historians we think it valuable to show continuity in this context within cruise ship behaviour, whether by crew or passengers. The P&O officers' manual has a delightful illustration of this in a description of how relief crews were positioned in India. Because at that time ships rarely docked at Bombay (now Mumbai), crews had to travel between Bombay and Colombo, a journey of some seven days by train and ferry. 'One of the problems associated with these journeys', states the manual, 'is the carriage of the large quantities of assorted gear, including sewing machines and bicycles, which Indian crew always manage to accumulate during their service abroad' (P&O c.1967, p. 3). An observant person on a 21st century cruise ship watching a crew change in port would be amazed at the personal accumulations of crew, especially in a port which is home for the crew members. The opportunity to purchase and transport goods which are either scarce or have great resale value within their own countries is evidently irresistible, and huge boxes of such items are trundled down crew gangplanks. Management is not unaware of this. During a cruise which included a call in Ho Chi Minh City, Vietnam, before arriving in Manila in the Philippines, Filipino crew about to sign off purchased huge quantities of ceramic elephants, vases, inlaid wall plaques and lacquer ware. When the ship sailed from Manila that evening, the captain commented on how much higher the hull was riding in the water now that all the trade goods had been off-loaded. This behaviour is not restricted to any one ethnic group. The goods accumulated, however, are those that have meaning or status within each society. Westerners are inclined to purchase the latest developments in audio and visual technology that are often available elsewhere before they are at home, while people from developing and emerging nations are more inclined towards tradable items from which they may eventually profit. Table 4.1 shows the diversity of crew nationalities on a Star Cruises ship in 2001, while our experiences on other ships have shown that they can have more than 30 nationalities represented on any one voyage.

Table 4.1   Nationalities of crew on *SuperStar Virgo*, November 2001

Nationality	Number
Philippines	520
Chinese from People's Republic of China	255
Indonesian	114
Malaysian	105
Thailand	68
Romanian	46
Swedish	25
Vietnamese	23

Source: Hotel manager, *SuperStar Virgo*.

An observant person on any cruise ship will very quickly be able to see 'who works where'. The various groups (officers, ship/technical and hotel) and subgroups within these will have their own designated quarters, kitchens and specific rules about the degree of interaction they are allowed with paying passengers as well as accessibility to public areas. For the majority of crew, interaction is very strictly controlled and, as indicated elsewhere, a ship can be described as two parallel worlds within a single hull. These worlds meet but rarely cross over. We suggest that a whole range of conditions and influences need to be examined to assist in understanding the situation.

Item 2

Item 2 refers to low wages and high costs, including illegal agents' fees to get the job. Cruise companies are usually reluctant to reveal the wage structures they use for a variety of reasons. Undoubtedly, wages for many categories of workers on ships are extremely low. Prager, in an article in the *Wall Street Journal* (1997, cited in Wood 2000), points out that however low the wages appear, they are usually much, much higher than the crew members could earn in their own country. A base rate for a room steward or waiter can be US$50 per month. These are people who have direct contact with passengers and for whom anticipated gratuities in a range of between US$1000 and US$2000 per month are considered the real substance of their earnings. When Americans made up 80 per cent of the cruise market (as they did until the mid-1990s) these employees could expect gratuities to be paid in the amounts promised, as tipping was a way of life for the majority of the passengers. Cruise companies provide clear guidelines to passengers as to how much should be paid to the appropriate person, per day per passenger. Commonly, it is paid at the end of the cruise. This information is received by passengers both in print and at verbal advisory sessions.

A dilemma has arisen, however, with a change in the balance of nationalities taking cruises. British, European and Australasian passengers are generally reluctant to 'pay the wages' of the crew on top of the cost of their holiday. They choose to offer gratuities at their own discretion for particular services rendered and often this falls a long way short of the amount a crew member anticipates. We have witnessed Italian waiters tossing back onto the dining table the little white envelope containing a passenger's gratuity. 'What is this? How you expect me to live? I have a wife and four children to support!', one remarked haughtily to the astounded passenger. Some people pocket their offering with an equally rude remark to the waiter; others are intimidated by the experience and fumble in their wallets to find additional notes, while mumbling apologies and 'I didn't know . . .'. A considerable time ago bar staff and drink waiters, feeling that their gratuities were not commensurate with the service they provided or were inconsistent, lobbied successfully to have a mandatory 15 per cent 'tip' added to the tab of every customer.

Some companies have tried to overcome these prospects by factoring the gratuities into the overall cost of the cruise and then using this as an advertising ploy with hooks such as 'No tipping onboard' or 'All gratuities included in price'. Others inform passengers that the estimated amount of gratuities for the days on board will be automatically charged to the passenger's account at the end of the cruise. Norwegian Cruise Line (NCL), having been rescued from impending oblivion by Star Cruises in 2000, is now experiencing a period of regrowth and is one such company. Its policy on tipping reads: 'For your convenience, NCL now automatically applies a service charge to your shipboard account: $10 per guest per day for guests age 13 and above, $5 per day for children age 3–12 and no charge for children under the age of three. All of the service personnel on board receive gratuities from this service' (<www.ncl.com/more/fp>). NCL's adoptive parent, Star Cruises, however, informs its passengers that 'Tipping is not encouraged' (e.g. Star Cruises 1999, p. 33).

We have seen passengers objecting strongly to the practice of obligatory 'gratuities' also. 'How can something which dictionaries define as a "small gift for services rendered" become a compulsory payment?' one unimpressed couple demanded of harassed staff at the purser's desk. 'We will decide who gets that small gift!' Some cruise lines have chosen to ignore the problem in the hope it will sort itself out. But the issue of gratuities certainly contributed to the demise of a cruise venture undertaken by Cunard, Australia in 1994. The company positioned a ship, *Crown Monarch*, in Australia in an attempt to break the virtual monopoly on cruising out of Australia into the South Pacific and South-East Asia held by P&O Australia. Among the challenges faced was the issue of gratuities supplementing wages. The passengers were mainly Australians and New Zealanders, neither of whose countries has a tipping culture. Consequently, Cunard found itself in a situation where crew members were choosing to break their contracts and/or requesting transfer to other ships because they were not receiving enough money. Other crew were refusing to take positions on this ship when the situation was passed along by word of mouth. The venture was unsuccessful, as we have detailed elsewhere (Douglas & Douglas 2001).

Most cruise companies operate through recruiting agents these days but this is no different from many other private sector and even some public sector enterprises. Even universities use agents to recruit full-fee-paying foreign students. It is unfortunate, to say the very least, that there are unscrupulous people operating on the fringes of this type of enterprise but, as long as there are people who will take almost any risk to escape the poverty/unemployment cycle, predators will continue to trap their prey. It is obviously in the interests of the companies and the employees that both parties check the credentials and terms of any recruitment agency. Company websites often direct hopeful employees to their preferred agencies. The complexity of the issue of overseas employment is illustrated in the example presented by the Philippines. Millions of Philippines citizens choose to work elsewhere, particularly within Asia and the Middle East, where they earn money to send back to their families. Remittance monies are the backbone of the economy. In 2001 remittances totalled US$5.56 billion, but by mid-2002 reports were indicating a 43 per cent surge: in the period January to June they had already sent home US$4.14 billion. Foreign exchange inflow from overseas workers contributes about 85 per cent of the gross foreign exchange earnings of the country and is seen as way to boost the peso and the overall economy. Thus the government agency Philippine Overseas Employment Administration (POEA) actively markets the labour pool internationally, citing their citizens' knowledge of English, reliability and cultural adaptability as major assets. The statistics from the Central Bank of the Philippines (Table 4.2) indicate that some 12 per cent of overseas workers are sea-based (including merchant shipping). About 205 000 are in the cruise sector. In the five months from January to May 2001, these cruise employees sent US$415 million back to the Philippines. They are the backbone of the cruise labour pool. A further indication of their perceived value is the establishment of a New Heroes bond specifically for people working overseas in which they can invest increments of US$100 for three to five year periods. These migrant savings, in turn, are directed to housing and other development projects across the country.

Table 4.2   Overseas Filipinos' remittances
(By country of origin and by type of worker: January to
October, 1999 to 2001, in thousand US dollars)

Type of worker				% change	
	2001	2000	1999	2001–2000	2000–1999
Land-based	3 944 460	4 347 671	5 164 254	(9.3)	(15.8)
Sea-based	893 453	754 049	692 245	18.5	8.9
TOTAL	4 837 913	5 101 720	5 856 499	(5.2)	(12.9)

Source: Central Bank of the Philippines.

However, while POEA (it deploys some 30 per cent of the sea-based workforce) and the Department of Labour and Employment attempt to regulate recruitment and conditions, examples of excessive fees and exploitation by private agencies persist.

Item 3

Item 3 refers to extremely long working hours and high work intensity, leading to fatigue. This sounds a reasonable comment to make. However, it is worth considering two very influential factors: the nature of a ship and the hospitality sector overall. The first factor obviously severely limits available space. To allow for what might be considered a better balance between work and free time, ships would need to accommodate twice as many employees as the general ratio of one crew member per two passengers currently established. Similar claims could be made by any worker in a contained and isolated environment including mining camps, island resorts and oil rigs. Secondly, the hospitality sector by its very nature is one of long hours, erratic shifts and high intensity, as any employee in a resort, restaurant, theme park or hotel would attest.

Items 4, 5 and 6

These items refer to poor management practices, including bullying and favouritism, plus racial and gender discrimination; high labour turnover, fatigue and inadequate training, giving cause for concern about safety; and employers who are hostile or resistant to trade union organisation and collective bargaining. Is there a workplace anywhere which has not had similar complaints laid against it? Again, we are not condoning the practices but indicating that they are not exclusive to the cruise business.

One further claim by Wazir and Mathiason (2002) is that workers are not allowed to 'mingle with their wealthy guests' or use passenger-allocated public areas. For the majority of crew this is quite true, if somewhat ingenuous. They have their own designated living and recreational quarters, just as staff do on isolated or island resorts. How many waiters, kitchen hands or room attendants have the above writers seen mixing freely with guests at large resorts elsewhere? However, certain staff, including photographers, entertainers, health-club personnel, hairdressers and casino employees, are permitted limited access to passenger areas. For example, they may use the deck buffet facilities at lunch but generally only in the last half-hour of serving. It is probably in this area that issues of discrimination are most often cited. We propose that this situation could be looked at from another perspective. In a high-intensity service environment such as a cruise ship, it may well be to the advantage of employees to have their own spaces where they can relax without scrutiny. Staff who do use some passenger spaces report that they feel that they are constantly on call or seem to be still working because they must follow strict rules on behaviour and appearance. There is no separation of work and relaxation environments. A further point is that passengers are forbidden from entering crew spaces unless with specific invitations and permissions from management. This is part of the maintenance of those 'floating parallel worlds', although some passengers, notably American female travel agents on familiarisation trips, seem to find the crew bar endlessly fascinating. It should also be pointed out that many short-term contract staff, usually in the broad 'entertainment' category, have passenger status, and are allowed use of all facilities.

Despite the widely published negative aspects, employment on cruise ships is likely to continue with strong growth and demand well into the 21st century. Increased scrutiny of terms and conditions will no doubt reveal examples of exploitation and abuse, but for the majority of people who choose to go to sea it will be a profitable and interesting experience which some will choose to develop into a lifetime career and others will use as a transitional or learning experience.

IMPORTANT! QUICK FACTS!

Any nationalities can work in the cruise industry!
100s of contracts become available on weekly basis!
Cruise companies are recruiting every day of the week!
Average contract is 6 to 9 months!
Earn up to US$4500 per month!

So reads part of the main page of Cruise Line Resources Pty Ltd, a Brisbane-based organisation. It also promises 'free accommodation and board', 'tax-free earnings' and (the ultimate teaser) 'see the world for free' to the successful applicant. The serious business begins with the applicant sending A\$59.95 for the *Cruise Employment Guide* and a 'free video' showing life on board a cruise ship. As evidence of its bona fides the company issues a disclaimer: 'We are not an employment agency . . . No promise or inducement is made to the successful procurement of employment in any cruise company . . .'. It also offers a '100% money back guarantee if materials are returned together with five letters of refusal from cruise companies or concessionaires' (<www.cruisecrew.com>).

There are many organisations which offer assistance with cruise ship employment. This example is representative. An Internet search engine will locate hundreds of related pages, and some cautionary sifting through the offerings is required. What emerges in a review of these sites is that many people are making money selling publications on how to get a job in the cruise business rather than providing an actual employment service. Very few, perhaps most notably <cruises.about.com/cs/cruise-jobs/>, managed by Linda Garrison, identify the drawbacks associated with this kind of work and acknowledge the less appealing aspects. Some are purely and simply scams. One such was reported by the *East African*, a Nairobi-based newspaper, in February 2003. It concerns an advertisement placed by one M. Arnoldus, of Sea Cruise Enterprises, and reads in part (<www.eastafrican.com>19 February 2003):

> The East African has learnt that many seafarers from Brunei, India, Saudi Arabia, Kenya, Tanzania, Liberia and South Africa have been cheated out of their money on being promised a tax-free income of over \$2000 per month, free food and a paid vacation. In press ads, job seekers are asked to fill up evaluation forms and send them to an address in Canada with an evaluation fee of \$69. The company then replies to paying applicants, regretting that they were not qualified.

The language of the advertisement, it will be noted, is already reasonably familiar from the example above, although no connection between them is suggested here. It may be useful to point out that almost everything one would need to know is available free of charge in the public domain of the Internet, although caution should be applied, as indeed it must with a great deal of information on the Internet. Individuals need to make their own decisions about how much money they need to outlay for this sort of advice. All major cruise companies have comprehensive and informative websites through which prospective employees can apply directly, either to a company's personnel department or to its own authorised agency.

5

A day in the life
of a passenger

Activities

One of the hurdles that cruise companies have worked hard to overcome is the perception, long held by many people, that 'There is nothing to do on a ship . . . I'll be bored'. Nothing could be further from the truth. A day at sea can be as busy or as boring as individuals choose to make it. When passengers return to their suites last thing in the evening, they find their bed nicely turned down, a chocolate on the pillow and, perhaps most importantly of all, a copy of the activities on board for the following day. Some read the program immediately, carefully marking what they intend to do. Others pore over it with their first cup of coffee of the day. However it is first consulted, it regularly appears out of handbags and back pockets throughout the day as people remind themselves where they should be or where they want to be.

Daily cruise life starts with tea/coffee either by room service or on deck. Before breakfast one can 'walk-a-mile' in the fresh air or join a stretch exercise class with a fitness instructor. Breakfast can be taken buffet style or in the formal dining room—or both, for those determined to get their money's worth. Organised mid-morning activities can include another fitness class, computer class, language group, beginners' bridge class, or a special-interest group such as gardening enthusiasts or needle-work. Specialist lecturers might be speaking on such topics as navigation by the stars, how to invest your money, or the history and culture of the next port of call. There may also be a presentation on the tours available in the next port of call. Cruise lines offer a variety of shore tours of differing degrees of energy level and length. Places are limited, and the necessity for the shore tour operators to make advanced reservations means that passengers must make their choices as far in advance as possible. For the passenger who does not want to join planned activities, the options to occupy the morning can include lying in the sun by the pool; sitting in a quiet corner reading; browsing in the library or through the shops; doing a self-directed gym program and workout; playing volleyball, shuffleboard, deck quoits or tennis; practising golf swings; or having a massage or other health or beauty therapy. Many people choose this time to do their laundry if they do not want to use the ship's fee-for-service laundry. A ship's self-service laundry is the place to meet people, catch up on some gossip and share some experiences from the last port of call. Others may choose to do absolutely nothing. There is something remarkably soothing about sitting on deck gazing out on a calm sea. In the tropics flying fish frequently break the water's surface. Dolphins may race alongside for a while. A whale may breach. In busy shipping lanes other ships pass by: cruise ships passing invariably salute each other with a blast from the ship's whistle. Nearer to land birds sometimes alight on the rails or swoop by, examining the ship. In many parts of the world small local fishing vessels always attract attention. Through his makeshift loudhailer we heard a Vietnamese fisherman call: 'Welcome to Vietnam, American boat people' as Princess Cruises' *Island Princess* made its first journey up the Saigon River in the early 1990s.

At noon the ship's bell rings and the officer of the watch reports on distance sailed since noon the previous day and any items of particular interest in the progress of the ship. A shipboard tradition related to these announcements is the cash prize offered in the daily tote. Last guesses and bets on how many nautical miles the ship has sailed since noon the previous day can be placed at 11:45 am. This is a longstanding tradition at sea, and was once a rare opportunity to place a legitimate bet on board a ship.

The noon bell also signals that it is time to eat, and the choices are deck buffet or formal. For many people the dress code required for the dining room—no singlets or bathing suits, for example—means that they choose to stay informal and to eat buffet style. On the other hand, many people enjoy the choices, service and style offered in the dining rooms. This is part of their holiday experience; they can eat at a buffet any day at home. Organised afternoon activities are generally less strenuous. A card game, usually bridge, another informative lecture, a first release movie or a dance class might be the choices offered. The computer rooms are busy with parents contacting children. (As an easy and swift means of communication, the Internet is challenging the postcard and the very expensive ship-to-shore phone call.) The hairdressers are busy repairing the damage of sun and wind and sea spray. Some ships offer afternoon concerts as a pleasant diversion. On many ships the afternoon bingo session is exceptionally popular, obliterating attendance at most other activities, with the stakes getting higher as the cruise proceeds. For many, afternoons at sea are a time for siesta. In 1877 the *British Medical Journal* espoused the therapeutic benefits of sea air, an endorsement that is held to have stimulated interest in the then novel activity, and certainly any cruiser is likely to acknowledge how well one sleeps at sea. Whether it is the properties of the sea air or the effect of the ship's gentle movement which can make it seem like a big cradle, sleep comes quite easily for most—weather, of course, permitting.

By 6 pm preparation for the evening's events are under way. Dress codes become more formal. Cocktail music plays in various bars and lounges; hors d'oeuvres are served with drinks; and somewhere there will be music to dance by. People emerge from their cabins and suites dressed for dinner and a show, and looking relaxed after a day at sea. The dining rooms are busy in the evening—the menu choices and service are generally preferred over informal options. After dinner is show time, with two performances for each of 1st and 2nd sitting diners. Beautifully appointed lounges or show theatres are the venues for expertly designed and produced Broadway shows or musical performances, many of them necessarily adapted in length or spatial requirements to suit the venue. Professional performers, excellent costumes, well-rehearsed dance routines and music entertain the crowd. After the finale they shuffle out to other diversions such as the casino, dancing, the nightclub or, amazingly, since many may have finished dinner only a couple of hours earlier, to the traditional midnight buffet. Some may even go to bed. Before they turn out the light, it is probable that the last thing they do is to read the daily program in preparation for another day at sea. A cruise ship holiday can be an active and learning experience or it can be as casually relaxing as one needs. Table 3.2 provides an illustration of the range of activities typically available throughout the day. Two-up, in which bets are placed on the outcome of two pennies tossed into the air, may be characteristically Australian, but the other events have counterparts on most cruise ships.

Gambling at sea

Research in this area is something of a gamble itself. Companies are coy about divulging details on facility management and profits connected with gambling on their ships. The researcher has to take a chance by talking casually to enough people serving in various positions on board and then assessing the responses for consistencies. Gambling facilities on cruise ships have been growing steadily in sophistication and opulence since the 1980s. Although this is a significant area of revenue-raising, most passengers, it seems, do not choose a ship largely because of the gambling opportunities. Nonetheless, this is an important and often controversial aspect of the cruise experience and is appropriately examined here. Industry insiders Dickinson and Vladimir (1997, p. 273) estimate that only about 30 per cent of passengers gamble while the rest watch. This may well be true for the majority of cruising Westerners, but in Asia the situation is quite different. Malaysia-based Star Cruises was founded on providing gambling opportunities. In 1993 Tan Sri Lim Goh Tong, Chief Executive Officer (CEO) of Genting Berhad, the company which had operated Malaysia's Genting Highland's casino since 1968, refitted a North Sea ferry to sail out of Singapore, beyond the three-mile limit (4.83 kilometres) into international waters where gambling restrictions did not apply. This activity was—and still is—known as a 'cruise to nowhere'. Indeed, the practice is not unlike that in the United States during the 1920s, when ships sailed out of New York into international waters so that patrons could sidestep the prohibition on alcohol of the time. Cruises to nowhere have been revived in the United States, where some states allow gambling vessels to go outside the three-mile limit to operate for one night or weekend trips.

All the ships of Star Cruises positioned throughout South-East Asia have gambling as their principal focus, with 24-hour casino opening and a full range of facilities to provide diversions for accompanying families. There is a qualitative world of difference between the 1920s 'booze cruiser' and the spectacular ships of Star Cruises. The Oasis (offering 'games of chance') on *SuperStar Virgo*, operating the cruises to nowhere at the time this was written, can accommodate 1800; this is twice as many as the next largest public room, the Lido Show Lounge: the ship's total passenger complement is 2171. A 'Grand' Oasis is provided for the really serious enthusiast. Three hundred dealers and other staff run the gambling operations and a number of the games are comprehended mainly or only by Chinese. We were unable to learn what the house limit was. Needless to say, security measures, with experienced staff often recruited from Australia, are extremely sophisticated and extensive.

For most Westerners, however, a cruise used to be one of the few places to find legitimate casino gambling outside of such major locations as Las Vegas or Atlantic City in the United States, certain locations in Europe or, much later, casinos in a few cities in Australia. It is still the case that the casino opens as soon as the ship is three miles offshore in international waters, a limit set in the 19th century as the boundary of the United States because it was the maximum distance that shore-based cannons could fire. Originally the activity had novelty value, with a cruise ship being the first place many people had exposure to gambling. However, as gambling restrictions have changed internationally, access to facilities for most people in Europe, the United States and Australia has increased considerably. In the South Pacific, for example, New Caledonia, a two-hour flight from eastern Australia, had the first casino in the Islands region. It was promoted as a major tourist attraction for Australians and New Zealanders, whose countries did not have legal casinos. But by the 1990s there were 14 major casinos spread throughout Australia and several in New Zealand. The mid-1990s also saw a nationwide expansion of slot machine legalisation in Australia. The presence of gambling facilities on a cruise ship consequently lost its impact as a motivator. In the United States the revival of riverboat facilities and the licensing of Native American tribes to open casinos under their sovereign nation status had a similar impact.

Despite this, in the 21st century cruise lines continue to build bigger and more elaborate casinos on board. Some are run by well-known operators; other companies, such as Princess Cruises which once franchised

Figure 5.1 The entrance to Caesar's Palace casino on *Crystal Symphony* (Source: Norman Douglas)

the operations, resumed control when they could see profits markedly increasing. Why get a percentage when you can take the whole lot! Crystal Cruises has Caesar's at Sea, a version of the famous Las Vegas casino with tables for blackjack, baccarat and roulette, a craps (dice) table and over a hundred slot machines. Carnival's Fantasy Class ships each have some 235 slot machines. Gambling participation is influenced to some extent by where the ship sails. On *QE2*'s trans-Atlantic crossings there is high use of the facilities, while on round-the-world cruises the casino staff get to spend a lot of time gazing at the passing seascape, although on sectors with a considerable number of Asian passengers—for example, Singapore to Mumbai—casinos may be very active. On short cruises out of Miami gambling is very popular. On South Pacific cruises out of Australia gambling has only limited appeal.

One interesting outcome of the corporate takeovers, which are a feature of the cruise business, relates to the takeover in 2000 of Norwegian Cruise Line (NCL) by Star Cruises. As noted earlier, Star was founded on gambling and the requirements of players. In 2002 the combined 300 000 readers of the popular magazines *Strictly Slots* and *Casino Player* voted NCL the best cruise line for gambling opportunities and facilities. NCL's Freestyle Cruising program, which allows guests to dine when, where and with whom they want was highly praised. 'This isn't only convenient; it's practically a necessity for gamblers, who won't leave a hot table just because some guy with a bell announced dinner', *Casino Player* editors pointed out: 'We're honoured to receive this award from the readers', said Colin Veitch, NCL's president and CEO. 'This outstanding recognition from the readers of these respected publications underscores NCL's commitment to providing the most enjoyable onboard experience possible and confirms Freestyle Cruising's broad appeal' (cited <www.cruises.about.com/library/weekly>). Star Cruises had introduced this dining style to its own fleet initially to accommodate the 24-hour opening of its casinos and its Asian clientele's cultural preference for 'grazing'.

6

Safety, health and supply

Safety and health are the most important considerations of all cruise companies: on board the captain has prime responsibility for his crew and passengers. International regulations control standards of equipment and systems which affect environments both on the ship and in the seas they sail. Breaches of standards and outbreaks of ill-health occur, nonetheless. A gastrointestinal or respiratory virus may strike many of the passengers and crew. Newspapers will gleefully report on the incident, tending, since 11 September 2001, to link it with terrorism (e.g. <news.nationalgeographic. com/news/12/1211>). Occasionally, and generally accidentally, a ship will discharge contaminating effluent into the sea. This is more likely to be noticed if it happens close to land rather than well out at sea. However, stricter monitoring of companies' adherence to rules and regulations and operating codes of conduct are seeing fewer breaches of health and safety standards. So aware are all major cruise business players of the need to protect both the marine environments and those of their ships and all who sail in them that a lengthy two-to-three-year cooperative research project was initiated in mid-2002. This has the goal of advancing applicable technologies to further improve the safety of passenger ship operations, while extending environmental controls to achieve as close to zero emissions as possible from ships while in operation. Termed the SAFENVSHIP project (SAF for safety, ENV for environment), this will be seeking advances in ship design and construction, personnel safety, clean seas and clean air.

SOLAS

In the meantime international regulations exist which govern safety and environmental protection at sea. SOLAS (Safety of Life at Sea), the requirements of the International Maritime Organisation (IMO) and the inspections provided by the US Vessel Sanitation Program (which is part of the US National Center for Environmental Health) are the principal regulatory watchdogs. SOLAS requires all ships to undergo a rigorous set of inspections by the US Coast Guard whenever a new vessel enters service or enters a US port for its first call. Inspections cover fire-safety drills, use of emergency equipment, crew drills and detailed examinations of the condition and safety of the vessel's hull and its machinery. Ships are inspected quarterly. The US Coast Guard has the power to detain a ship from sailing if it is deemed unsafe for passengers. Inspectors also investigate emergencies such as ships running aground, engine room fires and loss of electricity. In 1992 SOLAS requirements were made more stringent, a move which had significant impact on the cruise business, as companies were required to invest considerable sums of money in bringing older ships up to standard or replacing them. Costly alterations ranged from new sprinkler systems to freon-free air-conditioning systems and low-level lighting. Consequently, many older ships which proved far too costly to upgrade were scrapped or sold to operators who had no interest in US ports whatsoever and were therefore out of the jurisdiction of SOLAS. P&O's popular Pacific veteran *Fairstar* was one notable casualty of the more rigorous standards. By 1997 all existing ships, and from that year all new ships, had to be equipped with, or to have brought up to standard, the following installations:

- smoke detection and alarm systems in all accommodation and service spaces, stairway enclosures and corridors;
- heat detectors in galleys;
- low-level lighting;
- sprinkler systems in accommodations and service spaces, stairway enclosures and corridors;
- improved galley exhaust ducts;
- a general alarm system with a specific sound pressure level on all passenger, crew and open decks.

In 2002 it was reported by the Cruise Ship Forum, a group of international stakeholders in the business, that large passenger vessels employed safety practices and features above and beyond the current maritime safety requirements. Best practices include an onboard safety centre, a continuously staffed station that handles emergencies to prevent interference with navigational duties on the bridge, emergency lighting in cabins that kicks in during power loss, a damage stability computer that delivers up-to-the-minute information about the vessel's safety condition during an emergency, and a shore-based emergency operation centre providing full incident support and search-and-rescue information (Treacy 2002, p. 10).

All passengers must participate in lifeboat drill within 24 hours of embarking. Most often this happens just after sailing. Crew staff all emergency stations, and careful directions and instruction on emergency procedures are given to all passengers. Throughout a cruise crew have their own emergency drills and training sessions to prepare for all possible contingencies, including the launching of a lifeboat to search for a hypothetical person overboard. These are of only minor inconvenience to passengers but provide a sound sense of safety and well-being to all on board.

Sanitation

In 1975 the US Centers for Disease Control and Prevention (CDC) established the Vessel Sanitation Program (VSP) to assist cruise ships with foreign itineraries to maintain sanitation levels, to provide a healthy environment and to lower the risk of gastrointestinal disease outbreaks. They also provide hygiene education programs for staff, particularly those handling food. This is increasingly essential with multicultural crews, where language barriers and differing expectations can exist. Cruise ships are rated on water quality, food storage, preparation and handling, and general cleanliness. The following information is posted on the website of the National Center for Environmental Health and is updated regularly (<www2.cdc.gov/nceh/vsp/vspmain.asp>). Every vessel that has a foreign itinerary, carries 13 or more passengers and calls on a US port is subject to unannounced twice-yearly inspections and, when necessary, to reinspection by VSP staff. The vessel owner pays a fee, based on tonnage, for all inspections. In 2003 over 140 cruise ships participated in the program. The ships must meet the criteria established by VSP in the *Vessel Sanitation Program Operations Manual*, and are given a score based on a 100-point scale. To pass the inspection, a ship must score 86 or above. If the ship fails an inspection, it will be reinspected, usually within 30–45 days. The inspections are conducted by Environmental Health Officers (EHO) of the VSP, and take place only in US ports. The inspection may take from five to eight hours to complete, depending on the size and complexity of the vessel. The inspection focuses on the following:

- the ship's water supply—to determine how water is stored, distributed, protected and disinfected;
- the ship's spas and pools—to ensure adequate filtration and disinfection;
- the ship's food—to determine how it is protected during storage, preparation and service;
- the potential for contamination of food and water—to determine what interventions are needed for protection;
- the practices and personal hygiene of employees—to ensure cleanliness and the use of appropriate hygiene practices;
- the general cleanliness and physical condition of the ship—to ensure cleanliness and the absence of insects and rodents;
- the ship's training programs in general environmental and public health practices—to determine the scope and effectiveness of such training.

Inspection scores and reports are placed on the VSP website and are published monthly in the *Summary of Sanitation Inspections of International Cruise Ships*, commonly referred to as the 'green sheet'. This is distributed to more than 3000 travel-related services around the world.

In general, the lower the score, the lower the level of sanitation; however, a low score does not necessarily imply an imminent risk of gastrointestinal disease. Since the program began, the number of disease outbreaks on ships has declined despite significant growth in the number of ships sailing and the number of passengers carried. In the past, a score of 86 out of 100 or higher was reported as 'Satisfactory' and a score of 85 and below was reported as 'Not satisfactory'. Ships unable to achieve a score of at least 86 on a routine periodic inspection are given a reasonable time to rectify the problem depending upon ship schedules and an undertaking by the company to initiate corrective action. Slater and Basch (1996) comment that real value from green sheet scores can only be gained if a longitudinal study of the results is conducted. If a ship records consistently low scores then it may be assumed that its sanitation practices are inadequate. Occasionally a ship which has been a very high scorer will have a one-time infringement that temporarily affects its rating. In this situation the company seeks to rectify the problem immediately in order to protect its reputation.

Ships most commonly fail, according to Slater and Basch, when they are about to be sold, because the crew has little motivation to sustain standards. The change of ownership, however, may take some time to settle down. In 1998, following the transfer of *Norwegian Star* from

Florida-based Norwegian Cruise Line to Australia-based Norwegian Capricorn Line—ultimately, a failed regional venture—the ship received a score of 78 by the VSP inspectors before its repositioning voyage, and despite A$7.5 million said to have been spent on improvements and refurbishments (Douglas & Douglas 2001). P&O's *Fair Princess*, which was new to the South Pacific a year earlier, had to contend with its own series of misfortunes. Despite a A$10 million refit, flooded cabins, a fire in the casino, mechanical difficulties, faulty air-conditioning and an outbreak of typhoid among passengers which was traced to contaminated food served during a call at Port Moresby, Papua New Guinea, all challenged the company's reputation at the time. Both companies rectified the problems as quickly as possible. These examples indicate how unpredictable and diverse sanitation issues can be.

Health care

Although only ships registered in the United Kingdom and Norway are required to carry a licensed doctor or have hospital facilities, most ships carrying over 50 passengers have at least one doctor. Companies also have an obligation to care for the health of their crews. Although the nurses are employed by the company, doctors on board are more likely to be filling the position on a casual basis—a sort of working holiday. In the United States and Australia, for example, the medical associations have established systems whereby doctors can register their interest and availability in taking their skills to sea. Versatility rather than specialty is required: on *QE2*, a ship with kennels on board for traditional trans-Atlantic crossings, the doctor must also have veterinary skills. On a *QE2* cruise in which we participated there was a guide-dog on board, whose condition the doctor monitored. Health care at sea is meant to be essentially for minor ailments and accidents although serious complications can arise. Evacuation by helicopter is occasionally necessary if very serious complications develop, but for the captain this is a major decision as it places at risk everyone on the ship and full emergency procedures must be implemented. Prevention rather than cure is the guiding principle of health at sea. Spas, gyms, professional trainers, smoke-free environments and healthy menus are designed to satisfy even the most demanding health-conscious passenger and perhaps encourage others to attempt some changes to their normal routine.

Provedoring

This is an essential service which is derived from the verb 'to provide' and ultimately from *providere* (Latin: to prepare or supply), although the term doesn't appear in many dictionaries. A ship provedoring (sometimes 'providoring') company is one which provides specifically for ships. The major focus is on ensuring that food supplies are maintained for all on board; however, provedoring companies may have deck, engine, cabin and technical divisions as well. Shipping companies prefer, where feasible, to equip their vessels as far as possible where they are home-ported, but for extended periods—such as round-the-world trips—and for perishable items which cannot store for long periods on board, it is often necessary to use companies in convenient ports of call. Strict controls and guidelines determine the quality of any local produce taken on board and suppliers must work very hard to establish their credentials in the business and then maintain the quality of their goods. Reputations can be acquired initially by creating a demand for local produce. For example, Australian provedores can provide the unique barramundi fish, exceptional shellfish and crustaceans; New Zealand provedores market lamb and game as their specialty; and South-East Asian provedores can provide high-quality tropical fruits. These are not exclusive but are examples of what chefs can incorporate in the way of high-quality, local produce into their menus both as a special attraction and as fresh foodstuffs. Companies may also pack containers with supplies and send them on to await the arrival of the ship in port. This happens particularly with wines, spirits and beers, and non-refrigerated foods. Non-foods which require replenishing may include flowers, toiletries and cleaning products.

Given that much of the focus of cruising is on the quality and quantity of food, this section provides some examples of the quantities required to keep people well fed at sea. Cruise companies are aware that the decision to become a repeat passenger may be strongly influenced by dining experiences. Consequently, enormous attention is given to the planning, presentation and diversity of menus. Depending on the star rating and passenger profile of the ship, companies work on an expenditure of US$10 to US$50 per day per passenger. Obviously, the higher the per diem cost paid by the passenger, the higher the quality of the cruise cuisine. Crew meal budgets are considerably more restrained. An allocation of US$2 per day per crew member is not uncommon. In 2002 crew members on *QE2* were dismayed to learn that the parent company, Carnival, had halved their food budget in cost-saving measures (personal communications). Meals and provisions bought by crew members ashore when possible become quite important to staff wanting to add some variety or supplement their diet. Dietary considerations for both crew and passengers must be at the forefront of operational planning. Religious requirements such as those demanded by Jews and Muslims, as well as medical/health requirements such as diabetic needs, varieties of vegetarianism, and low-fat, low-salt and no-wheat diets must all be catered for among the varied collection of people who make up the human component of a 21st century cruise ship. It is instructive to read the galley fact sheet, which cruise lines issue at least once on every voyage (see Tables 6.1 and 6.2). Additional information which may illustrate the enormity of the task of feeding a ship's complement is that the plate-wash facility deals with 10 000 plates, 8000 glasses and 12 000 pieces of cutlery each day.

What is included is, of course, at the discretion of the company. These lists, although incomplete, help to illustrate the rating and passenger expectations of different ships quite well. Foie gras, cigars and champagne are practically standard on *QE2*.

Table 6.1   Galley facts: ten-day cruise of *Pacific Sky* in the South Pacific

Eggs	3000 dozen	Bacon	870 kg
Fish (assorted)	2500 kg	Chicken	2500 kg
Pork	730 kg	Beef	1300 kg
Steak	750 kg	Pasta	1350 kg
Rice	2000 kg	Lettuce	850 kg
Tomatoes	1000 kg	Cucumber	700 kg
Ham	500 kg	Cheese	900 kg
Pineapples	1200 kg	Apples	500 kg
Oranges	550 kg	Melons	1000 kg
Watermelon	1025 kg	Assorted beers	900 cases
Tea	60 000 tea bags	Wine	200 cases
Coffee	300 kg	Spirits	100 cases
Milk	40 000 litres	Soft drinks	750 cases

Source: *Pacific Sky*, P&O Cruises, August 2000.

Table 6.2   Galley facts: five-day Atlantic crossing on *QE2*

Cereals	3850 packets	Strawberries	535 lbs (243 kg)
Herbs, spices	50 lbs (23 kg)	Tomatoes	2370 lbs (1076 kg)
Marmalade/Jams	2765 portions	Portions of beef	2395 lbs (1087 kg)
Tea bags	12 800	Pork	4000 lbs (1816 kg)
Coffee	500 lbs (227 kg)	Racks of lamb	329 lbs (149 kg)
Caviar	75 lbs (34 kg)	Sausages	2000 lbs (908 kg)
Butter	2404 lbs (1091 kg)	Ducks	855 lbs (308 kg)
Ham	594 lbs (270 kg)	Potatoes	5 tons
Eggs	3582 dozen	Flour	4690 lbs (2129 kg)
Milk	1150 gals (5232 litres)	Rice	2000 lbs (908 kg)
Lobster	580 lbs (263 kg)	Juices	25 720 pints (14 609 litres)
Smoked salmon	420 lbs (190 kg)	Soft drink	4100 bottles
Bananas	1205 lbs (547 kg)	Wines	1850 bottles
Foie gras	60 lbs (27 kg)	Champagne	1000 bottles
Cigars	205 boxes	Spirits	900 litres
Cigarettes	50 000 cartons	Beer	12 000 bottles

Source: *QE2*, Cunard, March 2002.

Part 2

7

The historical growth of cruising

Purists insist that a cruise is a very specific type of ocean—or, more widely, waterborne—voyage, one in which the vessel begins and ends at the same place (i.e. a round trip), and that has as its main purpose the leisure and recreation of its passengers, rather than the aim of transporting them from one place to another, in which recreation is simply a diversion—albeit often an elaborate one—to take their minds off the inevitable monotony of the voyage. Indeed, a current primary definition of the term 'cruise' includes the concept of 'a pleasure trip' (*Encarta Dictionary* 1999). Earlier definitions which associated the term also with piracy or privateering (*Shorter Oxford Dictionary* 1969) seem to have gone out of favour. One must therefore consider the origins of cruising in relation not only to passenger shipping but also to earlier forms of tourism. As it happens, the accepted date of birth of modern tourism precedes the accepted date of the first cruise by just three years. Both were assisted initially by significant developments in industry and technology, especially by the steam engine. They would later be assisted by the greater availability of leisure time.

It is generally held that Thomas Cook was the father of modern tourism; that is, tourism for the people, rather than the aristocracy or the moneyed few. A 1991 book on the life of Thomas Cook names its first chapter 'The birth of tourism'. The story, writes author Piers Brendon, is a 'Victorian epic of achievement which began in 1841 with Cook's construction of a new industry out of nothing but a brilliant idea' (Brendon 1991, p. 1). It is a remarkable story of how one man developed an international network to facilitate the mass movement of holiday makers on the basis of a short train excursion from Leicester to Lough-borough, organised to promote the temperance movement. Cook's first excursion took place on 5 July 1841: within 46 years he had extended his business interests as far as Melbourne, Australia, where a Thomas Cook office began to produce its own Australasian edition of *Cook's Excursionist*. The 'penny periodical' had first appeared in May 1851, following the huge successes of his organised trips to the Great Exhibition in London's Crystal Palace. Although loudly criticised by the literary elite of the period, the *Excursionist* proved to be extremely popular reading and lasted in various forms for nearly a hundred years. Its chatty style was a combination of what, in the 21st century, might be called 'half-advertorial, half-experiential travel writing'. Descriptions of people, places and planned tours were interspersed with advertisements appropriate to the travel trade—hotels, clothing, steamships and travel sickness cures. The relationship between the Thomas Cook organisation (the 'inventors' of tourism) and P&O (the 'inventors' of cruising) at times would become quite close. Other early personalities now acknowledged to have been significant to the history of tourism, while of some interest, are not relevant here.

But another Victorian individual, generally less recognised for his part in the early days of mass tourism development, is also of importance. In 1835 Arthur Anderson, described by the historians of the Peninsular and Oriental Steam Navigation Company (P&O) as 'a colourful and adventurous person, likeable, kind and generous' (Howarth & Howarth 1994, p. 10), placed an advertisement in his own small newspaper for trips by ship around the wild coasts of the Shetland and Faeroe Islands and Iceland. That the ship did not exist was quite incidental. In this respect Anderson was certainly ahead of his time: in the late 20th century, with the increasing popularity of cruising, there were several instances of companies promoting cruises on non-existent vessels. Anderson's plan developed no further at the time, although he was clearly entrepreneurial by nature. Besides his local newspaper for Shetland Islanders (he himself was one), he was in partnership with Brodie McGhie Willcox in a small shipping business and could probably have produced an excursion vessel if required. That he had foresight and imagination is evident throughout the company's history. He and Willcox made a good team: the former saw the opportunities; the latter knew how to get the necessary finance no matter how risky the venture might have appeared initially. What is important here is that Anderson had the idea that people might like to go to sea because they were curious to see new places, not simply because they had to get from point A to point B and a ship was the only means of transport.

Early initiatives of P&O

The Peninsular Steam Navigation Company was officially founded in 1837. Initially the 'Oriental' component was absent, as the two men were concerned only with running services to Portugal and Spain. When they later expanded into the eastern Mediterranean, 'Oriental' was added. By 1844 P&O, as the company became known, had regular services to Alexandria in Egypt and connecting branch lines beyond. Their successes had been based on a number of innovations, but two in particular stand out. They introduced the concept of regular timetables to the world of shipping and they brought reliability to the delivery of mail in the peninsular and Mediterranean regions. The first was welcomed by passengers and merchants alike, who could now plan their voyages with some sense of predictability. Until Anderson and Willcox began to advertise confirmed timetables, the departure and arrival of ships had been 'time and tide permitting'. Adherence to advertised timetables is expected by modern travellers who invariably become indignant and angry when their plans are thwarted by weather, mechanics or industrial disputes. The second innovation was the guarantee of delivering mail to its destination. In the days before electrical and electronic means of communication, correspondence, whether personal or business, relied on the postal service. It was not uncommon, however, for mail to be loaded onto the ships of unscrupulous owners who often waved their vessels off under the command of rogues and scoundrels. The latter then moved into the fraudulent insurance claim business after tossing their cargoes into the sea or trading with privateers when at sea. P&O's apparent reliability made it a name to be remembered.

The first cruises, then, took place on mail ships; sometimes several ships might constitute a single cruise, as the experience of 19th century novelist William Makepeace Thackeray illustrates. The author of the first account of this kind of journey, Thackeray travelled on three different ships to produce his narrative. This raises something of a historical problem. P&O's own historians seem unable to agree fully on whether Thackeray's experience really represents the beginning of cruising. Rabson and O'Donoghue admit it 'was not a cruise in the modern sense' but acknowledge that 'with this voyage P&O **traditionally invented** cruising' (1988, p. 18: authors' emphasis). Howarth and Howarth, on the other hand, are happy to accept without qualification that 'as long ago as

1844, P&O invented deep-sea cruising' (1994, p. 47). This view, not too surprisingly, has passed into P&O's promotional literature. Later, vessels whose primary purpose was the carriage of cargo would also be inspired to offer cruises. Cruises—advertised as such or as 'excursions'—predated the appearance of cruise ships, even that of liners, by many years. This apparent paradox is of some historical significance, illustrating—among other things—the fact that the luxury usually associated with cruising was quite absent in the formative years of the activity. It also raises something of a problem, unacknowledged in the relevant literature, of how to fully distinguish between cruising and other forms of ocean travel, at least in the last years of the 19th and the first decades of the 20th century. *Titanic*, for example, whatever its other attributes and its historical significance may have been, was not a cruise ship—it did not survive long enough to become one—although because of the vessel's continual fascination for authors it manages to find its way into most historical surveys of cruising (e.g. Cartwright & Baird 1999; Dickinson & Vladimir 1997).

Geographical spread of cruising

After the first P&O cruises it was another four decades before, assisted by innovations in maritime technology, the geographical range of cruising began to expand with cruises advertised by small and large companies to destinations that included the fiords of Norway and the Caribbean Islands. The latter, promoted by Orient Line on its own *Lusitania* (a name later appropriated by Cunard) in 1895, may be seen as one of the earliest cruises to make use of a liner—that is, a vessel primarily concerned with the long-distance transport of passengers rather than mail or cargo. (See Figure 7.1.)

By the end of the century North American companies which ran regular services to the Caribbean had also entered the 'cruise' business, among them vessels of the United Fruit Co., which as the company's name indicates were essentially engaged in the transport of perishable produce. Doubtless, cruising on a banana boat had its points of interest—it may even have been regarded by some as 'romantic'—but United Fruit's passenger services paid mainly because they were subsidised by the US government. Closer to modern notions of cruising were the ships of the Quebec Line, which had 'given much attention to the development of tourist travel' to the West Indies and offered winter excursions of 22 days from US$100 (Lawton & Butler 1987, p. 330). It was 1904 before P&O thought it appropriate to introduce a ship 'specially fitted up as a [steam] yacht to carry about 150 passengers . . . on those Pleasure Cruises which have become popular . . .'. This was *Vectis*, whose conversion

Figure 7.1   An early (1895) Orient Line poster. Later versions were changed to read 'West Indies' (Courtesy P&O)

made certain that 'no expense has been spared' in adapting her for the new purpose of conveying recreational travellers to the Mediterranean, Atlantic Islands and Scandinavia (Rabson & O'Donoghue 1988, p. 82).

The euphoria of this activity was interrupted by the outbreak of war in 1914. The four-year international conflict resulted in widespread losses for shipping generally—P&O alone lost 17 vessels, and Cunard's loss amounted to 65 per cent of its fleet, including its own *Lusitania*, the world's largest ship at the time of its building in 1906. It was sunk by Germany in 1915, allegedly because it was carrying armaments.

The 'Golden Age'

After the necessary fleet restorations following the war, passenger services were resumed, but the effects of the war extended far beyond the loss of ships. The social consequences in the United States were great, particularly the prohibition on the sale and service of alcohol (introduced in 1920) and the restrictions on immigration (strengthened in 1924, but preceded by at least seven other restrictive Acts dating back to 1875). The first was a reaction to postwar excesses, the second a retreat into postwar isolationism. Perversely, both these restrictions had the effect of stimulating cruise activity. Prohibition in the United States gave rise to the short-haul 'booze cruise' to the Caribbean (special-interest tourism indeed); while trans-Atlantic shipping companies, much of whose prewar profits had been derived from the carrying of European immigrants to the United States, were obliged, as the flow dried up, to find other activities to make up the revenue shortfall.

The decades of the 1920s and 1930s have been dubbed in whole or part as the 'jazz age', the 'long weekend' and the period of 'boom and bust', and by historians of travel the 'Golden Age'. Pre World War I developments in shipping had been spurred by national rivalries and often sacrificed comfort for speed. The prestige attaching to the Blue Riband, an award dating from 1838 and made for the fastest trans-Atlantic service, appears to have driven German and British engineers particularly hard. Competition between the Hamburg-Amerika Line and Cunard was intense in the early years of the 20th century. 'Speed', according to Dickinson & Vladimir, 'sold more tickets than comfort back then because people didn't want to be at sea any longer than they had to' (1997, p. 11). The development of the steam turbine engine in 1884 ensured that they would not have to, although its widespread use did not take place for some years. Between the first award of the Blue Riband in 1838 and 1907, when Cunard reclaimed it for Britain from the Germans with its new *Lusitania*, the time for the Atlantic crossing had been reduced from 14.5 days to less than five days. Not long after, *Mauretania*, *Lusitania*'s sister ship, proved even faster and held the Blue Riband until 1929, losing it that year to a 'new generation' German vessel, *Bremen*. It is worthwhile recalling in this context that the reason most often advanced for the tragedy of *Titanic* was its owners' (hence captain's) obsession with trumping Cunard's achievement, to the point of disregarding warnings of ice in its path.

Speed, then, had been effectively conquered even before World War I. So too had size and comfort—the latter at least for first-class passengers. As for size, Hamburg-Amerika's answer to *Titanic* was the 4000-passenger *Imperator*, 'the biggest ship in the world' at the time of its launching in 1912, and referred to here mainly to illustrate the fact that the fondness for enormous ships is not entirely a late 20th- or early 21st-century phenomenon. But the huge vessel had little opportunity to establish a reputation beyond that. It was out of service for most of the war and was seized by Britain as part of the postwar reparations program: renamed, it became Cunard's *Berengaria*.

There was a major change in both the numbers and the nature of trans-Atlantic passengers as European immigration to the United States was curtailed. But the events of the war, especially America's involvement, helped to create a new interest in the Old World. Before the war much passenger traffic from Europe to the United States had been driven by necessity; now American voyaging to Europe was driven by curiosity and enhanced by a new prosperity. While much of Europe struggled to recover from the war, Americans, now more mobile than ever, travelled not only within the North American continent but also overseas. In 1928 alone, more than 437 000 people travelled *from* the United States by ship (Allen 1952, p. 157). Shipboard conditions were modified or changed to reflect this. Steerage accommodation, so named because of its proximity to a ship's steering mechanism, and deemed appropriate for impoverished immigrants, was improved and elevated, at least by name, to 'third cabin [class]' and ultimately to 'tourist class', thus reflecting—perhaps even inspiring—a new breed of passenger. The Italia Line, which emerged in the early 1930s from an amalgamation of three previous companies and aimed to attract American visitors to Europe, initially boasted four classes, with a 'special class' replacing the usual 'second class'. 'There are few people who do not regard the expression "second class" as a term of disparagement', wrote a contemporary. 'Mediocrity may be golden but it is certainly uninspiring' (quoted in Prior 1993, p. 85).

This was not the only change in amenities or facilities. The opulence that had characterised the leading prewar passenger vessels, causing both critics and enthusiasts of the period to refer to them as 'floating hotels', became more widespread and passenger comforts more hotel-like. 'If we could get ships to look inside like ships', wrote a contemporary maritime architect, objecting to the design trends, 'and get people to enjoy the sea, it would be a very good thing' (Arthur Davis, Royal Institute of British Architects, RIBA (1922), quoted in Prior 1993, p. 15).

Advances in style and imagery

Pleasure cruises became vital to shipping lines in the 1930s 'since trans-Atlantic business had been sharply affected by the great depression' (Server 1996, p. 37). Cruises to 'The Orient' were advertised by a number of lines, Hamburg-Amerika among them, but since for European purposes 'The Orient' began somewhere in the eastern Mediterranean, these need not have been of very great duration. P&O, on the other hand, having spread its influence to the Far East and beyond well before 1920, could advertise 'World Tours and Ocean Cruises' as far as India, Japan and Australasia without its tongue in its cheek. Of particular appeal to sophisticates was the company's *Viceroy of India,* built in 1929 for the Bombay (now Mumbai) service and perfectly named to represent the summit of P&O's fleet of vessels bearing names (*Rawalpindi, Ranchi, Rajputana*) that symbolised the imperial association. Like the others, *Viceroy*'s main purpose was to carry the servants of the crown to and from its most important jewel, but technological and design features made it 'a bench-mark ship' that 'brought the traditional P&O liner to new levels of opulence and comfort', including such passenger pampering features as an indoor swimming pool, the first on a P&O ship (Howarth & Howarth 1994, pp. 130–1). The sorts of passengers carried to and from Britain by *Viceroy* and other vessels in the Bombay service in the late 1920s and 1930s give some idea of the quality of life on board (Capt. D. G. O. Baillie, quoted in Rabson & O'Donoghue 1988, p. 172):

> Governors of Presidencies or Provinces of India; Maharajas and their enormous retinues . . . famous figures in politics or society going out to enjoy what was then a fashionable and popular winter pastime of the wealthy—cold weather in India.

The company's Eastern trade may have given rise to a neologism for the English language: 'POSH', an acronym for 'port out, starboard home', a request to agents from passengers who wanted to travel on the cooler side of the vessel (Howarth & Howarth 1988, pp. 66–7; Rabson & O'Donoghue 1988, p. 80). Whatever the precise origins of the expression, P&O long ago absorbed it as its own and continues to use it: the company's 'exclusive club' for frequent cruisers is called 'The POSH Club' (P&O 2003, p. 26). Between its Bombay runs the much admired

Viceroy and other P&O ships on the India service undertook cruises, 15 of them in 1929 alone, one of many indications of the increasing popularity of the vacation at sea. (See Figure 7.2.)

Figure 7.2   *Viceroy of India*'s swimming pool attracted participants and spectators (P&O art collection)

There were other signs. Not surprisingly, most of the visual imagery used in the promotion of passenger transport or cruising featured the ships themselves, emphasising their size and power, and often not in any particular geographical context. But P&O's advertising posters during this time were as likely to display the destination as the means of getting there. What could better encapsulate the appeal of a cruise to India, Ceylon (now Sri Lanka) and even further into the mysterious East, for instance, than caparisoned elephants? As if to reinforce the bond between them (begun in the 1880s) as agents of British imperialism, Cook's travel often used the same illustrations on its posters. In the 1935 season the Cook's/P&O combination sold 12 000 tours to India (Swinglehurst 1982, p. 110). The posters might have provided a visual symbol of their close association, but at bottom was a contract involving a sliding scale of commissions from Cook's to P&O. Cook's also undertook to provide P&O with free advertising in its travel publications and to make 'a special effort to push P&O's China trade' (Swinglehurst 1982, pp. 113–14).

Cook's, of course, was not wholly committed to P&O: as agent for a number of lines it could choose whichever seemed appropriate to its needs or those of its clients and even charter vessels for cruises under its own name, a practice it had initiated as far back as 1875. Swinglehurst notes that in its dealings with shipping lines, 'Cook's size and importance gave the company no little power in getting the terms they wanted' (1982, p. 109). The company, which had grown spectacularly as the means of travel became more efficient and leisure time became more extensive, advertised its services widely, including in the informative and well-researched destination handbooks produced by Orient Line as early as the late 19th century. In these it reminded passengers that it owned a number of visitor attractions in such places as Italy and Egypt and could facilitate tourist travel in the colonies: India, Ceylon, Australia and New Zealand (Loftie 1901, p. 325). Orient's handbooks are revealing also for the insight they give into the fundamentals of passenger ships, whether on line voyages or cruises, including notes for passengers that prescribed appropriate behaviour (Loftie 1901, p. xli):

> It will be well to remind readers voyaging for the first time, that in a ship everyone is dependent more or less on his fellow passengers for the comfort and happiness, or misery and wretchedness, of the voyage . . . People who cannot play are very fond of strumming on the piano. At home probably this matters little to anybody: on board ship it may annoy hundreds. Various other examples might be mentioned, but we may let this one suffice with the addendum that inopportune music is as annoying as bad music.

Passengers were also expected to be in a suitable physical condition, as the company reserved the right 'of rejecting any person who may be found on embarking to be lunatic, idiotic, deaf, dumb, blind, maimed, or having symptoms of disease or infirmity . . .' (Loftie 1901, p. xliii).

These days, although the language has been modified to suit modern sensibilities, the fundamental cautions remain (P&O 2000: authors' emphasis).

> A booking may be refused or cancelled after deposit for anyone whose state of physical or mental health renders them, **in the opinion of the company**, unfit for travel, or anyone whose condition may constitute a danger to themselves or any other passenger.

Other restrictions and possible exclusions are part of the fine print contained in most cruise brochures. In an era of both advanced political correctness and heightened legal liability, cruise and other travel organisations tread a fine line.

The restoration and proliferation of cruise activity in the 1920s and 1930s reflected not only new technological achievements in shipping but also new advances in maritime architecture and new styles in interior design. By the later 1920s interiors, from dining rooms and lounges to the surrounds of indoor swimming pools, were influenced by Art Deco trends. Similar influences were evident in promotional material such as posters and brochures, even in menus. The pinnacle of these developments was *Normandie*, introduced to the trans-Atlantic passenger trade by the French Line (*Companie Générale Transatlantique*) in 1935. It was followed the next year by Cunard's *Queen Mary*; both ships quickly assumed almost hallowed status. A contemporary view of *Normandie*, published in the *American Architect* (quoted in Prior 1993, p. 91), referred to the vessel as:

> an uncanny achievement for which the French have become famous. The speed of the ship and all its mechanical devices constitute in themselves a major miracle even in this age. But aside from these *Normandie* is unique as a travelling exhibit of native art and industrial design. Thus she is as truly noteworthy as any exposition acclaimed in Paris.

It also represented something of a dichotomy between the new holiday makers, at whom the 'tourist class' accommodations (an outgrowth of the immigrant-based 'steerage') were now directed, and the older, wealthier and more self-conscious voyagers, also keen to cruise but more demanding about the conditions, including their fellow cruisers. In 1927, at the height of the new era in cruising, P&O chairman Lord Inchcape referred to a letter from one such passenger (quoted in Rabson & O'Donoghue 1988, p. 173):

He thought we ought to have a strict list for those who proposed to go on our cruising voyages. He suggested that no man should be booked unless he could show that he was a member of a good London club and that no lady should be accepted unless she had been presented at Court! He also objected to retiring rooms being situated in the alleyways, protesting that no gentleman could possibly enter them if there were any ladies in the neighbourhood.

The trend to snobbery was also observable elsewhere. The appeal of cruising to the wealthy helped bring about greater diversity in the pastimes on board. Organised activities, including deck games (first introduced in the 1880s) and competitions, became more varied and popular. These often attracted large audiences of non-participating passengers, a phenomenon rarely encountered in the 21st century. With the widespread acceptance by the 1930s of a sun-darkened skin as an accessory to both fashion and sexual appeal for female and male alike (Turner & Ash 1975, pp. 78–82), 'Suntan Cruises' were promoted on such vessels as Canadian Pacific's *Empress of Britain*, 'the first big Atlantic liner designed purposely with off-season winter cruising in mind' (McCauley 1997, p. 75). The Italia Line is credited with having introduced the open-air swimming pool and the Lido, an outdoor recreational area, accessible only to first-class passengers (Prior 1993, p. 87; Dickinson & Vladimir 1997, p. 19). Cruising called forth appropriate apparel for both women and men. For the former, modified nautical gear was often fancied; for the latter—especially in the tropics—white linen suits and solar topees were essential. Masquerade balls ('fancy dress evenings' for the lower orders) became an essential feature of almost every cruise. The relatively staid P&O acknowledged—beneath a picture of flamboyantly dressed revellers—that 'Gaiety is the keynote of shipboard life during a P&O Pleasure Cruise, but provision is made for those who seek rest and quietness' (P&O 1934, p. 12). The features that eventually turned cruise ships into floating resorts were already becoming well developed by the 1930s.

The presence of well-to-do, even comfortably off, passengers encouraged another element in cruising—the appearance of professional gamblers and hustlers. These were present on trans-Atlantic crossings also, seeking to relieve the boredom that passengers almost invariably feel at some part of an ocean voyage by fleecing them. Professional gamblers have been made all but redundant by casinos on modern ships, but the hustlers are still in evidence on almost every voyage of a top-class vessel. Often they sell jewellery, from opals (particularly popular on US cruises to the South Pacific and often touted by Australians) to 'hand-crafted designer costume accessories', as one representative of the trade

Figure 7.3 P&O's *Stratheden*. The 'Strath Class' ships comprised unprecedented 'energy, speed and beauty', according to the company (P&O art collection)

described them to us. The sales venues for these vary from 'lectures', advertised in the ship's daily newspaper, and therefore apparently with the connivance of the company, to special in-cabin presentations, organised by word of mouth.

Before the coming of World War II and the disruption caused to passenger shipping on a global scale, many of the most identifiable attributes of the cruise experience were well in place. Until the much later era of purpose-built cruise ships, technological, architectural and cultural advances made in passenger shipping were largely for the benefit of line voyagers, although in the seasons when trans-Atlantic and other vessels were turned to cruising, leisure travellers gained the advantage of them.

Cruising in the Pacific Islands region

The majority of writings on the subject of early cruising are so strongly focused on activity in Britain/Europe and North America and their respective pleasure grounds, the Mediterranean and the Caribbean, that readers may be forgiven for thinking that the pastime did not occur elsewhere. In fact it quite early became a worldwide phenomenon, as did international travel generally. Two antipodean shipping companies, Burns Philp & Company of Australia and the Union Steamship Company of New Zealand, were offering cruises to the islands of the western and eastern Pacific respectively, as early as 1884, ahead even of P&O's re-entry into cruising. As did passenger ships elsewhere that turned to cruising for part of the year, they provided 'off-season employment for the company's [ships] and—most importantly—enhanced its public profile' (McLean 1990, p. 39). Staff members at the Islands branches of both companies organised shore excursions for passengers. The cruises contributed a great deal to both destination development and the imagery of tourism in the Pacific Islands. Furthermore, the first cruises in this region, far from being short-lived novelties, proved to be the precursors of very durable activities indeed, and may well have inspired the entry into the region of other more powerful, not to say predatory, shipping organisations.

Union Steamship Co. became a subsidiary of P&O as early as 1917, when the British company acquired all of Union's ordinary shares, a move attended by some popular controversy in New Zealand (McLauchlan 1987, p. 66). The action can be viewed as part of P&O's early expansionist phase that saw it take over other companies also, among them the British India Steam Navigation Co (BISN) in 1914 and Orient Line in 1917, both big names in shipping. Companies so acquired—by 'merger' in the official parlance—continued to function under their own names and their own flags, a practice still followed today: the mammoth Carnival Corporation, for example, boasts six 'brands' in addition to its own, to which have been added (as recently as mid-2003) those of P&O itself and its subsidiaries, including Princess.

This gives the consumer an illusion of choice, but the confusion generated occasionally makes life difficult for authors. If a takeover of Burns Philp also was ever part of P&O's plan, the details have been obscured by time, although there were certainly close associations between them. Lord Inchcape (James Mackay), chairman of BISN, became chairman of P&O and also sat on BP's board, and BP acted as P&O's agent in Australia, promoting that company's Pacific and international services strongly in its travel magazine. This is by way of suggesting that P&O could probably have had a stronger cruise presence in the region earlier than it did. The possibility of this is not mentioned in P&O's official histories (Howarth & Howarth 1994; Rabson & O'Donoghue 1988). Indeed P&O made its entry into Pacific cruising only in December 1932 with a tentative holiday excursion to Norfolk Island on *Strathnaver*. The following day Orient's *Oronsay* began a short cruise to New Caledonia, 'a complete success from every angle', and followed this by 'despatching representatives to various islands in the Pacific', to find which of them would 'prove attractive to cruise passengers', according to the company's Sydney annals (Orient Line 1943, p. 35).

The Matson Line to New Zealand and Australia

From north of the line the San Francisco-based Matson Navigation Co. contributed its vessels to the Pacific's leisure traffic, helping to introduce North Americans to Pacific Island destinations such as Fiji, the Samoas and French Polynesia, and adding its view of the Islands to the growing store of tourist images of 'paradise'. The main emphasis in Matson's trans-Pacific advertising was on the major destinations, Australia and New Zealand, but 'The South Seas', as the Islands region was popularly known, was prominently featured on the company's brochures. Matson's perception of the Islands was influenced to a great extent by its experience of Hawai'i, to which it had been operating services from San Francisco since 1901, and the tourist imagery of which it helped to define, if not invent. (See Figure 7.4.)

Matson absorbed the Oceanic Steamship Co. in 1926, and in 1932 replaced the latter's older ships on trans-Pacific service with two attractive modern vessels, *Monterey* and *Mariposa*, specially built for the Pacific run. (Two other Matson ships of similar standard, *Lurline* and *Malolo*, were less involved in trans-Pacific services.) Each carrying 715 passengers, two-thirds of them in first class, *Monterey* and *Mariposa* were regarded by many prospective passengers in the region as the definitive Pacific cruise ships, against which the smaller excursion vessels of Burns Philp and Union Steamship Co. failed to measure up. Aided by Matson's belief that, despite the economic depression, 'the affluent would respond to the new luxury liners to explore the exotic islands and ports of the Pacific', especially if encouraged by a vigorous promotional campaign, they quickly became identified with the region's ultimate cruise experience (Stindt 1991, p. 83).

Faced with the competition, Union, a long-time and bitter rival of US companies, especially over mail contracts, withdrew its ships from the trans-Pacific service in 1936. 'More passengers', wrote Matson's historian, 'switched from British [sic] operated vessels to the new US flag liners'. Passenger traffic also boomed on the trans-Tasman service 'as travellers in those countries wanted to experience the luxury, service and cuisine of the American ships' (Stindt 1991, p. 62). Importantly for this discussion, the majority of Matson's Hawaiian and trans-Pacific voyages were promoted as 'cruises', indicating that, among its passengers, travel largely for leisure rather than merely transport was a very significant factor. Among the

Figure 7.4   Matson's *Mariposa* in Pago Pago, American Samoa. The location is authentic. The dancers and spectators were air-brushed in (Courtesy Matson Navigation Co.)

novelties introduced by the company was an exchange of passengers at Tahiti or Pago Pago, achieved by having both ships—one north-bound and the other south-bound—arrive at these ports at the same time, so that passengers could experience the facilities of both vessels. The point of this is somewhat obscure, since the ships appear to have been all but identical in terms of service and quality. Along with the rest of Matson's organisation, they were turned to US government service following the outbreak of war in the Pacific on 7 December 1941. The vessels named *Monterey* and *Mariposa* which cruised the Pacific under Matson's flag between 1956 and 1970 were actually newer and smaller ships and were only moderately successful. Ironically, Matson withdrew from passenger services in 1970, on the very eve of the revival of cruising.

World War II and beyond

The global reach of hostilities during World War II affected vast areas of the Pacific and Asia which had been relatively safe from the conflict of World War I, and had grim effects on passenger and cargo shipping. The losses of the P&O group (which included Orient, British India and other smaller lines) totalled 182 ships, eight of them from P&O's own passenger fleet. Because of its close involvement with the western Pacific, the main theatre of war with Japan, losses were heavy also for Burns Philp & Co. of Australia, less so for the Union Steamship Co. of New Zealand. Many surviving passenger ships the world over had been used as troop transports during the war and immediately after, and bore the evidence of hasty conversions and refits that sometimes trebled their carrying capacity. 'In the circumstances', P&O Chairman Sir William Currie told the first postwar general meeting of the company, 'it is to be hoped the travelling public will bear with us if the facilities and opportunities offered are not quite up to prewar standard . . .' (quoted in Howarth & Howarth 1994, p. 151).

To complicate matters further the costs of ship building had increased enormously because of both the great demand and the temporary reduction of facilities resulting from wartime damage. For British companies an additional obstacle was about to emerge—the dissolution of the empire itself, resulting in the loss of a great part of the passenger traffic between Britain and the East on which so much had previously depended. To make up for this loss of passenger trade, however, the postwar years saw a considerable increase in the movement of migrants from Britain to other parts of the empire dominated by Europeans, such as Canada, Australia, New Zealand and South Africa (Broeze 1998, p. 106; Plowman 1992, *passim*). There was also a smaller but no less culturally significant flow of people of British or part-British parentage from India and South-East Asia to the above countries or to Britain itself. Migration from other parts of war-torn Europe to countries such as Australia was also encouraged, if at times cautiously. As a consequence Italian and Greek shipping companies, including the Lauro, Sitmar and Chandris lines, in addition to British, took up the lucrative trade, benefiting from government contracts or subsidies. Importantly for this study, between migrant voyages they were frequently turned to cruising: at the end of a run to Australia, for example, cruising out of Sydney to the South Pacific Islands became a standard seasonal program. For almost a decade and a half after the war, long-distance travel remained the prerogative of the passenger ship. This encouraged optimism on the part of shipping companies, which responded with new buildings appropriate to both cruising and line voyages: Cunard's *Caronia*, which entered service in 1948, was one of the first of the new postwar breed and one of the first to introduce *en suite* bathrooms for every cabin, an innovation that heralded later trends towards the democratisation of cruising and the cruise ship as a luxury 'resort'. In the 1950s, celebrating its new confidence, Cunard's advertising team coined the slogan 'Getting there is half the fun' to describe the joys of an Atlantic crossing, and perhaps to imply that the company was no longer interested in competing for new speed records.

Having largely overcome the ravages of the war by the early 1950s and with the trans-Atlantic trade, world voyaging and cruising restored, passenger shipping was about to encounter another threat: not this time from enemy destroyers or submarines, but from jet aircraft capable of carrying large numbers of passengers. Although the first commercial jet flew in 1952, it was 1958 before Pan-American Airways' 140-passenger Boeing 707 began to make shipping companies nervous, particularly those with trans-Atlantic operations. Even the fastest Atlantic crossing by ship, set in 1952 by the new *United States*, took three-and-a-half days— a record that still stands. In a passenger jet the time was reduced to a matter of hours. The first such flight 'effectively sounded the death knell for the trans-Atlantic steamship business' (Dickinson & Vladimir 1997, p. 23). The bells also tolled loudly elsewhere. A final blow was delivered to passenger shipping by the appearance of the Boeing 747 in 1969, which, together with the oil crisis of 1973, managed to send an impressive number of vessels to the breakers.

Themes of the late 20th century

The student wanting to recall the history of cruising over the next half century or so can think of it as a sequence of overlapping themes, all beginning with the letter 'A':

- **Attrition**, of passenger fleets;
- **Accommodation**, as cruise companies and airlines realised that cooperation rather than mutual antagonism was the way ahead;
- **Activity**, as new fly-cruise ('air-sea' in the United States) programs broadened the product and the revenue base of both;
- **Ascent**, as new companies entered the market, encouraged by a resurgence in the popularity of cruising;
- **Acquisition**, as small or economically vulnerable companies were 'merged' or swallowed whole by large corporations, a process still in evidence.

The attrition of passenger fleets resulting from the threat of the jet was a worldwide phenomenon. A regional example of it comes from the Australian run of P&O and Orient, which together had 15 passenger vessels on that service in the early 1950s (compared with 21 just before the war). By 1970 these had been reduced to seven and by 1974 to only five (Fitchett 1977, pp. 72–3). In 1960, the year of the complete merger of the two companies, the new chairman had expressed his disbelief in the notion that sea travel would be seriously threatened by improvements in air services (Fitchett 1977, p. 71). His predecessor had believed that 'air and sea can and should be complementary' (Howarth & Howarth 1994, p. 151). But by 1970 P&O services to India and the Far East had ceased too, although these had also been affected by the second closure of the Suez Canal in 1967 (Rabson & O'Donoghue 1988, p. 217).

The concept of the 'fly-cruise', said to be have been introduced by Chandris Lines in the Mediterranean in 1960, is widely held to have saved cruising, though why the collaboration between aircraft and ships should have been thought quite so innovative is curious: after all, passenger shipping and passenger train services had been cooperating in leisure travel for decades, as early advertisements show. The 'fly-cruise', however, put paid to the long-held belief that cruising necessarily involved a round trip entirely by ship: it was now possible for one to join a vessel in any of the world's major cruise regions with a little additional effort and expense, rather than having to live conveniently close to a port of embarkation.

This is not to suggest that, following immediately on the Chandris example, there was a deluge of fly-cruises on offer in the new market. What was most observable during the 1960s and early 1970s was the succession of passenger vessels being re-created as cruise ships, changing owners or simply going to the breakers. A number of ships went through all three processes. In 1968 P&O/Orient was uncertain whether 'to continue with or to phase out from the passenger ship business' having built both *Oriana* and *Canberra* less than a decade earlier (Rabson & O'Donoghue 1988, p. 216; Howarth & Howarth 1994, p. 169). Yet within only a few years the rapid rise of a US market for cruising inspired a new confidence in the industry and encouraged a wider deployment of cruise ships, many of them now purpose built. New cruise regions were opened, and existing ones expanded. Alaska began to see its first large cruise ships; and the Caribbean cruise circuit was intensified.

The South Pacific, although regional operators Burns Philp and Union Steamships had moved out of passenger services, maintained its seasonal popularity with vessels that exchanged a European winter for a cyclonic Pacific summer. *Oriana* and *Canberra* established their long-standing reputations with Australian cruise passengers during this period, although the latter's early entry into Caribbean cruising was unsuccessful. Indeed, the arrival of these ships in Australia was of such importance that the construction of a new shipping terminal at Sydney's Circular

Quay had been largely influenced by the building of both (McCart 1987, p. 226). But the North American market was expanding geographically as well as demographically, and with the fly-cruise well in place by the mid-1970s, US-based companies, led by Princess and Royal Viking, brought their ships into the South Pacific during the northern hemisphere winter also, for the benefit of mainly American passengers. They were joined occasionally by other companies, whose vessels ranged from the fundamental to the adequate but all of which enjoyed popularity for a time. These included the Italian Lauro line, the Swire Corporation of Hong Kong and CTC Cruise Line, which used Russian vessels in a number of budget programs. As more variety in the cruise product became necessary, themed cruises, which promoted a particular activity or special interest as the main focus, grew in popularity. One such interest—the Pacific War (1941–45)—was promoted as a theme by both Princess and Royal Viking, and centred on the presence on board of a leading US military figure from the period of conflict, attracting considerable numbers of American veterans for whom the campaigns were vague, youthful memories. It is arguable that during this time there was—as far as island ports of call, themes, length of voyages and variety of vessel were concerned—a greater range of cruise product available in the South Pacific, with Sydney as the hub, than there has been since.

The last of our themes, acquisition, is sufficiently complex to require a full-length book study and perhaps is of even more interest to the student of business and corporate activity than to the student of cruising. However, as the early history of P&O shows, it is by no means a recent phenomenon, since that company had been engaged in the elimination of its rivals throughout the 20th century, ultimately merging them completely out of existence. But the exceptionally rapid growth of cruising in the 1980s and 1990s, at all levels of quality, and the international scope of the activity, necessarily intensified competition: P&O, not surprisingly, was in the forefront, as was its traditional rival, Cunard.

Even by the early 1980s the trend towards what some observers call 'consolidation' was under way. In 1983 Cunard, itself owned by Trafalgar House since 1971, paid US$73 million for the five vessels of Norwegian American Cruises. (The sum now seems paltry: in 2003, two of P&O's newly built vessels, *Aurora* and *Oceana*, each cost US$30 million.) A little more than one year later Klosters Rederi, the Oslo-based owners of Norwegian Caribbean Lines, took over Royal Viking, a company that had been established only in 1970 and was in the forefront of the trend towards luxury cruising. Cunard had also shown interest in acquiring P&O itself, an event which, had it taken place, would certainly have altered the face of international cruising at an earlier stage

(Maxtone-Graham 2000, pp. 442–3). But P&O's own acquisition of Los Angeles-based Princess Cruises in 1974 had not only given the British company a strong position in the American market but also enlarged its fleet considerably, making it a formidably expensive proposition. It is worth pointing out here that throughout their association P&O and Princess have maintained separate brands and separate marketing strategies. Princess Cruises' own reputation—hence economic value—rose rapidly with the advent of the famous *The Love Boat* television series in 1975, the influence of which was far longer lasting than could have been predicted. P&O also added Sitmar International to its fleet in 1988, and by doing so provided its Australian branch with a year-round Pacific cruise ship in the shape of *Fairstar*. The above details illustrate something of the flavour of the period and the sometimes giddying speed with which changes occurred. But the efforts of such long-time players in this expensive game were to be eclipsed by the rise of another organisation: this was Carnival Cruise Lines.

Don't stop the Carnival

The corporation, now the world's largest cruise company, was founded shakily in 1971 by Ted Arison, an Israeli with a background in the transport business best described as 'unsound'. Projects he had initiated since 1966 had come to nothing. In 1971 a ten-year contract he had entered into with Knut Kloster of Norwegian Caribbean Lines was cancelled when Kloster decided that Arison was making an insufficient contribution to the partnership's profits. With the combination of luck, guile and borrowed money characteristic of so many ventures that ultimately succeed, Arison then obtained the financial backing to buy the out-of-service *Empress of Canada*, which, renamed *Mardi Gras*, ran aground on the first voyage for its new owners. The one-ship cruise line, operating in the Caribbean, which has been Carnival's main home ever since, made its first profit in 1975 (Dickinson & Vladimir 1997, p. 33). Within the next three years two more ships, neither of them new, were acquired. By this time Carnival had adopted the slogan 'Fun Ship', and the accompanying policy of classless, good time, largely informal cruising, in which the main attraction was the vessel rather than the port. As the now president Bob Dickinson put it: 'With the Fun Ship positioning, the ship itself became a destination and the ports of call became green stamps' (Dickinson & Vladimir 1997, p. 33). Carnival's financial advance was assisted by the application to its vessels of economically competitive 'flags of convenience' registrations. Liberian and Panamanian registry stopped being a bad joke that had been previously applied to decrepit cargo ships and became an apparently essential part of the economics of cruising, as more and more companies availed themselves of it. The prestige value and marketing significance of First World registries has continued to the present, however. P&O's Australia-based *Pacific Sky* maintains a British registry, as do the company's other P&O—as distinguished from Princess—vessels, such as *Oriana*, *Aurora* and *Oceana*, also Cunard's *QE2* and *Caronia*.

In the late 1980s Carnival entered a vigorous period of fleet expansion by both new building and acquisition, in 1988 taking over Holland America Line and its subsidiary Windstar, in 1992 Seabourn, in 1997 the Italian company Costa Cruises, and in 1998 Cunard. All of these are now represented under Carnival's banner 'World's Greatest Cruise Lines', but are marketed under their own distinctive brand names. Carnival's acquisition of Cunard was said at the time to have been made for the latter's brand name rather than its 'eclectic mix of ships that didn't fit' (Douglas & Douglas 2000). Not long after the takeover, the eclectic mix was reduced to only two vessels, *QE2* and *Caronia,* although a *Queen Mary 2* was expected in late 2003. In 2001 Star Cruises of Malaysia, which had learnt its operational methods by closely studying those of Carnival, took over the ailing Norwegian Cruise Line (NCL), having entered into the transaction originally in partnership with Carnival.

In November 2001, apparently concerned at the expansion of Carnival, which in a relatively brief period had become the largest cruise company in the world, former rivals Royal Caribbean International and P&O Princess (respectively the second and third largest) announced their own merger. The news was received with a counter-bid for P&O Princess by Carnival, which by that time had a documented history of 'spoiling' the intentions of other cruise companies by making counter offers followed by withdrawals, a tactic it had partly applied to the Star Cruises venture above (Waples 2002b). P&O chairman Lord Sterling announced to colleagues that, as financial regulators in both Europe and the United States were certain to block Carnival's bid, its main purpose was clearly obstruction (Waples 2002a).

But in late 2002 P&O announced that it had advised Royal Caribbean of the receipt of a 'superior' offer from Carnival and, failing a better one from the former, would be accepting it. When none was forthcoming negotiations went ahead, not without strenuous objections from Royal Caribbean. In early February 2003 P&O and Carnival issued a joint announcement that the proposed transaction had received 'unconditional clearance' from the European Commission in Brussels, which, together with an earlier clearance from the US Federal Trade Commission, removed any antitrust obstacles to the plan. The decision to terminate its proposed deal with Royal Caribbean resulted in P&O Princess having to pay a 'break fee' of US$62.5 million to its erstwhile merger partner (www.ananova.com/business/story/sm).

The language used in various announcements and documents relating to the proposal left no doubt that Carnival was 'acquiring' P&O Princess. The latter would be representing only 26 per cent of Carnival's total group and at least part of the P&O Princess identity would be subsumed by Carnival: 'Upon completion of the transaction, P&O Princess will be renamed Carnival', although 'the existing well-established brands operated by P&O Princess will not be affected by the change to the parent company name' (P&O Princess Cruises 2003b). The transaction was expected to increase Carnival's total fleet to 50 vessels, making the combination 'one of the leading global vacation companies; [with] a whole array of leading consumer brands in every major cruise market in the world', according to Princess CEO Peter Ratcliffe (P&O Princess Cruises 2003a).

There is on one hand considerable irony in this outcome—largely unexpected by industry watchers, compared perhaps with industry insiders—and on the other a degree of predictability, given the relative positions of the leading players at the beginning of the new millennium. The company that 'invented cruising', and throughout its history had done its best to absorb its competitors, had itself been absorbed by the company that had revolutionised the activity and was now seeking ultimate control of it. The arrangement resulted in 50 vessels operating under Carnival's many brands.

It had been suggested that diehard loyalists among the P&O shareholders would oppose the takeover by the American giant, but no opposition of any consequence had met Carnival's takeover of Cunard and, in any case, the combined P&O Princess organisation was, in terms of vessel numbers and berths, largely US-dominated. Sentiment is not so evident a quality in the cruise business, despite the age-old tradition of personifying vessels and referring to them in feminine gender terms. Captains and crews may become emotionally attached to their ships, and so may passengers: there would be far fewer repeat cruisers if this were not the case, and repeat business in any aspect of tourism is essential to survival. Directors and shareholders (many of whom have never set foot on a cruise ship) are less concerned with sentiment than profit potential. This was made overwhelmingly obvious at an Extraordinary General Meeting of shareholders of P&O Princess on 16 April 2003. They voted 99.7 per cent in favour of the merger (P&O Cruises 2003c). The following day P&O Princess became yet another of Carnival's brand names. The transaction, which cost Carnival a reported US$5 billion, was undoubtedly a watershed in the recent history of cruising, probably the most significant event since cruise ships and passenger jets decided to cooperate, and so provides a perfectly appropriate conclusion to this brief history.

8

Destination development in the cruise industry

The dictionary definition of the term 'destination' is 'the predetermined **end** of a journey or voyage' (e.g. *Collins Dictionary* 1985; *Encarta Dictionary* 1999), but in tourism its meaning is somewhat broader, perhaps vaguer. Thus, in a recent book devoted to the subject of visitor destinations: 'The term "destination" is commonly used for any location to which people make a journey, but in the present context it refers to the area in which visitors conduct their leisure or business activities' (Kelly & Nankervis 2001, p. 13). Similarly, the word is often used in cruising to refer to the ports of call: e.g. 'a five-destination cruise'; or to the geographical region in which the ship cruises: the Caribbean, Mediterranean, South Pacific and so on. However, just as tourism sometimes renames geographical features or locations to suit its own needs, so the application of the term 'destination' may vary according to marketing strategy. Robert H. Dickinson, president of Carnival Cruise Lines, writes: 'Since the early 1970s, we have been marketing our "Fun Ships" as destinations in themselves, with the ports of call as secondary considerations' (1995). The following discussion, therefore, must take all these uses into account.

Cruise destinations: a contemporary overview

The Caribbean, although it has declined slowly in significance over the past decade, continues to maintain its position as the world's most popular cruise destination. In 2002 it attracted nearly 47 per cent of total cruise passenger capacity. But changing passenger preferences, rising competition from other destinations as they court itinerary planners, and the need to redeploy growing fleets may contribute to the steady decline of the Caribbean and the slow rise in popularity of other regions. On the other hand, it may simply result in greater congestion in Caribbean ports. One of the biggest challenges for many destinations is their distance from the primary generating markets. While the fly-cruise product has revolutionised the cruise business in many ways, the majority of people still resist very long flights to join relatively short cruises. The cultural variety of the Asia–Pacific region has a lot to offer cruisers, but sustained growth depends on moving away from reliance on the American and European markets to develop a stronger and more consistent regional demand. Away from the Caribbean, Europe accounts for some 11 per cent of passenger capacity, the Mediterranean over ten per cent and Alaska eight per cent (and growing steadily). Within the Asia–Pacific region Hawaii attracts about three per cent of capacity, the South Pacific (including Australia and New Zealand) 1.3 per cent, and South-East Asia and the Far East about half a per cent each, although the last two may grow under the influence of Star Cruises. It should be noted that the destinations listed here are fluid and represent what seems appropriate to the Cruise Lines International Association at the time of its surveys. See Table 8.1. They have been different in previous years. Trans-Pacific and Indian Ocean, for example, seem a little spurious, as they are not destinations in themselves.

Table 8.2 indicates the growth in cruise capacity for the Asia–Pacific region. It necessarily incorporates around-the-world cruising, which has significant impacts on the region in the southern hemisphere summer, when a number of ships are repositioned to a warmer climate for the duration of the northern hemisphere winter.

In the first years of the 21st century the cruise business in Asia–Pacific has seen some changes which have not yet been fully evaluated. Star Cruises has been redeploying its fleet after testing out certain Asian markets that have not been as successful as the company had hoped. In late 2002 P&O introduced two new ships into the South Pacific in order to broaden its market and consolidate its presence in the region.

Table 8.1   Selected destination growth, 2001–02

Destination	2001 % of capacity	2002 % of capacity
Caribbean	36.4	40.0
Europe	8.12	10.9
Mediterranean	12.67	10.2
Alaska	7.89	7.95
Mexico West	1.96	5.33
Bahamas	7.89	4.52
Trans-Canal	4.02	3.29
Hawaii	2.61	2.99
South America	2.39	2.19
Trans-Atlantic	1.9	1.93
South Pacific	1.94	1.31
Far East	0.36	0.57
South-East Asia	0.72	0.54
Trans-Pacific	0.11	0.22
Indian Ocean	0.38	0.15
Antarctica	0.08	0.12

Source: CLIA (2002).

Table 8.2   Cruise growth capacity in Asia–Pacific

Destination	1992 '000	1994 '000	1996 '000	1998 '000	2000 '000
South Pacific	401.8	763.8	283.0	369.6	1155.2
South-East Asia	164.9	282.8	415.6	157.7	244.6
Trans-Pacific	11.0	51.2	85.1	99.8	52.4
Far East	189.0	305.1	200.8	219.0	201.6
Around World	117.9	148.2	239.5	181.7	138.1
Total	884.6	1551.1	1224.0	1027.7	1791.9

Adapted from G. P. Wild (International) 2001.

Major destinations

The ever-increasing number of ships has encouraged a parallel increase in the destinations on offer. In one year, 1998, Crystal Cruises added 24 ports of call to its itineraries; Cunard added 55. However, although these are usually described by the cruise lines in question as 'new' ports, they are generally new only to that particular line, not necessarily new to cruising. The larger ships are most commonly found in the traditional Caribbean, Mediterranean, Alaska (see Figure 8.1) and Atlantic Europe regions, where waters are more protected, large target markets are easily accessible and there is a plethora of suitable ports within a few hours' sailing time. Ships of less than 70 000 GRT are being located in other areas where the design of vessels must take into account more unpredictable seas and greater distances between ports, with longer cruises the result.

Figure 8.1 Princess Cruises' *Regal Princess* in Seward, Alaska (Courtesy Bert Plenkovich)

The major cruise areas are subject to seasonal variations. The Mediterranean, Alaska and Atlantic Europe, for example, are northern hemisphere summer itineraries when ships are repositioned from the Caribbean. The South Pacific and Asian regions see their greatest activity during the southern hemisphere summer, when ships from both UK- and European-based fleets as well as US-based fleets are repositioned for a series of short cruises, or the regions are visited as part of round-the-world voyages. The latter exercise enables cruise lines to sell wholly South Pacific or wholly South-East Asian itineraries as individual sectors, naming and promoting them accordingly. For example, the Los Angeles to Sydney sector on the 2003 world cruise of *QE2* became the 'Idyllic Polynesian Passage' in the hands of Cunard's destination spin doctors, while for *Crystal Symphony*'s inaugural world voyage, the very well-travelled route between Hong Kong and Bombay (now Mumbai) became the 'Mystic Passage'.

Destination determinants

Present cruise destinations, as the examples below of the Mediterranean, Caribbean and South Pacific illustrate, may be the result of various

factors: regions that had appealing climates, interesting geographical features, historical monuments or other cultural attractions were obviously
far more likely to attract leisure travellers. But in the early days of cruising it was the convenience of the shipping companies that was the first
consideration. The Mediterranean ports to which P&O's earliest cruises
sailed were on the company's new mail services. Many of the first
cruisers to the Caribbean Islands were taken there on vessels otherwise
engaged in freight runs or normal short-haul passenger services from
nearby North America, sometimes both. South Pacific cruising was introduced by companies based in the region on ships that were far from
purpose-built for vacationers, sailing to ports on the vessels' regular
schedules. All these occasions were promoted as 'cruises', nonetheless.

Modern destination planning is a somewhat more complicated business. Itinerary preparation may often involve a former ship's officer,
hence someone more likely to be familiar with such necessary nautical
details as distances between ports, speed of travel required by the vessel
to maintain its schedule and seasonal weather variations. Although the
procedures vary from one company to another, the itinerary is usually
then considered by a group which may include representatives from
various company departments: marine, sales and marketing, air/sea and
shore excursions. The discussions would probably be chaired by a senior
management figure, since senior management approval is necessary
before the itinerary is accepted.

Reasons for itinerary changes also vary from line to line, but generally are based on the marketing and sales consequences of including a
new port or eliminating an established one. Industry sources say that a
cruise has more appeal to Americans if it contains a generous number of
ports relative to sea days. British cruisers, on the other hand, are happier
to accept fewer ports and more sea days. A balance has to be struck
between these for an itinerary such as QE2's World Cruise, which is marketed to both British and Americans, who together make up the great
majority of passengers, although passengers of a dozen or more other
nationalities may join the cruise for short sectors. Because of the importance of repeat business to cruise companies and the need to retain the
frequent travellers' market, world cruises need to provide variety as well
as maintaining those parts of an itinerary that are either popular with passengers or necessary for logistic reasons to the company. Ports that are
'firm favourites' are the framework around which variations in itinerary
can be constructed: they include ports of embarkation or disembarkation
and ports which are necessary for bunkering or provedoring. Among
these are Los Angeles, Hong Kong, Singapore, Honolulu, Sydney, Cape
Town and, in the South Pacific Islands, Noumea.

Cruise itinerary planners work on a minimum lead-in time of two years; that is, a cruise is promoted at least two years ahead of its intended occurrence. But a destination which appeared quite desirable and popular in 2003 may well be off-limits by 2005 for a number of reasons. The first priority of captains is the safety of their ships and all that sail in them. They do not hesitate to sail right past a scheduled port of call if there is any chance of danger to either vessel or passengers from foul weather or social and political unrest. The weather and seasonal variations pose itinerary planning challenges. For the South Pacific, the best time to cruise is during the middle months of the year when monsoons, cyclones and heavy seas are out of season. However, the lines based in the United States and the United Kingdom want to send their ships to this region during the northern hemisphere winter, which coincides with the November to April southern hemisphere monsoon and generally wet seasons. Even the most modern innovations in stabilisers can find the swells of the Pacific Ocean a challenge, and landing, especially at ports requiring tenders, presents problems. Despite having taken quite a number of South Pacific cruises, we have never once put in at 'Mystery Island' in Vanuatu or Amedee in New Caledonia, notwithstanding their being featured as ports of call each time. Weather conditions were on each occasion deemed unsuitable. On one cruise a crew member who had been with the vessel for many months admitted that landings in either place were quite rare. During his time on the ship he had never been to them either.

Civil unrest or doubtful safety at a destination may have very far-reaching impacts in terms of whether that port is included in itineraries planned several years ahead. In 2003 neither the eastern Mediterranean (including Israel and Lebanon) nor the Gulf States were considered appropriate destinations. The eastern Mediterranean, though some distance from the area of actual conflict, was also avoided during the Gulf War of 1991 because of 'perceived risk'. 'The American market is more susceptible to unrest in a region than the British', according to an industry source (personal communication September 2002). In South and South-East Asia, ports avoided in recent years for reasons of passenger safety include Colombo, because of continual domestic strife in Sri Lanka, and—following the attack by Moslem extremists on New York on 11 September 2001—also ports in Indonesia and Malaysia, because of their Moslem affiliations. After the attack certain US-based cruise companies chose to cruise closer to North America in the belief that their passengers would feel more secure. The reaction to perceived risk can take curious forms. During a cruise in South-East Asian waters in early 2002, on which we were engaged as lecturers, a schoolteacher from New

York made an official complaint to the cruise director that our survey of religions in the region had included references to Islam, causing her considerable grief and anxiety. 'I didn't expect I would have to hear anything about Moslems on this cruise', she said. The gradual removal, almost to extinction, of ports in Papua New Guinea (PNG) from cruise itineraries provides a further illustration of official caution. In the mid-1970s there were as many as six ports in PNG visited by cruise ships. By the late 1990s the perpetually troublesome capital, Port Moresby, was being avoided, and other ports once regarded as not merely safe or convenient but interesting in their own right had also been excised because of lingering uncertainties. The current attitude of cruise planners to PNG is in sharp contrast to that of earlier times. Solomon Islands, at least in the short term, is likely to suffer the same fate.

The notion that passenger preference might play some part in destination choice and development by the cruise company is a relatively recent one, dating back probably no further than the revival of cruising in the 1970s but gaining strength in the bitterly competitive atmosphere of the 1990s and early 2000s, when passenger satisfaction and the repeat bookings resulting from it have become extremely important. Just before the end of a cruise passengers are invariably requested to fill out a questionnaire or assessment form on almost every aspect of their cruise experience. Port preferences are carefully noted from the results of these. In addition, companies are said to take note of passengers' comments to such personnel as captains, hotel managers, cruise directors, cruise sales consultants and shore excursion personnel. A captain's farewell address to passengers often includes a summary of ports visited, the names of which are usually greeted with acclamation or vociferous dissatisfaction. This input, however, is still subject to the requirements of the cruise line: no number of passenger complaints about Noumea, for instance, seems able to dislodge it from P&O's regular South Pacific itineraries. In ports that are widely unpopular or overfamiliar, passengers often show their indifference by staying on the vessel during its time in port. A shore excursion manager told us of one female frequent traveller who, despite her tendency to remain on board while in most ports, made a practice of leaving the ship entirely during its cruises to South America, such was her dislike of that continent.

The long flight time from the US market to join fly-cruises in such distant places as the Asia–Pacific region remains a constant difficulty. Australia-based cruise lines constantly cite the '14-hour hurdle' as a major obstacle to their growth, referring to the flight time from the west coast of the United States to Sydney. This factor has also brought about a slower than expected expansion of the major cruise lines into the Asia–Pacific region. The long haul to ports of embarkation such as Singapore, Mumbai, Hong Kong, Bangkok and Sydney is a significant deterrent to growth in this area. Attempts by US-based companies to reposition ships on a semi-permanent basis within Asia–Pacific have so far not been successful because of the difficulties in maintaining passenger numbers. Those who have made the journey may spend the first few days of their cruise recuperating from the effects of flying across several time zones or the International Date Line. Proximity of market to destination, therefore, is another significant determinant in destination development. It is widely accepted that the statistics on destinations produced by the CLIA, even though they focus on the US market, can be used as reliable indicators for what is happening elsewhere in the cruise world.

The rise and fall of destinations

The process by which **tourism** destinations rise and fall in popularity has been examined by a number of writers, each of whom has tried to find a recognisable sequence or pattern in destination growth and decline (e.g. Plog 1974; Butler 1980). That none of these has included any specific reference to **cruise** destinations may suggest either that they have not thought about them at all or that they don't consider them to be distinctive. But cruising introduces factors that differ markedly from other forms of tourism—for example, the extraordinary numbers that can arrive at a port of call all at the same time, placing serious strains on all kinds of services there. Increasingly, also, there are destinations at which cruise passengers represent the overwhelming majority of visitors, sometimes the only visitors. The end product of this tendency is 'Our Island', the 'destination'—a beach, or bay or small island, or even an artificial island—that is actually owned by, or wholly under the control of, the cruise company and considered exclusive to it. The practice was introduced by Norwegian Cruise Line in 1977. They have since appeared in both the Caribbean and the South Pacific, under the auspices of such companies as P&O, Princess, Royal Caribbean and Disney. On the latter's Castaway Cay in the Bahamas, Disney characters welcome visitors, and the diversions include 'Searching for Hidden Mickeys'.

Cruise destinations: some historical factors

The examples that follow are intended to illustrate some aspects of the historical growth and change of certain cruise regions over the past century or so, rather than to imply that the same process is at work in all of them.

The Mediterranean

The Mediterranean is historically the most significant of cruise destinations. It was here that Arthur Anderson, one of the founders of P&O, is said to have 'invented' cruising in 1844, a detail dutifully recorded in almost everything written about the Peninsular and Oriental Steam Navigation Co. (e.g. Howarth & Howarth 1994, p. 47). It is also the most highly developed, many would say overdeveloped, of all. This, however, is not the fault of the cruise companies: unlike the South Pacific and the Caribbean, in both of which it could be argued successfully that cruising represented the origin of tourism, the Mediterranean had been exposed to leisure travel since antiquity. It reached one of the historical peaks of tourism development in the age of the Grand Tour in the 18th and early 19th centuries, and another with the operations of the Thomas Cook organisation from the mid-19th century onwards, which saw European touring taken out of the hands of the aristocracy and democratised. The cruise companies have been able to take great advantage of what was already there.

The reasons for the perennial popularity of the Mediterranean are not hard to find: it is an enclosed body of water, making it safe for even large vessels of shallow draft; it has a series of scenically attractive coasts; it is

Figure 8.2 P&O's new *Oriana* in Venice, a perennially favoured
destination (Courtesy P&O)

bordered by no fewer than 15 countries, all culturally distinctive; much of its maritime infrastructure was first established in the pre-Christian era and has been developed over centuries; and it offers more accessible and culturally significant visitor attractions than any other comparably sized region on earth. In the course of a 12-day cruise from east to west one may visit Turkey, Greece (mainland and islands), Italy (several ports), France (several ports), Monaco and Spain. (Portugal, strictly speaking, is not a Mediterranean country.) Those are but a few, and all on the Mediterranean Sea's northern coast. If the Levant (east coast) and the North African coast are also taken into account, another eight countries may be added to the Mediterranean's variety, but many of these are nowadays considered politically risky and no longer figure strongly in destination planning. Mediterranean cruising has been frequently interrupted by military, social or religious strife: the Crimean War, World Wars I and II and the conflicts between Palestinians and Israelis, and between factions in Lebanon, have all affected cruise activity since its introduction.

One of P&O's ground-breaking early cruises in 1844 was recorded in detail by the English author William Makepeace Thackeray, who had been invited on the voyage in the expectation that he would have good things to say about it, an early example of the sort of deal travel writers have been engaging in ever since. What the company thought of Thackeray's almost relentlessly critical view of most places and people he encountered is not known. Certainly there is not much evidence that the book which resulted from his trip 'greatly helped the company to popularize cruising', or that he 'eulogized the company and the cruising experience at great length' (McAuley 1997, p. 130). But his detailed description of the places visited—Lisbon, Cadiz, Gibraltar, Malta, Smyrna (now Izmir), Constantinople (now Istanbul), Beirut, Jaffa (now Tel Aviv-Yafo), Jerusalem, Alexandria and Cairo—however caustic his comments about many of the things he saw (Thackeray 1991), give a good indication of the geographical scope of even the earliest kind of cruise, and make it apparent why the innovation became quickly popular.

But less than a decade after their introduction, P&O's Mediterranean cruises were suspended because of war in the Crimea from 1853 to 1856. When they resumed they received a boost from an unexpected quarter. The staid but widely respected *British Medical Journal*, having become aware of the curative possibilities of ocean voyaging, drew attention to P&O's low scale of charges for accommodation on its 'magnificent ships', pointing out that ocean travel of this kind had 'a special interest for medical men and their patients' (quoted in McAuley 1997, p. 131). As an apparently unsolicited promotion for their cruises, P&O could hardly have asked for better. By the latter part of the 19th century, parts of the

Mediterranean, especially the French Riviera, were attracting a great deal of attention from British and Northern Europeans for their salubrious, almost miraculously healing qualities (Douglas 2001). Cruising also benefited, therefore, by gaining added custom from the infirm and the consumptive.

The period between the World Wars (1919–39) saw remarkable developments in the design and comfort of passenger ships and hence cruising. Both the North Atlantic crossing services and the already established cruising grounds such as the Mediterranean gained in popularity and prestige. The concept of the ship as a resort or destination in its own right can be traced back to this time, if not earlier—notwithstanding the more recent claims of Carnival Cruise Line—especially for passengers travelling first class, where food, facilities and entertainments were influenced by, and often equal to, that found in the great hotels of Europe. Ports of call may have provided a diversion, but they were often of far less consequence than the comforts and amusements to be found on board. The interiors of the grander vessels exceeded the grand hotels in opulence, and swimming pools became more and more evident on larger ships, with Italia Line vessels simulating a beach resort by adding real sand around pools on the Lido deck. The term 'Lido' was itself Mediterranean, having been derived from the name of a bathing beach near Venice. It is still used on tradition-conscious vessels: 'This hedonistic approach to ship travel became all-encompassing with the development of the "pleasure cruise"—long lingering journeys on vessels designed for the sunny skies of the tropics . . .' (Server 1996).

The Caribbean

The Caribbean area is shown in Figure 8.3. For the purposes of cruise destination statistics the Bahamas are at times regarded as a separate region from the Caribbean, and at times not. This is true of Bermuda also (CLIA 2002). The distinction is not recognised by some researchers (e.g. Lawton & Butler 1987) because of the 'numerous similarities' of both the Bahamas and Bermuda to the Caribbean, a view that seems somewhat more practical and is accepted here. As the Caribbean is the most convenient cruise region to the world's largest market, the United States, and remains the most popular with cruisers, it is not surprising that it has come in for the most scrutiny. The Bahamas are close enough to lend themselves to weekend cruising from Miami, the main US cruise hub. It is possible to depart Miami at 4 pm on Friday, spend 24 hours in Nassau, the Bahamas capital, followed by a day at sea and be back in Miami at 8 am on Monday. Weekend vacationers who have less time to spare may leave Florida's Port Canaveral at 4:30 pm on Saturday, spend most of

Sunday in the Bahamas port of Freeport, and be back at their point of departure at 8 am on Monday. Geographical proximity to the United States is certainly part of the reason for the perennial popularity of the Caribbean: it is often claimed that among the obstacles faced by Australia's cruise industry is the amount of water between Sydney and the nearest foreign port, Noumea in New Caledonia, requiring more than two days' sailing time. No quick, and proportionately cheap, weekend cruise getaways to 'exotic' destinations are possible in the South Pacific.

But history also contributed a good deal to the Caribbean's popularity. According to Lawton and Butler (1987), as early as the late 19th century 'the emphasis of the cruise ship industry gradually shifted to the Caribbean from the Mediterranean and Europe'. If we leave aside the detail that the activity hardly constituted an 'industry' at that stage, this seems reasonable if one considers mainly the services from mainland United States, which those writers do. But it overlooks the fact that some of the most successful cruises to the Caribbean in the late 19th century originated in England. One of the earliest cruise posters extant, from Orient Line, advertises a 60-day cruise to the 'West India Islands' via Madeira, Tenerife and the Azores, departing London on 16 January 1895 (see Figure 7.1). Subsequent posters for the same service referred to the

Figure 8.3 The Caribbean: the most popular cruise region
(Source: Pacific Profiles)

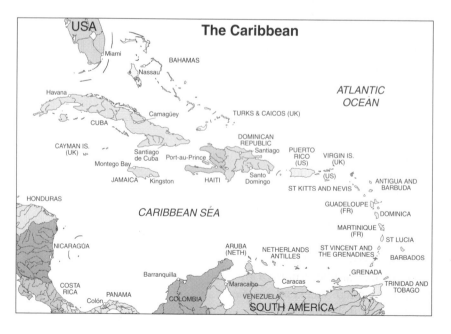

'West Indies' apparently to avoid misunderstanding. The departure date is significant: what better way to avoid the miseries of a winter in Britain than a two-month cruise that included island destinations in both the Atlantic and the Caribbean—an island-hopper's dream. British influence in the Caribbean region was very strong in that period and remains so today, despite the nominally independent and self-governing states that have emerged from former British colonies. Indeed, the 'Britishness' of such places as Bermuda and the Bahamas has become part of their advertised appeal for visitors (e.g. Carnival 1999). In addition, if one were seeking warmth and attractive and varied scenery, the Caribbean was the tropical region most easily accessible from Britain, with colonies in Africa or Asia being considered more suitable for colonial administrators and commercial agents than for vacationers at that early stage.

European vessels offering cruises were not slow to follow, a standard being set in 1901 by the Hamburg-Amerika Line's *Prinzessin Victoria Luise*, a ship fashioned after the royal yachts of Europe but capable of carrying 400 passengers. It inspired a number of developments in cruising, most immediately the conversion to regular cruise activity of another vessel from the same company which was given almost the same name— *Victoria Luise*. In addition to ports of call, some of which no longer appear on cruise itineraries, *Victoria Luise* offered to its passengers a close-up of the Panama Canal in its final stages of construction. The visit aroused so much interest that the canal and passage through it became one of the major attractions of the region and eventually a cruise destination in its own right: trans-canal now ranks seventh in passenger capacity out of the world's 16 designated cruise destinations (CLIA 2002), and some lines offer cruises that transit the 80-kilometre-long waterway twice, so popular is the experience.

If popular fascination with industrial initiative provided one early stimulus to Caribbean cruising, popular fondness for alcohol provided another. World War I (1914–1918) not only brought about a decline in regional shipping but also indirectly led to a prohibition on the sale or consumption of alcohol in the United States in 1920. This curious and ultimately futile law not only helped create the appropriate conditions for the rise of criminal gangs in the United States but also gave an enormous boost to short cruises to the Caribbean. Once out of US waters, bars on the vessels could trade openly, and alcohol was readily available also in nearby British territories such as Bermuda. The excursions quickly became known as 'booze cruises' and helped to further popularise a number of Caribbean ports. One of these was Havana in Cuba, also very near the United States, where entertainment of most kinds, including (in addition to drinking) gambling and prostitution, was largely controlled and regularly patronised by American gangsters. The irony in this is evident, but there is greater irony in the fact that Havana, so close to the United States and once considered one of the region's most desirable tourist destinations, has been out of bounds to American cruise ships (indeed, to all American tourists) for more than 40 years because of the US political and economic blockade against Cuba. In the meantime, smaller cruise operators are taking advantage of the US intransigence by running short cruises to Havana from departure ports such as Cancun in Mexico or Puerto Plata in the Dominican Republic. According to the seavacations website, 'the Cuban government is taking a more positive position [to future cruise visitors] and is devoting a lot of energy and money to the renovation of docking facilities and passenger terminals. Already, Cuba receives over 300 passenger ship calls a year with a total of about 140 000 passengers' from cruises originating in Europe (<www.seavacations.com>).

Cultural variety, another consequence of the region's history, also added to the appeal of the Caribbean for cruise tourists. Within a small compass it was possible to see and briefly experience the colonial cultures of Europe—Spain, France, the Netherlands and Britain—as well as the small, politically independent states within the region. The survival of these vestiges of colonialism provided much grist for the cruise marketing mill and continues to do so, as these extracts from a brochure of Carnival (Carnival Cruise Lines 1999), the dominant cruise line in the region, illustrate:

'The half-French, half-Dutch island of St Maarten impresses with its architecture . . .'
'The very French island of Martinique offers the serenity of secluded beaches . . .'
'Barbados in the West Indies has all the flavour of Great Britain in the tropics.'
'Curaçao is a mini Holland in the tropics . . .'

A number of factors, then, related to both geography and history, in addition to the region's favourable climate for vacationers, contributed to the popularity of the Caribbean. They are all now essential elements of the marketing strategy applied by the cruise lines that operate there. There are indications, however, that saturation and overfamiliarity with the Caribbean as a cruise destination is breeding indifference on the part of passengers. Declining numbers provide one illustration of this: from over 52 per cent of capacity in 1994 to 47 per cent in 2001 (CLIA 1994, 2002a). One could suggest that the more and more elaborate distractions offered on the ships themselves is a way of dealing with destinations that are falling from favour: it hardly matters where the cruise is taking place, or whether the passengers are indifferent to ports of call, if the vessel itself constitutes the destination. Another is the attempt by cruise lines to introduce variety by conjuring up their own exclusive destinations, some constructed for just that purpose. The ultimate tourist dream destination, it seems, if not a cruise, is a tropical island. The *reductio ad absurdum* of this has been reached on the Internet with an advertisement for Kastaway Island, 'the first cruise ship that, with the creative use of paint and fibreglass, will be renovated to look like a lush tropical island floating along the water'. A picture of the vessel, complete with palm trees painted on its hull, a waterfall and an erupting volcano where the funnel should be, and resembling nothing so much as the hallucination of a theme park designer on LSD, is displayed on the site. The caption reads: 'This ship may not look "exactly" like the final ship due to extensive renovations to be carried out' (<www.kastawayisland.com>). In the tourism 'life-cycle' model propounded by Richard Butler (1980), the search for additional novelties such as these may be interpreted as representing the beginning of serious decline. It seems unlikely, however, that there will be very many to compare with this remarkable effort. At a more credible level, the concept of the cruise ship itself as destination/resort seems to be catching on. 'Think of it as a floating seaside resort', says P&O of its *Pacific Sky* (P&O Cruises 2002).

Destinations and diversions in the Pacific Islands

'So, I said, why can't *Fairstar* go to some of those unspoilt island paradises for a change?' (Phil Young, managing director, P&O Australia, personal communication 1996).

The manner in which cruise destination determinants change over time from being motivated by company convenience to being motivated to some degree by passenger leisure considerations finds an ideal illustration in the South Pacific region and in some respects is a capsule history of regional cruising.

Perhaps encouraged by the early success of P&O in the Mediterranean, in February 1884 Burns Philp (BP), an Australia-based company trading in the South Pacific Islands, advertised its first cruise from Thursday Island in the Torres Strait to Port Moresby. This brief voyage, whose importance was long overlooked, heralded not only the beginning of cruising in the Islands region but also the effective beginning of tourism there. BP's counterpart in New Zealand, the Union Steamship Co., followed soon after with a cruise to the eastern Pacific Islands.

Whatever unusual delights were promised excursionists by the advertising, the main aims of the early Burns Philp vessels were to load/unload cargo and deliver mail. The presence of passengers was profitable but incidental to the real purpose. The astonishing (by today's standards) number of island ports visited by BP ships in the first decades of the 20th century illustrates the extent of the company's copra depots rather than its desire to provide variety for passengers. The 'capital shooting and fishing' advertised in connection with BP's second cruise to Port Moresby in September 1884 required no real organisational effort on the part of the company. For some years, however, the very novelty of this kind of travel to the Islands was reward enough for many, even if the promised colourful savages were not always forthcoming, or were only to be seen loading copra. But after watching the loading of copra at perhaps up to 15 ports on one cruise, passenger interest may well have waned.

By the beginning of the 20th century BP's cruising itinerary included, in addition to Papua and New Guinea (then separately administered), Vanuatu (then the New Hebrides), Solomon Islands, Lord Howe Island and Norfolk Island. Regular ports of call included, in addition to the capital towns—Port Moresby, Tulagi (Solomon Islands) and Port Vila— remote out-stations such as Yule Island in Papua and Herbertshoe (later Kokopo) in New Britain; Ugi, Santa Anna, Makira and the Santa Cruz group in Solomon Islands; and a plethora of ports in Vanuatu, including at least four on Tanna Island and seven on Malakula. Freight contracts entered into with both Catholic and Protestant missions augmented the itineraries considerably. The Australian islands, Lord Howe and Norfolk, were initially part of BP's Vanuatu route, until they developed an importance of their own on the company's 'conducted tours' schedule (Buckley & Klugman 1981).

In 1911 a second edition of BP's lavish tourist publication, *Picturesque Travel*, added—to what were still basically cargo runs—the gloss of promotional language that helped to define Melanesia for many tourists in terms that anticipated the travel brochures of a much later era. The Solomons was made up of 'wild islands', yet at each anchorage 'one is free to wander through the native villages', comforted by the fact that the 'picturesque simplicity of the natives is not yet destroyed by influence of civilisation' (*Picturesque Travel* 1911). By the late 1920s a new publication—*The BP Magazine*—was exploiting the myth of the South Seas for all it was worth. Full-page advertisements for the company's cruises spoke of the 'Wonder Isles' and 'The Enchantment' of the Pacific and invoked the writings of Tennyson and Robert Louis Stevenson (e.g. *BP Magazine* 1928).

The entry of P&O into the Pacific, a five-night cruise with only one port of call—Norfolk Island—appears in retrospect tentative, as though the well-established company was merely testing the market and, away from Melanesia, the main area of operations of its major regional competitor, Burns Philp. Norfolk Island was an interesting destination, its popularity already proven by BP, and sufficiently far to appear exotic to mainlanders, but, with its exclusively European population, free of the chances of mishap still possible among the less civilised islands to the north. With so many more passengers to consider than were carried in BP's ships—1166 in all—risk minimisation seemed appropriate.

The success of the first P&O cruise probably exceeded all expectations. Enthused by it, the company dispatched its representatives to various parts of the Pacific to check out port facilities and onshore attractions for passengers with a view to establishing a series of cruise itineraries for the Australian winter. Suva (Fiji) and Noumea (New Caledonia), the first pioneered as a tourist port of call by the Union Steamship Company of New Zealand, the second by the French organisation Messageries Maritimes, and broached only occasionally by Burns Philp, were brought into P&O's orbit. Despite their declining popularity with cruise passengers, they have remained immovable from most Pacific Islands cruise itineraries ever since. P&O also moved deeper into BP territory, adding Port Moresby, Samarai and Rabaul in Papua New Guinea, Port Vila in Vanuatu and Tulagi in Solomon Islands to its ports. Within a few months of P&O's first cruise to Norfolk Island in December 1932, Burns Philp & Company, as P&O's agent in Australia, was in the incongruous position of promoting the growing cruise activities of its major competitor in the region, carrying vivid poster-style advertisements and articles on P&O's port visits in its house journal (e.g. *BP Magazine* September 1933).

The primary purpose of each BP voyage was to deposit stores and collect cargo, thus ensuring that the tourists got to see many small and often isolated bays, trading stations and villages. In the case of the Solomons: 'There are no townships or settled communities, but a charming series of visits to Barbaric Islands' (*Picturesque Travel* 1921). The advent of P&O with its larger vessels introduced a marked change in emphasis in Pacific cruising. Although even passenger ships carried mails and some cargo right up to the days of containerisation in the 1960s, the size of P&O's ships meant that they could not have called at many of the smaller ports, even if the company had wanted them to. In any event, P&O, lacking BP's close involvement in island commodity trading, had no need to anchor off every copra shed in the islands. Furthermore, with passenger complements up to six times that of many BP ships, a higher degree of onshore organisation was required. This was most likely to be found at the rapidly growing port towns in the South Pacific. Passenger priority, therefore, rather than cargo priority influenced the choice of ports of call for P&O. Thus was established the fundamental South

Pacific 'cruise circle'—Sydney, Noumea, Port Vila, Suva and return—which, with occasional augmentations and accretions, has remained the main framework of regional cruising ever since.

The sudden appearance of the larger P&O vessels with their several hundreds of passengers was regarded as ominous by some observers, including Sir Hubert Murray, lieutenant-governor of Papua, who wrote to the captain of *Strathaird*, strongly suggesting that tourists were causing some social disruption within the Papuan community and encouraging beggary among the children. Murray thus became an early participant in the continuing debate on the effects of tourism on indigenous cultures (Douglas 1996, p. 82). In 1934 a party which cruised to Papua on the P&O ship *Mooltan* claimed that the Papuans were profiteers. Having found that each influx of tourists eagerly sought to take their pictures in full feather dress, the natives were quick to apply the principles of supply and demand. The price for posing rose quickly from 1/- to 2/- to 3/- and then to 5/-. 'The indignant passengers refused to pay this exorbitant price', reported the *Pacific Islands Monthly* of August 1934, 'and boycotted the natives until the price returned to the 1/- level'.

In Suva, which had been receiving tourists since the late 19th century, there were diversions enough by the mid-1930s. The practice of farewelling or greeting passenger ships with a brass band, already established in Honolulu, was introduced about this time, organised drives could be taken to the hinterland, and at least one hotel—the Grand Pacific—had been built two decades earlier essentially for tourists by a shipping company: its interior design reflected this. Noumea provided, as it still does, 'an outpost of French culture' in the Pacific. In Vanuatu and Solomon Islands onshore entertainment was often restricted to watching the loading and unloading of cargo and having afternoon tea with the plantation manager or mission sisters. In Tulagi and Port Vila it was possible to be invited to the Resident Commissioners' houses for tea. In the latter, then part of the jointly governed New Hebrides Condominium, it may have been morning tea with the French Commissioner and afternoon tea with the British Commissioner. Burns Philp's early command of the south-west Pacific as a cruise region was gradually overtaken by P&O. Finally, with the withdrawal of its well-appointed *Bulolo* from service in 1968, BP withdrew from passenger shipping, hence cruise services, completely. Its New Zealand counterpart, Union Steamship Co., abandoned passenger services in 1973, when its *Tofua* was 'sold to foreigners' (Brewer 1982, p. 229).

After the disruptions to shipping caused by World War II (1939–45), cruising in the South Pacific was slow to resume. A number of lines made seasonal cruises in the islands region either between line voyages to and from Europe or, as in the case of the revived Matson Navigation Co., as part of a trans-Pacific voyage to New Zealand and Australia from the west coast of the United States. Matson helped to repopularise destinations such as Tahiti and Samoa, generally omitted from cruises out of Australia because of their distance.

P&O's seasonal cruise presence in the region was strengthened by its use of vessels such as *Oriana, Himalaya* and *Canberra*, the tremendously popular superships of their day, against which the competition provided by other players in the South Pacific cruise game appeared feeble, though all had their devotees. But P&O did not establish a permanent year-round presence in the South Pacific until 1988, when it took over the operations of a rival cruise line, Sitmar International, whose fleet included *Fairstar*, which had been cruising in the region since 1973 on well-established itineraries. (See Figure 8.4.) It is not too much to claim that *Fairstar*, built as a troop carrier but never actually used as one, and in service for many years as a migrant ship before it was turned to full-time cruise activity, established a new era in South Pacific cruising. P&O acquired not only four ships and many of Sitmar's personnel but also, importantly, the reputation of its vessels, in particular *Fairstar*, the 'Funship'. It says a good deal for *Fairstar*'s reputation that it was the only Sitmar vessel not renamed by P&O after the takeover.

Changes to various aspects of the management and marketing of *Fairstar* had begun in the 1980s, before its acquisition by P&O. Among them was a revamping of its earlier itineraries. In 1976, for example, *Fairstar* offered a number of cruises of between 24 and 45 days. Not long afterwards cruises of a fortnight or less became standard, with the result that such countries as Tonga were omitted. In 1975 Tonga had received more than 62 000 cruise visitors (though certainly not all from *Fairstar*); in 1988 it received only 7500. But other itinerary modifications were about to take place. On his first cruise with *Fairstar*, Sitmar's new marketing manager, Phil Young, was disappointed that the vessel called only at established ports with well-developed berthing facilities. 'I had hoped to go to the South Sea Islands paradises I'd heard about', he told the authors (personal communication 1996). He discussed the matter with Sitmar's Sydney-based operations manager, Luigi Nappa, former staff captain of *Fairstar*, and found that Nappa shared his views. Against odds, which included opposition from Sitmar's head office in Italy and a lack of precise nautical information about some of the imagined 'island paradises', Young and Nappa went scouting for 'unspoilt' destinations, testing the market reaction with the inclusion of Dravuni, a southern outlier in Fiji. 'The passenger response exceeded our expectations', said Nappa. 'Many of the larger destinations were based on the belief that passengers wanted shopping. They didn't; they wanted to relax. Places like Dravuni were perfect'

Figure 8.4 *Fairstar*'s leaping dolphins were a metaphor for the activity on board (Courtesy P&O Australia)

(personal communication 1996). There followed a flurry of 'unspoilt island paradises' as the list was enlarged to eventually include Champagne Bay, 'Mystery Island' (Inyeug) and Lamen Bay in Vanuatu, Lifou in New Caledonia's Loyalty Group, Yasawa-I-Rara, Rotuma and Kioa in Fiji, though by no means all of them on every cruise. Some of these were P&O innovations after the company had acquired *Fairstar* in 1988, and with it both Nappa and Young, who became managing director of P&O Australia.

The exclusive nature of their 'discoveries' has been jealously guarded by the company, against attempted intrusions by other cruise ships. A few of them were experiments that failed: Rotuma was dropped after one call because of disputes between local chiefs over the division of landing fees, and the prevalence of rough seas. Kioa, in an isolated part of Fiji, was tried only once before 'we realised the impact on the local community would be too great', according to Captain Steve Hunt, P&O Australia's operations manager (personal communication 1999). The first visit to Lamen Bay was attended by considerable misunderstanding between P&O and the local Islanders. The successful ones have been maintained well after the retirement of *Fairstar* from service and are proving generally more popular (weather permitting) than the longer-established 'town calls' such as Noumea, Suva or even Port Vila, for years the favourite of Sitmar and P&O passengers. Surveys conducted in 2002 showed that, on itineraries which included both, small ports such as Lifou were beginning to displace Port Vila as a favourite call for South Pacific cruisers.

The great majority of the 'new' ports mentioned above are 'beach calls'. Finding variety in shore activities in the Pacific presents something of a challenge for destination planners. Duty-free shopping is no longer the attraction it once was; the number of attractions is limited compared with those of other destinations, and contemporary wisdom advises caution against overexposure to the sun, even on the beaches of 'unspoilt paradises'. In any event, passengers may already have had a surfeit of sun on the open deck of the ship before arriving at a port of call that offers little else. But if passengers are cautious, the advice evidently has little effect on crew members who, denied exposure to the sun by mostly indoor activity during their 12–14-hour working days, hit the beaches with a vengeance during their precious three or four hours of shore leave, with predictable results. The effect of the South Pacific sun on the normal below-decks pallor of a British or East European member of the crew can be dramatic, even frightening.

Part 3

By far the great majority of writings on the cruise experience deal with ocean cruising. There are a number of obvious reasons for this. Ocean cruises account for many more people annually; hence, they are more important in economic terms. Indeed, annual international statistics on cruising are usually derived from ocean cruising alone (e.g. CLIA Market Reports). Ocean cruising, which grew out of passenger shipping, is thought to be more significant in human terms because of the numbers involved and because it has a far greater share of public attention directed to it. To a great extent this is a result of the vast amounts of money spent on publicity by ocean cruise organisations and the glamour and 'romance' associated with large cruise ships (see Part 4 for a discussion of these aspects).

But with the growth in popularity of waterborne activities over the past three decades, including kayaking and whitewater rafting, other forms of cruising (some of which had been neglected or lain dormant for years) were revived, given a new gloss and sometimes even a new name, and presented as new or alternative forms of recreation. What is now referred to as 'freighter cruising', for instance, was once simply 'travel by cargo ship', and 'river cruising' is a refined and leisure-oriented version of a type of transport essential in countries that have navigable inland waterways but are often lacking in roads—parts of Africa or South America for example. Although probably more limited in their growth potential than ocean cruising, a discussion of some of these alternative types of cruising is necessary to an understanding of the total cruise experience, particularly as they are now being promoted as 'more satisfying', 'more relaxing' or even in some instances 'more romantic' options to ocean cruising. For all that, in global terms ocean cruising is still the dominant form. This series of case studies, therefore, begins with an examination of one of ocean cruising's leading players in the Asia–Pacific region, Star Cruises.

9

Star Cruises

If the last decade of the 20th century saw remarkable developments in the character of international cruising, few were more remarkable than the rise of the South-East Asian company Star Cruises. Historically, cruising had been dominated by Western companies: British, European or American. Even if the company names had an exotic touch—Orient Lines, British India Steam Navigation, Oceanic & Oriental Navigation—ownership was Western, as was the market. Cruising was merely another aspect of Euro-American paramountcy over the sea lanes: Britannia, herself, ruled the waves for a considerable time. Until the early 1990s it could hardly have been imagined that an Asian cruise company would be established successfully, let alone become—in the space of seven years—one of the major players in this enormously expensive and competitive game. Crystal Cruises, while owned by the veteran Japanese company Nippon Yusen Kaisha (NYK), is to all promotional and marketing purposes an American organisation.

Almost equally remarkable are the circumstances of Star Cruises' birth. Unlike a number of other cruise companies, Star did not grow from an already established maritime venture or out of trading and mail services, but from a far less likely background: the company that established it operated a casino in the Genting Highlands of Malaysia.

The Genting Corporation

The rise of the Genting Corporation itself must be mentioned here, in order to understand the context in which Star Cruises began to operate. Inspiration for the original resort development is said to have come from the experience of Tan Sri Lim Goh Tong, Genting's founder, in 1964, in the British hill stations of Malaysia's Cameron Highlands. Tan Sri Lim envisioned, according to the company's website, 'a cool mountain resort within the reach of all Malaysians'. The Cameron Highlands, however, being further than he thought convenient from the country's capital and major visitor market, Kuala Lumpur, Tan Sri Lim managed to find a more suitable spot only 58 kilometres—barely an hour's drive—from the capital. There he set about transforming 'a remote mountain into Malaysia's premier holiday destination' (<www.genting.com.my>).

In 1965 Tan Sri Lim managed to obtain approval from the Malaysian state governments of Selangor and Pahang for the alienation and development over a five-year period of a total of 6000 hectares of land, which included the top of the 1800-metre mountain Ulu Kali. Four years later, the country's first prime minister, Tunku Abdul Rahman, officiating at the laying of the foundation stone for the resort's first hotel, declared himself so impressed by the initiative of the private company in wanting to build the resort and its supporting infrastructure, without government assistance, that he granted the resort a gaming licence 'to help accelerate the development of this remote area' (<www.genting.com.my>). The fact that gambling of any kind was forbidden to most Malaysians for religious reasons, the majority of Malays being Islamic, was apparently of no concern to either the prime minister or the resort's entrepreneur. The real market for the casino, it was thought correctly, would be the predominantly ethnic Chinese population of Singapore.

The first hotel was completed in 1971. Together with its casino, it was so successful that over the next two or three decades an entertainment city grew around it. Tan Sri Lim's memoir records that he was inspired to invest a considerable amount of money in order to facilitate access to the Genting resort area by constructing a new highway (<www.genting.com. my/en/mydream/index.htm>). By 2000 the complex boasted four hotels, two apartment blocks, and cable-car access described as 'the world's fastest' and 'the longest in South-East Asia'. The 324-hectare Genting Awana Kijal, a ranch and country/beach resort, was established on Malaysia's east coast. The original organisation was restructured in 1989 to become primarily an investment holding and management company, while the resorts and related businesses became a new subsidiary. By the late 1990s the Genting group contained seven divisions, including leisure and hospitality, plantations, power, paper, and oil and gas (<www. genting.com.my>). Genting Berhad was acknowledged by the *Far Eastern Economic Review* as Malaysia's top company for the fifth consecutive year in 1998.

Star rises

Star Cruises was founded in 1993—'a bold initiative to tap Asia–Pacific's potential as an international cruise destination', according to the company's website (<www.starcruises.com>). It may have been that in part, but the main aim in the beginning was to tap South-East Asia's potential for, and interest in, off-shore gambling. If a land-based resort in what was originally a fairly remote destination could attract customers on such a scale, what might ocean-going ships devoted largely to one specific activity achieve? The founder of Star Cruises, however, had a considerable interest in ocean cruising and more than a little knowledge of its history.

The 40 000 GRT *Star Aquarius* was the first of two ships bought by Star Cruises in 1993. The purchase of its twin, *Star Pisces*, followed shortly after. Although Asian-based ocean cruising was not entirely novel, the marketing capability of the Genting Corporation, together with astute study of the practices of US companies Carnival and Royal Caribbean, put Star almost immediately ahead of the game in Asia. Both ships were Scandinavian ferries before their purchase by Star Cruises. There is nothing unusual about the conversion of large ferries to cruise ships, especially if they possess accommodation facilities and are already well-fitted for recreation and entertainment, as are many European and Channel ferries. These ships were of quite recent construction, having been built in 1990. Under their previous Swedish ownership the vessels were named respectively *Athena* and *Kalypso*. Before long three more ships were acquired, including Cunard's *Crown Jewel*, which was renamed *SuperStar Gemini* and until 2002 was promoted with great success in Australia and New Zealand. This caused no little concern to P&O Australia, which had long regarded the small antipodean market as its exclusive property. A third category of vessel, MegaStar, was created with the renaming of two small (72-passenger) German ships as *MegaStar Aries* and *MegaStar Taurus*.

The titles 'Star', 'MegaStar' and 'SuperStar' were not mere whimsy. They were intended to reflect distinct 'product labelling', although in this context it is difficult to say what 'Mega' is supposed to have meant, since the MegaStar ships were the smallest vessels in the three categories. It didn't aid understanding when the new range of SuperStar vessels acquired later, including *SuperStar Leo* and *SuperStar Virgo* (see Figure 9.1), were referred to in Star's promotion as 'megaships'. Nor were the SuperStar ships all that close in size or quality of facilities. *Gemini* was 19 089 GRT, *Aries* (once MS *Europa*) was 37 301 GRT, while *Leo* and *Virgo* were each 76 800 GRT. There is a temptation to think that in its eagerness to get into the cruise business, in the beginning Star simply acquired the vessels it could afford, or those conveniently available, and rationalised its purchases later. Nonetheless, some product differentiation became apparent, at least between the SuperStar series and the two Mega-Stars, which might more appropriately have been called MiniStars to reflect their size. Both only 85 metres long and 3264 GRT, they were ostentatiously refitted and 'designed to appeal to the niche market with their rich, luxurious décor'; that is, to expensive charter clients, corporate or private (www.starcruises.com). One tourism personality, having inspected the opulent nature of the lounges and the suites with their mirrored ceilings, remarked that they resembled nothing so much as 'floating brothels', although their quality was far more extravagant than that of other ships which had gained that description (personal communication 2000).

Acquisitions such as these built up a fleet of quite impressive size for Star within a relatively short time, and the inroads made into the Australian and New Zealand family cruise market by *SuperStar Gemini* gave the company a gloss that helped to obscure its image as essentially a gaming

Figure 9.1 Star Cruises' *SuperStar Virgo* (Courtesy Star Cruises)

operation. By 1999 Star had moved close to international cruising's big league and was extending its ambitions. 'The leading cruise line in Asia Pacific' (a slogan it had used successfully in its largely competitor-free regional environment) sought to become 'the first global cruise line', an ambition it could best achieve by another acquisition; not, this time, by simply adding a few ships but by taking over an existing major league company. This it did in early 2000 when, to the amazement of a number of industry watchers, it absorbed Norwegian Cruise Line (NCL).

NCL and Star Cruises

It had been common knowledge for some time within the trade that a takeover of NCL was imminent, although it seemed unlikely to observers that an Asian upstart would be responsible. The takeover had been initially planned jointly by Star and the massive US-based Carnival Corporation on a 60/40 basis, and was announced to the press as 'the start of a long-term global alliance' in a Star Cruises press release on 2 February 2000. Within two weeks, however, the would-be allies failed to agree on aspects of the venture and Star decided to proceed on its own (Star Cruises PLC, Annual Report 1999). Opinions differ as to whether Carnival was serious about the takeover or was acting in its fairly familiar role as 'spoiler' by delaying the actual takeover by another party, a technique it had used previously and applied again in 2002 when it sought to intervene in the proposed P&O merger with Royal Caribbean. Norwegian Cruise Line, since it had not grown for seven years, was 'a sitting duck', according to Braydon Holland, Star Cruises' director of sales and marketing for Australia and New Zealand (personal communication 20 October 2000). Indeed, Star had acquired a 50.2 per cent interest in NCL in mid-December 1999, two months before it closed in fully in February 2000 (Star Cruises PLC, press release, 17 December 1999; Star Cruises, Quarterly Report, May 2000).

Star's long-held determination to obtain a foothold in the US market obliged it to target a leading American line, but one that showed signs of economic vulnerability. This was NCL, which ranked fourth in the global cruise hierarchy but apparently was not growing. The decision to go it alone in the takeover was evidently an expensive one, costing Star more than US$1 billion (personal communication 28 May 2001) and obliging it to obtain a bridging loan of US$600 million from Barclays Bank and the Bank of Hong Kong and Shanghai (Star Cruises, press release, 31 May 2000). For its money and trouble, Star acquired not only NCL with eight ships but also Orient Line, a small (two-vessel), albeit well-known, subsidiary, which NCL itself had not long before taken over in an apparent attempt to bolster its own presence. In the manner of Carnival, whose operational style Star had long sought to emulate, the brand names of both NCL and Orient were retained as were their apparently individual identities. As part of the package also came Norwegian Capricorn Line, a joint venture between NCL and Australian interests, which had been plagued by operational and financial problems since its inception in 1998 and had lost a reported A$22 million in its first year of operation. Star emerged from the expensive process with a total of 22 ships, almost certainly more than were really needed. A couple of earlier purchases were shed without much delay.

The acquisition of Norwegian Capricorn Line and its sole vessel, *Norwegian Star*, had a number of interesting regional consequences, among which was the sudden removal of the last possibility of survival for that financially troubled company (Douglas & Douglas 2001) and the abrupt shrinking of choice for Australian would-be cruisers. Many of these now began to regard Star's *Gemini* as the only alternative to P&O's Australia-based product. P&O, however, regained the monopoly on Australia–Pacific cruising that had been briefly disturbed, if not seriously threatened, by Norwegian Capricorn.

Star claims the highest crew-to-passenger ratio of any cruise line and has introduced a number of technical innovations, including the building of its own ship training simulator located within the company's Port Klang complex. Used to train officers, this was completed in 1998 and is said to be the only one of its kind in the world owned by a shipping company.

Further fleet rationalisations and redeployments followed the events of 11 September 2001 and the consequent downturn in international tourism. By early 2003 Star was operating eight cruise vessels under its name; its subsidiaries, NCL and Orient, were operating eight and two respectively. NCL's own fleet had been enhanced by the transfer of vessels originally intended for Star. The extent to which Star itself could be regarded as a 'global cruise line' as a result of its acquisition of NCL remained conjectural, as did the extent to which Star was introducing Asians to cruising as a travel choice, rather than merely facilitating their access to gambling. In early 2003 the deployment of vessels carrying Star's own brand—as opposed to that of NCL or Orient—indicated that very brief cruises and 'cruises to nowhere', both of which have gambling as their main rationale, were still the staples of the company's Asia-based operations. The popularity of these cruises contradict the sweeping assertion made by Dickinson and Vladimir (1997, p. 273) that it is 'a myth that the casino is the biggest money maker on the ship . . . In truth most people do not take a cruise to gamble'. In truth, most of the passengers on these cruises were there for little other purpose. A partial exception was *Super-Star Virgo*, which replaced *Gemini* as the main product for Star's international market, but whose enormous casino (capacity 1800 people) was still packed almost around the clock on its weekend 'cruise to nowhere' out of Singapore. The other facilities on board ships home-ported in such places as Hong Kong, Taiwan, Japan, Pyongtaek (South Korea) and Laem Chabang (Thailand) were there essentially to support the major revenue earners, the vessels' casinos. There were also signs that some areas of the Asian market were still proving difficult, even perhaps resistant to Star's innovations: finding the right vessel to represent the company in Thailand, for example, appeared problematic. Whether this meant that Thais were less interested than other Asians in gambling or merely more conservative in their travel choices was difficult to say. In any event, long-distance cruising for which travel itself provided the major rationale was in the hands of the Star subsidiaries, NCL and Orient Line.

10

Small ship cruises

As cruising has grown in significance as a sector of tourism its terminology has widened to include new or revived concepts. The expression 'small ship cruising', for example, is a fairly recent one that requires some explanation. What constitutes a 'small ship'? As the new entries into cruising become larger and larger (Princess Cruises' *Grand Princess* is 109 000 GRT and 290 metres in length, for example, and Carnival Cruises' *Carnival Conquest* is 110 000 GRT and 291 metres), should anything below 23 732 GRT, the size of the famous P&O Strath class liners, be thought of as 'small' or merely smaller? It is worth noting that Crystal Cruises has won 'best cruise ship' awards in both the 'large' and 'medium-size' categories, with the same ships!

To what extent is the use of this terminology influenced mainly by promotional considerations? Seabourn Cruises, whose three ships are uniformly 10 000 GRT and carry some 200 passengers, rejects the description 'small ship' completely and refers to its vessels as 'The Yachts of Seabourn'. Its nearest rival, Silversea Cruises, prefers the expression 'intimate ships'. A website (<www.smallships.com>) devoted to the subject of small ship cruising defines the term as ships with fewer than 500 passengers, although this definition is questionable:

These ships typically accommodate 500 or fewer passengers in comfort. Medium ships are frequently viewed as those carrying 500 to 1200 guests. These may offer passengers a happy medium between a small adventure cruiser and a huge ocean liner carrying 2000+ passengers. A large ship is considered to carry from 1200 to 2700 passengers. These ships frequently offer the amenities such as large auditoriums with nightly entertainment, vast sports facilities, casinos, numerous dining opportunities . . .

Unfortunately, this rather confuses things, as 'small ships' are not necessarily 'adventure ships', as we see in chapter 11, on 'adventure cruises'. A more appropriate passenger capacity might be 300 or fewer. Small ship cruising, however, is defined by its practitioners and publicists not only by size but also by policy to some extent, the terms of which are expressed here by the US company Cruise West (<www.cruisewest.com>), but are probably applicable to any similar organisation. The major emphases are on informality and ecological interests:

A cruise on a small ship is not filled with elaborate distractions, sleek resorts and packaged tours [this qualification immediately excludes the 'yachts' of Seabourn and the 'uncompromising luxury' of Silversea] . . . we don't overwhelm the local communities—our largest vessel [*Spirit of Oceanus*] hosts just 114 guests [who] would rather watch for whales . . . than spend the afternoon in a casino . . . On a small ship the focus is very often outside, on what Nature has provided for entertainment . . . The casual style on board all of our vessels encourages relaxation and congenial interaction between guests and crew alike. And the experience is personally enriching, you're not just a visitor, you're a participant.

Cruising range is also a major consideration. Seabourn and Silversea prefer to assert their big league status by engaging in long-distance cruises that cover the majority of the world's cruise regions, but a significant number of small ship companies cruise only in limited, sheltered areas. Cruise West, for example, cruises in such areas as the coast of British Columbia and nearby islands, and Mexico's Sea of Cortez; Fiji-based Blue Lagoon Cruises concentrates on the Yasawa and Mamanuca Islands of western Fiji, a destination it shares with Sydney-based Captain Cook Cruises. The latter also has a small ship based in the North Queensland city of Cairns for cruising the islands of Australia's Great Barrier Reef.

Small ships or large, market promotion is still of major importance. The larger cruise brands reinforce their own promotional mythology with constant reference to their historical or sociocultural significance. P&O is 'the company that invented cruising'; Cunard has been 'advancing civilisation since 1840'; Princess Cruises, at least until its slogan changed relatively recently, claimed that its operation was 'not just a cruise, it's the Love Boat'. Small ships must often celebrate more modest achievements to give credibility to their less flamboyant approach to the industry. Cruise West is 'American owned, family operated', a claim that might equally well be applied to a grocery chain or a trucking company. It was named not after the geographical location of its main activities but after its founder Charles B. ('Chuck' or 'Mr Alaska') West. A mythology is apparently essential in this highly competitive field and, as though to best illustrate the qualities of dedication and perseverance, may centre on the personality of the company's founder. This personalisation of the product's history, especially if there is an element of adventure or risk associated with it, suits certain modes of travel and tourism well. Two South Pacific-based small ship cruise lines have used this approach, with apparent success: Fiji-based Blue Lagoon Cruises and Sydney-based Captain Cook Cruises.

Blue Lagoon Cruises

Whatever the extravagant claims made on behalf of tourism in the Pacific Islands, the business aspect of it is not easy. 'Paradise' has a way of ruthlessly culling operators who lack initiative, stamina or staying power. So much more credit, then, to the ones who make it against the apparent odds by transforming their dreams into reality with sound business and social practices. Like a few other successful Pacific tourism enterprises, Aggie Grey's Hotel in Samoa and Fiji's Turtle Island among them, Blue Lagoon Cruises started from very little and became in time one of Pacific tourism's major success stories, a tourism legend. Along the way it also developed its own promotional mythology, much of which centres on Blue Lagoon's founder New Zealander Trevor Withers, who established the company in 1950.

Withers had come to Fiji some years earlier with his friend Harold Gatty, an Australian aviator, hoping to establish a tuna-fishing industry. Fiji, then a British Crown Colony, had an underdeveloped tourism industry, although it had a long history of recreational visitors. Most of the time, however, visitors arrived in Fiji on their way to somewhere else by air or sea. Withers and Gatty set up headquarters in Suva, and began to assess the potential for tuna fishing using two small boats. Fijian protocol and tradition demanded that they make a special visit to the islands to pay their respects to the local chiefs before proceeding with their venture.

At Yalobi village on the island of Waya in the Yasawa Group, Withers found that the chief and his people could speak neither English nor a dialect understood by his crew. At the nearby island of Waya Lailai they enlisted a young villager as an interpreter. With his help Withers obtained the full support of the Yasawa people for his fishing venture and established firm friendships with the chiefs and the people of the Yasawa Islands. Later this association became crucial to Blue Lagoon Cruises.

Four years later Withers and Gatty were obliged to admit that their hopes of establishing a tuna-fishing industry in Fiji had come to nothing. But both had become fond of Fiji and decided to remain. Gatty went on to establish Fiji Airways, the forerunner to Fiji's national airline, Air Pacific. Withers began to consider taking visitors on cruises through the Yasawa Islands. His enthusiasm for the new project was not shared by many. Tourists were still few. Determined to realise his aim, Withers returned to the Yasawa Islands to request again the support of the chief and his people. To his delight, they met his cruise proposal with promises of cooperation. Pondering a suitable name, Withers recalled his association with the original version of the film *Blue Lagoon* shot partly on location in the Yasawas in 1948. He had lent a hand on the set, and had met English star Jean Simmons. 'Blue Lagoon' seemed the ideal choice of name for the cruise he had in mind.

Withers purchased his first boat from the New Zealand Civil Aviation Authorities in Fiji and christened it *Turaga Levu* (Great Chief, his local nickname), launching it in Suva's Walu Bay. The first cruise date was scheduled and advertised, and brought a complete lack of response. As the hour of its first departure drew near, it appeared that *Turaga Levu* would sail empty. Withers, though tempted to cancel, was reluctant to disappoint the islanders awaiting its arrival. He invited six Fijian men on the wharf who had previously assisted him to become *Turaga Levu*'s first cruise passengers. For the first month, Withers sailed every Monday, often carrying Fijians to their Yasawa villages but lacking any paying passengers. Ten days into his second month of operation he secured his first charter.

During the following three months, however, only 27 passengers were carried on the cruise. Facing bankruptcy, Withers made a final gamble. After obtaining an agreement with airlines flying the Pacific to undertake a joint promotion in North America, he sold his possessions for £7000 to finance a whirlwind visit to travel agents in the United States and Canada. The gamble succeeded. By 1966 Blue Lagoon Cruises had established an international reputation and Withers, suffering poor health, retired after selling the business to Captain Claude Millar of NZ. Withers died in 1981 (<www.bluelagooncruises.com/story.htm>). By then the company had changed hands twice, and Blue Lagoon vessels were being purpose-built.

Among the joys of small ship cruising is the opportunity to talk to everyone—passengers and crew—on the vessel. If the crew on a Blue Lagoon vessel is more or less homogeneous, the passengers are invariably an assorted international group; the company's vigorous overseas promotion guarantees that. On a typical cruise one may find North Americans (including Canadians), Germans, British, Australians, New Zealanders and even the occasional Italian or Spaniard.

Itineraries vary only slightly from year to year. The Yasawa and Mamanuca chains contain 33 islands in all, but the majority of these are never visited, although many unvisited ones can be seen relatively close by. Experience has shown that, for visitors, there are some islands and villages that are far more appealing than others: the beaches are better and easier of access, they contain significant natural features such as underwater caves, or some villages are deemed more hospitable than others or have more to interest visitors. With the increasing number of locally operated budget resorts in the Yasawas and elsewhere in Fiji, itineraries may become more variable if local operators feel that a visit from a cruise ship is a valuable way of drawing attention to their enterprises.

Blue Lagoon helps to support the Yasawa Islands community financially, as do other tourism businesses in the area. The company is an important factor in the cash economy of these islands, providing the opportunity for the people to earn revenue from the company's payments to access beaches and visit villages, from performances of traditional Fijian entertainment, and from the sale of shells and artefacts. Assistance in times of emergencies is also given freely. In May 1999 a Blue Lagoon ship was instrumental in the rescue of 23 people, many tourists among them, when their unregistered, overcrowded boat capsized in rough weather.

In 1986 the company enlarged its investments, purchasing freehold title to a 23.5-hectare plantation on the island of Nanuya Lailai in the Yasawas, as well as a commercial property adjoining their Lautoka headquarters. A new F$3 million headquarters complex was formally opened in 1993. It contains a passenger preboarding lounge, small café, bar, boutique, executive offices, engineering workshops, stores and refrigeration facilities, shore galley, staff association office and training rooms.

In early 2003 the Blue Lagoon fleet consisted of four vessels with a total passenger capacity of 230. The largest, *Mystique Princess*, had a capacity of 72 (see Figure 10.1). The company reported that its passenger base continued to grow at a rate of about 10 per cent annually, but declined to provide actual figures. Company staff totalled 176, the majority of them Fijians. In-house training is regular, and food and beverage

Figure 10.1 Blue Lagoon's *Mystique Princess* in Fiji's Yasawa Islands
(Source: Norman Douglas)

training is continuous. Other training courses include upgrades in engineering, international safety management practices, first aid, fire fighting and cooking. Employees also participate in courses conducted by the Fiji National Training Council, which range from those concerning seamanship to aspects of hotel and catering. The company's sailors and engineers study, with company support, at the Fiji Marine College.

In Blue Lagoon's promotion, much continues to be made about the company's association with films, some of which is, to say the least, peripheral. Under the heading 'A Hollywood Obsession', the company's website (<bluelagooncruises.com/obsession.htm>) lists a number of cinema-related events, a part of which reads:

1999 MOVIE: CASTAWAY—BOX OFFICE HIT FILMED IN YASAWA ISLAND
The box office hit, *Castaway*, starring Tom Hanks was filmed in the very waters Blue Lagoon Cruises operates in. In fact the film crew & stars used 3 of Blue Lagoons ships at different times over a two-year period, often utilizing the food & beverages of our luxury vessels.

Mimi McPherson
Sister of supermodel Elle McPherson spent her recent holiday aboard a Blue Lagoon Cruise.

Captain Cook Cruises

The evident success of Blue Lagoon Cruises inspired the Australian company Captain Cook Cruises to want a share of the island cruise market in Fiji. Whether or not the market was really large enough to accommodate both operators the year round is still debatable. In 1995, the year of Captain Cook's entry into cruising in Fiji, tourism there was expanding impressively, having grown from 189 866 visitors to 287 462, after earlier setbacks following the political coups of 1987. The effects on tourism of a third coup in 2000, however, were still being felt in 2003. The actual relationship of cruising to other forms of tourism is not always clear; many countries omit cruising entirely from their annual summaries of visitor activity, and we have been told by executives of tourism marketing in widely different locations that they had little interest in the sector. But in order to cruise among the smaller islands of Fiji, the great majority of visitors must come from other countries, since, as the founder of Blue Lagoon Cruises soon learnt, there is little or no local market. This means that visitors must necessarily, if only briefly, use a number of other services also, making the official indifference to cruising difficult to understand.

An Australian identity

The Australian identity of Captain Cook Cruises is a quality the company stresses. If the language is already familiar from the Cruise West example, the nationality has necessarily changed. 'An award winning Australian family owned and operated company' declares its website (<captaincook.com.au>), while brochures identify it as 'Australia's cruise line', at least partly in order to distinguish it from both P&O's Australia-based operation and the since failed Norwegian Capricorn Line which, despite promotional literature implying otherwise, was effectively controlled from the United States (Douglas & Douglas 2001). To what extent this identification has contributed to the company's success is impossible to estimate: effectively, Captain Cook is Australia's **only** cruise line, with no serious competition either in its geographical range or the number of its vessels. Not all of these, however, qualify as small ships for the purposes of this discussion, since only four of the total fleet of 20 provide sleeping accommodation for passengers, while one of these is a Murray River paddle-steamer and another cruises only in Sydney Harbour.

The name of Blue Lagoon's founder, Trevor Withers, remains indelibly associated with that company although he died in 1981. Similarly, most promotional materials for Captain Cook Cruises ensure that readers will be made aware of its founder, Captain Trevor Haworth, who was still living when this was written. A message from Captain Haworth introduces the company's website (<www.captaincook.com.au>). The public stories of both Withers and Haworth are those emphasising initiative and perseverance. Haworth, an Englishman, commenced training in Britain in 1946 for the merchant service and subsequently served on cargo and semicargo ships, obtaining his master's certificate in 1957 and becoming master of the Australian-Oriental Line vessel *Taiping* in the same year. His affection for the 120-passenger semicargo ship and what the official history of Captain Cook Cruises refers to as 'the traditional grandeur of ship life' was to greatly influence his concept of small ship destination cruising (Goldsack 1995, pp. 17–18).

Haworth retired from the merchant service in 1961, married and settled in Sydney, taking a job as marine surveyor and loss assessor. Less than happy with his new occupation, he bought a boatshed with slipways and shortly after became partner in a ship-delivery business. Meanwhile, he was making a number of personal and business contacts that would serve his later aims well. A brief but successful period as partners in a restaurant in Edgecliff, a prestigious Sydney suburb, awakened the business-minded Haworths to the possibilities of closer involvement with tourism and hospitality. They were further inspired in 1969 by a Circle Line cruise on New York's waterways, an experience that helped point them more precisely in the direction their own tourism enterprise should take. In 1970 Trevor Haworth chartered *Daydream II*, a World War II Fairmile B motor gunboat that had been first converted for use as a whaler and later converted again for day cruising on the Barrier Reef. He renamed it *Captain Cook*, registered a company in that name, and was able to take advantage of a few already scheduled charter cruises on Sydney Harbour.

Vigorous promotion and canny public relations made a success of the Haworths' coffee cruises and lunch cruises over the next few years, but the business was already outgrowing the old chartered vessel. In 1975 it was replaced by a purpose-built craft, *Captain Cook II*, which cost A$500 000 and was capable of taking 250 passengers. By the end of 1978 two more ships had been added to the fast-growing fleet, and in late 1981 they were joined by the purpose-built *City of Sydney*, constructed in New Zealand at a cost of A$1.2 million, with space for 300 passengers and a better-equipped galley than its predecessors.

But these vessels were all operating exclusively in Sydney Harbour, where cruises of very short duration, with or without meals, had grown rapidly in popularity with both overseas visitors and domestic tourists. There was as yet no small ship in the fleet able to accommodate sleeping passengers on cruises of several nights, nor evidently a need for one. This changed abruptly in 1988, the year of Australia's bicentenary celebrations, with the acquisition of not one but three vessels with accommodation, two of which were Murray River paddle-steamers, the type of craft that initially appeared an incongruous choice.

The decision to acquire the accommodation vessels, however, had two major consequences: it expanded the operations of Captain Cook Cruises geographically and also set it on a more ambitious path towards small ship cruising. That direction received additional impetus in 1989, when, to capitalise on a rapid growth of interest in the Northern Queensland city of Cairns and its access to the Barrier Reef, the Australian flag carrier, Qantas, proposed a joint venture to Captain Cook Cruises. The airline had already acquired Dunk Island and the less developed Lizard Island and approached Trevor Haworth to discuss 'the advantages to be gained by placing a small liner in Cairns to explore the Great Barrier Reef' (Goldsack 1995, p. 91). Given the dynamic growth of tourism in North Queensland following the change of management and expansion of the Cairns airport, the advantages seemed obvious, but serious obstacles, legal and technical, delayed progress on the construction of the vessel because of economic events in Fiji. Work on the 'small liner' at the Fiji government shipyards in Suva began in 1989 but was not completed until 1995, by which time the original cost of A$10 million had expanded to A$15 million. Marketing of the Barrier Reef cruiser, which had begun in early 1990, resulted in bookings for the schedule of cruises for 1992 having to be met by the remodelling of an existing Captain Cook vessel, *Lady Hawkesbury*. This emerged some months later with a new, taller funnel more appropriate to its new status as small liner and a new name— *Reef Escape*. It was eventually replaced in late 1995 by the Fiji-built *Reef Endeavour*. The entry into the market of the reef cruisers could hardly have been better timed.

'There is very little else in life that needs to be achieved after experiencing the Barrier Reef', writes the company's official historian (Goldsack 1995, p. 92). The immediate success of the enterprise, however, seemed to suggest that the market was certainly ready for it. *Reef Endeavour* was the first vessel purpose-built for the company that fully met the now accepted concept of small ship cruising. Its appearance was, without modification, that of a modern liner, necessarily scaled down; it had permanent ocean-going capability; it had sleeping accommodations of various qualities for 168 passengers; its itinerary included scheduled destinations; and it carried on- and off-board recreational facilities and engaged the appropriate specialists to enhance passenger experience, including a marine biologist and a diving instructor.

The problem of what to do with the now surplus *Reef Escape* was

Figure 10.2 Captain Cook's *Reef Escape* passengers take a coral-viewing trip (Source: Norman Douglas)

solved quickly. The idea of collaborating with Qantas to build and position a small ship in Fiji to compete with the very successful Blue Lagoon Cruises had been put forward in 1989 by an earlier partner in *Reef Endeavour*, but the airline had shown no interest, preferring to concentrate on the domestic market. In 1995, therefore, with Fiji's visitor industry recovering and tax holidays being offered to new investors in a number of employment-generating industries, especially tourism, the opportunity for another small ship to cruise the Yasawa and Mamanuca Islands still existed. After negotiations with the Fiji government and other appropriate authorities, *Reef Escape* (see Figure 10.2) was deployed to Fiji, to the chagrin of Blue Lagoon Cruises, which had already suffered the market downturn from the earlier political coups.

Extending the range

In an apparent desire to vary its product and extend its geographical range, Blue Lagoon was advertising in mid-2002 the 'ultimate new historical & cultural cruise' aboard its flagship, *Mystique Princess*. This was to take place in 2003, visiting the north-eastern islands of Fiji, including Vanua Levu, Taveuni, Ovalau, Kioa and Rabi, the latter two with small Micronesian populations and very rarely visited by tourists of any kind, let alone cruise ship passengers. 'Kioa & Rambi [sic] do not have a tourism infrastructure', the company advised, 'with these visits requiring an invitation from the Chief'.

Passengers were promised 'a series of experiences that will give them a true understanding of the many facets of Fiji' (<www.bluelagoon cruises.com/press4_new7dd6nn_historical.htm>). Not to be outdone, Captain Cook offered an almost identical program that was subsequently scaled down. Early 2003 proved to be one of the Pacific's worst cyclone seasons in recent years. 'We have cancelled 2003 sailings', a Blue Lagoon representative informed us, 'due to the devastation caused to Taveuni, Rabi and Kioa by Cyclone Ami in early February' (personal communication).

The largest Cruise West vessel, *Spirit of Oceanus*, accommodates 114 passengers; Blue Lagoon's largest, *Mystique Princess*, accommodates 72; and Captain Cook's largest, the Barrier Reef cruiser, *Reef Endeavour*, accommodates 168.

11

Adventure cruises

The difference between 'small ship' cruising and 'adventure' cruising may at first seem rather slight. Adventure cruise ships are also necessarily small, in order to fulfil their aim of 'getting off the beaten track'. But at times, as it tends to with all forms of advertising, promotional terminology gets in the way of accuracy. Also, what may seem an adventure to one person may seem predictably tame to another. For many of the passengers on the American cruise ships that visit Vietnam, crossing the street in Ho Chi Minh City (Saigon) constitutes an adventure—that is, 'an exciting or extraordinary event' (*Encarta World English Dictionary* 1999). Indeed, for many American passengers on the first cruises by US ships to Vietnam in the early 1990s, simply cruising up the Saigon River became an emotional adventure—a 'heart of darkness' experience, since very few knew quite what to expect from a former and relatively recent enemy. Other expressions, introduced by cruise companies in an effort to distinguish their product from that of others, may confuse rather than enlighten the potential customer. The terms 'expedition' and 'expeditionary' are two. Is an expedition also an adventure, or is it something grander? If one cruises to the Antarctic, is one engaging in an adventure, an expedition or both? *Berlitz complete guide to cruising and cruise ships* (Ward 1992), widely regarded in the trade as an authoritative work, seems to use the terms interchangeably, speaking on the same small page of 'adventure cruises', 'expedition cruises' and 'adventure/expedition cruise companies', but their formal definitions indicate a considerable degree of difference. Here are some comments from Lindblad Expeditions ('Share the extraordinary on our world-wide adventures') on the subject (<www.lindbad.com>; <www.expeditions.com>):

> Join one of our expeditions, and you may find yourself on deck listening to the songs of whales as they play over the hydrophone, or, from the comfort of the lounge, watching live video of the world beneath the waves as an Undersea Specialist utilizes the underwater video camera to capture the sights.

Surely, one would assume, an expedition requires a little more effort on the part of those engaged in it than sitting on the deck or in the comfort of the ship's lounge in order to listen to or view the natural world.

Lindblad

Lindblad: the man and the myth

Nonetheless, Lindblad was an early starter in this field of cruise activity, has been a survivor, and consequently must be regarded seriously. On the company's website (<www.lindblad.com>) the current president introduces its credentials as follows:

> Any discussion of the history of Lindblad Expeditions has to begin with my father, Lars-Eric Lindblad, the pioneer of expedition travel. In the introduction to his autobiography, *Passport to Anywhere* [Lindblad 1983], my father's friend, the ornithologist Roger Tory Peterson, wrote: 'If Lars-Eric Lindblad had lived in the year 1000, he probably would have set foot on the North American continent before Leif Ericson. Or, turning eastward, he might have reached China before Marco Polo.'

We have already referred to the practice of identifying small ship cruise companies as 'family owned' operations, as though in being so they were somehow more deserving of customer support than 'corporations'. But here the family connection is embellished in a way that makes its importance almost unassailable. In the space of a short paragraph we find weighty terms such as 'discussion', 'history', 'pioneer', 'expedition', 'autobiography' and 'ornithologist', making the seriousness of the claims beyond dispute. As though that were not enough, we then find that the founder of the company was an explorer of even greater initiative than the semilegendary figures Ericson and Polo. Unfortunately, there is no way of verifying this. Thankfully, the remainder of Lindblad Expeditions' survey of its achievements to date is a good deal less excessive and, hence, more credible.

Whether or not Lars-Eric Lindblad was an explorer of the same or greater magnitude than Leif Ericson and Marco Polo, there is general agreement in the travel business that he pioneered 'expedition cruising' to the hitherto unlikely tourist destination of Antarctica. This is not to say that he was responsible for taking the first tourists there. In 1956 a Chilean airline, using a Douglas DC6 aircraft, took 66 sightseers over Antarctica and two years later a combined Argentinian–Chilean enterprise made two voyages to the South Shetland Islands, carrying in all some 500 fare-paying passengers. In Antarctica prior to this, according to Dr Bernard Stonehouse of the Scott Polar Research Institute, University of Cambridge, 'dangers abounded and heroics were essential: with no human population of its own, Antarctica was a continent for real men. Tourists were unthinkable' (Stonehouse 1997). The implications of these observations should perhaps not be dwelt on too long.

Distance from the main tourism markets, however, particularly North America and Europe, together with other inhibiting factors meant that Antarctic tourism was not an overnight success. But in late 1966 Lars-Eric Lindblad, who specialised in travel to less visited areas such as Seychelles, Papua New Guinea and East African countries, combined his 'expedition cruising' concept with an educational purpose and took a group to Antarctica on a chartered vessel. The idea proved such a success that Lindblad designed a ship specifically for the purpose of carrying tourists to Antarctica. It made its first voyage there in 1969. This was *Lindblad Explorer*, a vessel which in the view of many represented the birth of the modern expeditionary cruise industry.

Lindblad, an early example of the environmentally conscious travel entrepreneur, once said, 'You can't protect what you don't know'. According to an admirer, 'he believed that by providing a first-hand experience to tourists you would educate them to the ecological sensitivity of the Antarctic environment and promote a greater understanding of the earth's resources and the important role of Antarctica'.

Like many similar pronouncements concerning the natural environment, this was probably both visionary and naïve. As other travel promoters began to broaden their horizons and those of their clients, flights over the frozen continent became suddenly popular. In the three years between 1977 and late 1979 Qantas and Air New Zealand flew some 11 000 sightseers over Antarctica, an exercise that ended tragically, but only temporarily, with the crash of an Air New Zealand DC10 on Mt Erebus in November 1979, in which all passengers and crew died. By late 1983, however, flights from Chile had become regular. In the 1992–93 season more than 6000 ship-borne tourists visited Antarctica, and during the 1999–2000 season almost 15 000 did so. In the latter season no fewer than 17 travel operators were taking tourist ships to Antarctica. The likelihood of **all** their passengers being ecologically sensitive and pursuing educational goals seems remote. As with almost any tourism undertaking, the seekers after novelty may one day be in the majority, if they are not already. The road less travelled is in danger of becoming a superhighway.

Lindblad Expeditions

The company known in early 2003 as Lindblad Expeditions was established in 1979 as Special Expeditions, a division of Lindblad Travel, which specialised in group travel to less well-known parts of the world, in many of which facilities for tourists were minimal. The parent company deliberately sought out relatively obscure destinations; its offshoot varied the approach somewhat by emphasising also obscure parts of better-known countries in, for instance, Europe and the Americas and visiting them on a regular basis. 'We made something of an art of returning to the same regions year after year and really getting to know them', according to Sven-Olof Lindblad, current president and heir to the family philosophy. Having settled on a more or less different approach from that of the company's founder, Sven-Olof Lindblad decided in 1982 to

Figure 11.1 A Lindblad team prepares the huskies for an Antarctic adventure (Courtesy Lindblad Expeditions)

distinguish between them completely by making Special Expeditions independent of its parent company. It was not long before it became apparent that, although many travellers were happy to be able to visit the world's less touristed areas, they were often less than overjoyed about the prospects of fundamental accommodation and dubious dining choices. 'I also came to understand', says Lindblad, 'that ship-based travel offered a unique way to reach out-of-the-way places, while allowing our travellers comfortable accommodations, good food, and the convenience of not having to pack and unpack'. It also, of course, offered a practical way of limiting—if not controlling completely—the possibility of illness or severe discomfort to passengers arising from unpredictable lodgings and food and thus disrupting the proceedings, because it had early become apparent that most of the people able to afford both the time and the not inconsiderable expense of joining 'expeditions' such as these were seniors and retirees, 55 years and over, curious in a number of respects but conservative in many others—'Lifelong New Englanders', in the words of one cruise guide (Slater & Basch 1996, p. 711).

Lindblad's earlier practice of chartering vessels gave way, as success grew, to purchase: in 1987 the 80-passenger *Polaris*, which travelled initially to such places as Arctic Norway, Greenland and Hudson Bay and was later repositioned to the Galapagos Islands; and 1989–90 the 70-passenger sisters, *Sea Lion* and *Sea Bird*, which concentrated on the eastern coast of North America, varying seasonally from Alaska to the Sea of Cortez. The fleet grew further with the acquisition of *Caledonian Star*, a veteran ship with an impressively loyal following, mainly of British cruisers. Renamed *Endeavour* by Lindblad to emphasise its exploratory credentials, the 120-passenger vessel was placed on the company's Antarctic run during the 1998–99 winter.

In June 2001 Sven-Olof Lindblad was honoured by having his name included in the United Nations Environment Program's (UNEP) Global 500 Roll of Honor, the first occasion on which the founder of a tourism company had been so distinguished, in recognition of outstanding achievements in environmental protection and improvement. In the same year another vessel, the 65-passenger *Sea Voyager*, was added to the fleet, to concentrate on Central American itineraries.

The capacities of Lindblad's vessels all illustrate one essential of expeditionary or adventure cruising: it is necessarily a low-key exercise in terms of passenger numbers, far lower than the size that generally identifies 'small ships' in the cruise world—300 to 500 passengers. Size, however, is by no means the sole determinant. The ships of the defunct Renaissance Cruises carried only about 100 passengers, and called at smaller destinations, such as Krakatau in Indonesia, but were almost as distant in concept from Lindblad as it was possible to be. Cruise ships carrying more than 1000 passengers are now visiting Antarctica, though without making landings. Although one might argue that even up to 100 people arriving simultaneously at a little-visited site are still capable of inflicting environmental damage or having a cultural impact, there seems little likelihood of this occurring, given such factors as Lindblad's concern for its own reputation, which is evidently a major reason for its success.

Other distinctions between ships of this nature and less specialised cruise vessels are more tangible. Instead of the after-dinner shows regarded as standard on larger ships, there are lectures, briefings or 'recaps', sometimes a combination of all three. In place of the typical cruise director and support staff, whose primary concern is passenger entertainment, are specialists on cultural or environmental matters, whose primary concern is education, though this is often delivered in an entertaining way. The casino, a feature of most cruise ships, is absent—so for that matter is bingo. The time taken up by the afternoon bingo game is more profitably spent on a shore excursion (though doubtless the term 'expedition' is preferred) or on allowing additional time for observing natural events. Flexibility in the timing of itineraries is therefore an important aspect of these cruises as, to a great extent, is passenger agility. Methods of landing used by these cruises—inflatable landing craft and kayaks, for instance—tend to preclude passengers with physical disabilities; and there is neither elevator nor special wheelchair access on a number of vessels. Partly because of the flexible nature of itineraries and variable schedules, excursions are usually built into the cost of the cruise, another feature that generally helps to distinguish between these and more conventional vacation cruises.

12

Freighter cruises

In the decades before the revival of cruising in the 1970s, the distinction between passenger ships and cargo ships was not always as clear cut as is sometimes thought. Although the main business of so-called passenger vessels was transporting humans, and that of cargo vessels was carrying freight, the former—even ocean liners—usually carried cargo of some kind, often mail, while the latter generally had room to accommodate passengers who, though rarely on pleasure trips, had business of some kind, as traders, missionaries or teachers in remote places. The so-called semicargo or semipassenger ships were universally known and made up a significant proportion of the fleet of some shipping lines: the P&O subsidiary British India Steam Navigation Company, for example, or Burns Philp of Australia. The first ocean voyage taken by one of the authors was on a British India semicargo ship that carried fewer than 100 passengers and on which the swimming pool was improvised from canvas and filled by a fire hose.

With the advent, throughout the 1960s and 1970s, of more specialised forms of cargo shipping, such as container, bulk carriers and roll-on roll-off vessels, and more advanced forms of maritime technology, the carrying of freight underwent a series of major changes. Being able to carry more cargo on container ships and bulk carriers meant having less space for passengers who, in any event, might sometimes be a nuisance and get in the way of the vessels' operations. As a result, many shipping lines, making the change from earlier forms of freight carrying to the more advanced methods, completely ceased carrying passengers on vessels whose essential purpose was the movement of cargo. For many years after the introduction and global spread of the container ship or bulk carrier, it was difficult, if not impossible, for people to obtain passage on freighters.

But advances in ship design and construction were accompanied by advances in navigation and communication technology and in the operational methods of loading and unloading ships. This meant that fewer people were now required to crew a vessel. One consequence of this was that many cabins, including some once used by senior officers, became vacant. Their potential for raising additional revenue, however, soon became obvious and the longstanding objections to passengers on cargo ships gradually disappeared. This does not mean that all freighter companies now accept passengers, but many do and the number is increasing. Restrictions on the type of vessel are still applied. Container ships are more likely than bulk carriers to accept passengers, and oil tankers are generally not regarded as suitable for carrying passengers.

Not surprisingly, the standards of the amenities for passengers vary considerably from ship to ship, but the typical cabin on a freighter of recent build is likely to be a good deal larger than the bottom-end passenger cabins on many cruise ships, and on some freighters may consist of two rooms and bathroom—a suite, in effect. The 'owner's cabin', so-called whether or not the actual owner ever occupies it, is necessarily the largest and best equipped. It will probably contain comfortable furniture, a small refrigerator, a TV set and a VCR. The ship itself may have a swimming pool, a library and exercise facilities. The latter are thought necessary for the crew also, because although it is usually possible to walk most of the way around a freighter, there is very little open deck or recreational walking space compared with most cruise ships. The food will be adequate in quality and plentiful in amount, if lacking in choice, and there is unlikely to be any provision for special diets. As with cruise ships, meals are included in the cost of the voyage and sometimes include wine. In the evening drinks are available in the lounge/bar, where passengers pay the same low prices as crew. There is usually a small facility on board which sells basic necessities, including liquor. There will normally be from two to eight passengers. Numbers are deliberately kept low, not only because accommodation is limited but also because carrying more than 12 passengers requires the presence of a medical doctor. There is usually an age limit for freighter passengers. Most often this is 75, but it is occasionally 80. The minimum age is 13, but some lines do not accept passengers younger than 18. Some companies require passengers over 65 to have a medical examination certifying to their fitness to undertake the trip; others require one from every passenger.

The ports of call on a freighter voyage are determined, of course, not with passenger diversion and amusement in mind but by the nature of the cargo. As ships have become larger (some container ships are 350 metres in length; *QE2* is 293 metres) and their freight-carrying capacities have become huge, requiring special facilities for their loading or unloading, there are fewer places where they can berth. In earlier times smaller cargo ships were able to visit ports, especially in the Pacific or parts of Asia, which are no longer accessible to today's vessels. As a result, a round-the-world freighter cruise may call at fewer ports than a cruise ship, thereby limiting one of the professed aims of ocean voyaging, which is to 'see the world'. On a typical round-the-world cruise, *QE2* calls at 36 ports, including overnight stays at such places as Honolulu, Auckland, Sydney, Hong Kong and Cape Town. A container ship may call at 18–20 ports, some for only a few hours. The popularity of freighter travel has increased so rapidly within the past few years that the authors of a 1999 publication could write: 'Today this form of cruising has all but vanished . . .', and name only two examples, neither of which were on freighters in the sense in which the word is usually understood (Cartwright & Baird 1999). In fact, freighter travel was quite active even then, but the activity has become more widespread, with several freighter companies offering passenger berths and a growing number of travel agencies advertising the experience.

Experiences of freighter cruising

Three first-hand experiences of freighter cruising, provided by Maris Freighter Cruises of Westport, Connecticut, United States, are reproduced below. They have been edited for reasons of length, repetition or clarification, but are otherwise in the words of the passengers who wrote them. It was decided to present them in this form, because they not only personalise the experience but also provide answers to many of the questions raised about this sort of travel.

A trans-Atlantic cruise from Montreal to Antwerp

My quarters . . . would be the envy of many a passenger on a five-star cruise ship. The sitting room, bedroom and bathroom were all tastefully furnished, and I had two windows on the starboard side of the ship which provided lots of sun on the eastbound voyage.

Furnishings included two easy chairs, a sofa, coffee table, a desk with an upholstered swivel chair, and a console containing drawers, shelves and a liquor compartment. The quarters had wall-to-wall carpeting throughout. The twin-bedded sleeping room provided ample space for storing garments, and each bed had its individually controlled reading light.

The pleasant accommodations were more than matched by the warmth and friendliness of the Captain and his officers who greeted me in the handsome lounge for a welcome-aboard drink. The curved bar, television set and VCR promised many happy hours at sea.

Dinner was served by Antoni, the steward, who always ensured that we were served with professionalism that would put to shame many a waiter on a cruise ship. The first meal, consisting of an assiette froide [collation of cold meats], salad, wiener schnitzel and frites [chips or french fries], let us know that there was a pro at work in the galley as well. The homemade bread and carafes of red and white wine reassured us that every meal on this crossing would be satisfying . . .

The next morning's light revealed a sparkling bay outside my starboard-side window while the port side revealed the impressive gigantic plant of the Wabush Mines facility where we were to pick up the last of our cargo: 68 000 tons of processed, pea-sized, iron pellets. The amazing sight of two black streams of what appeared to be ore pouring from mile-long conveyor belts almost made me decide to skip breakfast and continue to watch the remarkable feat of engineering. [The writer evidently travelled on a bulk carrier] . . . The time in port also offered an opportunity to visualize our shipboard vocabulary: holds, hatches, windlasses, winches, bollards, hawsers, etc. all became more real. Floors became decks and walls, bulkheads.

. . . The eternal question from friends whenever I tell them how much I enjoy freighter cruising. No floor shows, no dancing girls! But plenty of time for reading, walking on deck, watching the endless motion of the sea, good eating and lots of relaxation.

Entertainment is replaced by an opportunity to learn the ways of the sea . . . We started with the bridge—the wheelhouse and the chartroom—where the chart showed our pencilled-in position every four hours. Not that this was really necessary in these days of electronics and satellites—for example, the automatic pilot which meant no-one was actually at the wheel steering the ship.

There was, of course, an officer on watch but only to observe rather than control. The radar was probably the most important electronic device as it revealed any potential dangers to the ship such as other vessels, icebergs, etc . . . there is a mind-boggling array of electronic devices including the GPS (Global Position System) Navigator . . . one push of a button provided a digital reading of our exact position, speed (13.5 knots), course, and estimated arrival time at the next chosen point.

By pushing another button, our entire route, containing every change of course from Montreal to Antwerp, could be brought up. And should there ever be a man overboard, the push of another button would permanently show the location of the person, until the vessel had been turned around and returned to the exact spot.

On another day we decided to visit the galley where the chef and his able assistants still prepare meals the traditional way, using only the freshest ingredients. We were welcomed there, as we were everywhere else . . . The scent of the sauce he was preparing and the smell of the freshly baked bread were tempting enough for me to want my lunch then and there.

And so the days passed by . . . But every day was special.

But we made our passage through with no problem and soon were in the North Sea heading for a rendezvous with our Belgian pilot ship off Ostend. A spectacular electrical storm was our entertainment that night and the entrance to the river, enshrouded in fog, was our entertainment for the following morning. I was tense watching both phenomena but it was nothing, apparently, for the pilot and captain. They treated both as calmly as any other experience. Once on the river the clouds lifted, the sun shone and we had a summery cruise upstream, all the while enjoying the varied scenery.

Frank Nicholson, August 1996 (Maris Freighter Cruises 2001)

A trans-Pacific cruise from Savannah, Georgia, United States, to Australia and New Zealand

After months of planning we finally left Calgary on February 5th 2001 for Savannah, GA. We learned that the *Queensland Star* would be leaving on February 9th which gave us the opportunity to witness a shuttle launch from Cape Kennedy Space Center. The day after, we drove back to Savannah, walked through the historic city and set sail the next day . . .

In the afternoon of March 2nd we saw Pitcairn Island coming up. Pitcairn is a British territory and is also the island where the mutineers of the *Bounty* settled in 1789. We had a number of people come aboard on the rope ladder to sell wares, like T-shirts, small carvings, booklets, stamps. They also traded fruit for soft drinks and meat.

After we left Pitcairn, the weather changed abruptly. We passed the centre of cyclone Paula at a distance of 100 km and were suddenly in the 8-meter-high waves. The ship was rolling 20–25 degrees. During mealtime we had to hold onto the table, and sometimes hold onto our food as well. All the chairs and tables were tied up. The next day was quieter.

But by the evening of March 5th we were heading towards another cyclone, Rita, which was even more severe than the first, with 9–10 force winds and waves about 10 meters high. The ship was rolling and pitching. Our speed was reduced from 17–18 knots down to 8. It was not until the afternoon of March 7th that we reached calmer seas.

Thursday, March 8th was non-existent as we crossed the dateline and, since the beautiful weather returned, we could spend time out on deck again. On March 10th we arrived in Auckland, then sailed again early afternoon of March 11th towards Melbourne.

I did quite a lot of needlework (made a quilt top) and Bill walked 210 km around the deck as part of his daily exercise during the voyage. We enjoyed numerous visits to the bridge and learned how to read the radar screen. We didn't have to do any work, not even make our own beds! We did our own washing, though.

Allie and Bill Janson, April 2001 (Maris Freighter Cruises 2001)

A round-the-world voyage

We took a cabin close to the dining room, two decks apart, which meant that we had to climb four flights of stairs for every meal . . . the improvement in the shape of my thighs by the end of the trip was worth it all! On an average day I climbed up or down thirty flights of stairs . . .

Because we were going through the Suez Canal, we had to be immunized against cholera and yellow fever. So part of your preplanning should always include the medical aspect . . .

Our cabin had two rooms. The main room contained a pullout sofa, coffee table, desk, two armchairs, refrigerator, glass cupboard, bookshelf, and some storage space . . . There was an adequate medicine cabinet. The steward cleaned the cabin once a week [every day on cruise ships], when fresh bed linen and towels were provided.

Meal times were at 7:30 A.M., 11:30 A.M. and 5:30 P.M. and coffee was served at 10:00 A.M. and 3:00 P.M. The meals are more than ample and nourishing as they are prepared for hard-working sailors. For breakfast eggs are always available, as well as some kind of breakfast meat, several kinds of bread, fruit, juice, cheese and cereal. The noon meal is the main meal of the day, usually including soup, meat, a starch dish, vegetables, salad and fruit. Wine is included. The evening meal is usually a ragout of some sort, often over rice, with platters of cold cuts, crudités and cheese.

When we first boarded, meals were adequate but completely uninspired and boring. In Hong Kong we picked up a new chef and what he could do with the same ingredients was a revelation! Passengers and officers shared the dining room, but sat at separate tables.

As for wardrobe, take one 'very nice outfit' to wear ashore and put it in your closet immediately. Then wear all your oldest clothes. We quickly found out that we were on a working ship where the men are constantly washing, scraping, painting, and greasing cables. Unless we were willing to remain in our air-conditioned cabin, we had to cope with all this activity including smudges of whatever was being used on the ship, as well as occasional soot deposits from the smoke stack.

The 'very nice outfit' for going ashore included pants and shirt in a lightweight silk. After a day in the hot sun you can walk into the shower carrying your silks with you, wash everything, hang them on a plastic hanger, and they're ready to wear the next day. We also brought several soft hats that either sat down well on the head or were tied on in some way as a ship running at 18 knots an hour creates its own wind. A few heavy sweaters and two pair of lightweight wool pants took care of the cooler weather in Australia and on the Atlantic in September. We wore boat shoes constantly since the decks are frequently wet and slippery.

There was a comfortable lounge and bar, usually empty during the day, with games and a small library of paperbacks. The floor below had an indoor swimming pool which was filled with sea water every day. It also had a sauna, ping-pong table, dart board and self-service laundry. And then there was the bow! By walking all along the main deck we would reach it, and there, peace and isolation reigned. There was no sound from the engines, only the occasional creaking of the container lashings, which made one think of the rigging on a sailboat, and the empty, endless sea.

As no hairdresser was available for over three months, I took headbands and combs and let my hair grow, which took away the temptation to hack at it myself. The ship has a limited amount of items for sale including toilet soap and washing powder for the laundry and, best of all, liquid refreshments!

The final question to consider before you go is your own attitude and temperament. Lewis and I owned a sailboat for years . . .When once we decided we were too old to climb the rigging, we tried a conventional cruise. While it was very nice, dressing for dinner every night, eating sumptuous meals, watching a lavish show before the plentiful midnight buffet, it did not really excite us. On the freighter, we would mix our own scotch and soda, take it out on the deck right outside our cabin, sit on a deck chair, and watch the sun go down.

Unless you enlist some friends to go with you, the passenger list is in the lap of the gods. Upon leaving the United States we were six: a delightful couple from Paris, who left in Tahiti, a lovely lady who had worked in London for many years and was returning to her native New Zealand, and a retired German sea captain. For the New Zealand to Hamburg leg, our only companion was Captain Gerhard Reichelt. [He] had spent his life at sea as a captain on cargo vessels . . . He answered every question we asked about the ship's cargo and navigation. We were lucky beyond description to travel with him.

English is the lingua franca of all these ships. The senior officers are German and use their mother tongue among themselves. The crew is Filipino, and they speak Tagalog. But when speaking to each other, or to the passengers, they all speak English.

An important thing to keep in mind is that this is a working ship. The officers and crew were always very friendly and polite to us, but they were hired to run the boat, not to entertain passengers or act as tour guides. When we arrived at a port there was no tour bus carrying thirty passengers, or a lady holding her umbrella in the air to show you the sights or guide you to souvenir shops. From the moment we walked down the gangplank, we were on our own.

The overriding and exciting part of the trip is loading at each port. And every port is different! From the few cranes in Tahiti, where the men manhandle the monster containers from the end of the hoist into position on the ship, to the miles of docks and gantries in Singapore with immense equipment reminiscent of Star Wars. Each port has its own character: fast and efficient or slow and disorganized.

We provided the rest of the entertainment ourselves. Lew brought his new PC and unravelled most of its secrets. I brought plenty of cross-words, my knitting and a large stash of paperbacks, mostly murder mysteries and intrigue.

In the evening we often went down to the lounge for a Campari and soda for 59 cents, and watched a video, which had been chosen by the crew. If the Filipinos chose, it was English. If the German chose, it was dubbed in German. Hearing Bruce Willis moan 'Ach, mein Gott!' as he crawled the ventilator pipes made quite an evening. We've discovered a wonderful way to travel and we hope it catches on.

Vivienne Knapp, September 1997 (Maris Freighter Cruises 2001)

Comments

There are a number of observations in these accounts worth drawing attention to. Passengers are to a great extent expected to be self-reliant. Nothing in the way of organised entertainment is provided. Apparently, lots of reading is done, but one is entitled to wonder if it is really worth paying all that money ($US12 750 was a typical round-the-world fare in 2003) to spend most of one's time reading or doing crossword puzzles. Cruise ship passengers engage in these pastimes also, but out of choice rather than necessity. Watching the loading and unloading of cargo and other harbour activities fascinates quite a number of people, and has done so since the earliest days of ocean voyaging, but the majority of passengers on a cruise ship would probably find something else to occupy their time. Food becomes an important part of the experience, as does weather, but so they do on a cruise ship, or on any vacation for that matter. Many travellers find themselves unable to deal with even mildly rough conditions at sea, and those who have been on board a cruise ship in a cyclone will know what an unsettling experience it is. At least cruise ships are equipped with stabilisers to reduce the roll (side-to-side motion). Freighters are not, since the distribution of their weight and their low elevation in the water is supposed to steady them. But these features do very little to stop pitching (the forward/backward motion), and since freighters are so low waves need not be of exceptional height to break over the bow, as the author of the second account would have found. The tendency to compare the relatively Spartan experience of the freighter with that of a cruise ship reads a little like self-justification, especially since there is really no obligation on the part of cruise ship passengers to engage in all or any of the scheduled activities provided on a cruise, although finding a consistently quiet spot on many cruise ships can be difficult.

Freighter travel is clearly growing in popularity, especially with experienced travellers and the appearance of newer, more comfortably designed cargo ships that are actively seeking passengers, while making few concessions to them. There is even a growing literature on the subject, exemplified by the works of Gavin Young in *Slow boats to China* (1981) and *Slow boats home* (1986). But it is unlikely that it will ever capture more than a small fraction of the total cruise market. Although freighter travel is assumed to be cheaper, in economic terms there is often little difference between a cruise in a freighter and one in a cruise ship, because of the competition and heavy discounting that apply to the latter—there are no 'two for the price of one' deals to be found with any of the freighter companies. It appears that the informality of freighters, rather than any financial consideration, is a major reason for their appeal. The point at which 'travel by cargo ship' became 'freighter cruising' is obscure.

13

River cruises

Fascination with the world's great rivers has long been a feature of European exploration and, later, tourism, which one may regard as exploration with the hazards of the unknown removed. The Nile, the Amazon, the Congo, the Yangtze, the Mekong and the Mississippi continue to draw tourists, many of whom believe that they are travelling in the wake, if not the footsteps, of the world's great explorers. Lesser waterways also draw their share of sightseers, whether they are streams of history, both natural and constructed, or have little to show except mangroves and sandbanks.

River cruising craft vary enormously in size and degree of pretension, perhaps far more so than ocean cruise ships. They may range from super-annuated commuter ferries—large and small—to multistoreyed creations bearing at least a superficial resemblance to some of the more ambitious ocean-going vessels. The Yangtze and the Nile, for example, are home to vessels that can accommodate 160 or more passengers, and the traffic may be heavy at times. One company, Yangtze River Cruises, has no fewer than 28 ships on its list. It is of interest to note that the promotional language commonly applied to ocean cruising is also being employed by the river cruise specialists. The craft are regularly referred to as 'floating hotels', a term obviously preferred to the more mundane 'ships' or 'boats'. They are necessarily of shallow draft to handle the river conditions, but in many other respects include features and facilities found on ocean cruise ships: shops, beauty salons/hairdressers and nightly entertainment, which may include Dixieland jazz, belly dancing or karaoke, depending on which river one finds oneself. Within the South Pacific region, one of the most distinctive river cruises has been presented for many years by a Papua New Guinea (PNG) company, Melanesian Tourist Services, owned by the Barter family.

Melanesian Tourist Services

The Barters' involvement with tourism dates back to 1967, when Peter Barter established Talco Tours, then owned by Territory Airlines and based in Goroka. By 1975 Talco had become the largest inbound tourist operator in PNG and pioneered tourism to many regions in PNG. It also operated a number of tourist hotels and lodges. In 1975, having acquired Talco, the Barters moved their operation to Madang and shortly afterwards acquired the Hotel Madang (now the Madang Resort) and the ownership or management of other lodges and visitor services.

Maintaining something of the adventure mythology of small ship operations, the Sepik River cruises are said to have started in 1972 with two dugout canoes tied together and covered with canvas and mosquito netting to form a 'houseboat'. In 1976 the company, now known as Melanesian Tourist Services, purchased the first of four vessels to operate expeditionary cruises in PNG, naming it *Sepik Explorer*. This began a progression of expeditionary vessels, gradually becoming more sophisticated and comfortable until, in 1988, the twin-hulled *Melanesian (MTS) Discoverer* was constructed in Perth, Western Australia, especially to meet the needs of river and open-water cruising in PNG. The ship, registered in Madang, has accommodation for 42 passengers at capacity, a cruising speed of 15 knots, a range of 2000 nautical miles, state-of-the-art communication and navigation equipment, and the facility to make its own drinking water—from either the sea or the Sepik—which is a valuable resource if the copious supply of liquor on board ever runs out. It also carries auxiliary craft such as inflatables and a speedboat, and at times a small helicopter. Earlier successes inspired in 1989 the appearance of a smaller competitor, the 18-passenger *Sepik Spirit*, which offers a slightly different itinerary.

Apart from operating its own facilities, Melanesian Tourist Services has assisted many locally owned tourist enterprises, and has received a number of awards for cultural preservation and sustainable tourism through the work of the Melanesian Foundation, an organisation which directly and indirectly provides assistance to people living in remote rural areas of PNG. The directors of the company are mainly Barter family members, although a number of managerial positions are held by indigenous Papua New Guineans. Peter Barter, who has held ministerial posts in the national government of PNG at various times, was most recently minister for intergovernmental relations. He received a knighthood some years ago.

The nature of tourism enterprises in the Pacific Islands and the generally successful record of the company mean that the Barters are not without their public critics. In 1987 Australian film-maker Dennis O'Rourke produced *Cannibal Tours*, having taken several trips on *Melanesian Discoverer* to secure the footage he required, according to Janet Barter (personal communication). The resulting 77-minute film presents a fairly cynical view of the vessel's 'typical' passengers and the brief relationship between them and the villagers on the itinerary, implying strongly that the visitors are guilty of both cultural ignorance and exploitation, implications that reflect on the management of the enterprise.

In addition, for the past three years or so, Sir Peter Barter has been the subject of a constant campaign of vilification directed at his various interests in PNG. Readers with an interest in this kind of personal vendetta may find examples of it on a number of Internet sites, all of which appear to emanate from the same source and carry much the same information: <www.peterbarter.com> is representative. It may be suggested that their real value is mainly to illustrate how easy it is to post scurrilous, possibly defamatory, material on the Internet. The views they convey are not relevant here.

The *Discoverer*

MTS Discoverer offers two basic cruise itineraries: to the Trobriand Islands, an archipelago situated just north of the eastern tip of mainland PNG, and up the Sepik River, its best-known operation. The itineraries of both are variable, in order to allow for changes in both the social and natural environments. Papua New Guinea, it should be pointed out, is a volatile place politically and culturally as well as geologically. Manam Island, for example, close to the mouth of the Sepik, contains an active volcano, a feature that inhibits regular visits.

The relatively small size of *MTS Discoverer* precludes the sorts of passenger amenities available on the Yangtze and Nile vessels mentioned above: no-one is likely to refer to it as a 'floating hotel'. Accommodation is very comfortable and reasonably spacious rather than 'luxurious', a term applied with misleading frequency to cruise vessels. There is no bingo on board; instead there is a large library of books and an impressive collection of videotapes on the country. The dining room also serves as the venue for nightly briefings on aspects of

PNG or on the following day's activities. Visits to villages are included in the price of the cruise, and are supervised by a staff member thoroughly familiar with local conditions.

Travellers to the Sepik generally agree that there is a quality about this region of PNG, shared by only a few other parts of the Pacific, which makes most visitors feel that they are the first outsiders to be privileged to see it. This is partly due to the nature of the villages, whose layout and architecture appear indifferent to the introduction of modern designs and materials, and partly to the inhabitants of them, who look very much as though they have emerged from another era and have no need for such irrelevancies as electricity or motor vehicles. Only the T-shirts bequeathed by previous visitors and the occasional outboard motor powering a dugout canoe remind one that this is now the 21st century.

The contrasts between villages, even those fairly close to each other, add to the impression of isolation from the rest of the country, let alone the world. The river itself is wide, flat and meandering for most of its 1100 kilometres, bordered by numerous oxbow lakes and with narrow tributaries or channels that give access to wider bodies of water. It suggests timelessness, and is one of the region's most distinctive natural features, despite the efforts of mostly American tourists to force comparisons on it. It pays the researcher to eavesdrop in such company. 'This is

Figure 13.1 Sepik villagers perform a crocodile dance for visitors on *Melanesian Discoverer* (Source: Norman Douglas)

just like the Panama Canal', said one, responding to her first dawn on the Sepik. 'It reminds me of the Amazon', insisted another. 'We were there last year, you know.' A male passenger standing nearby thought it resembled the Nile (Douglas 1995, p. 59). Cruises to the Trobriands are usually of seven days, and Sepik cruises from four to six days, depending on whether the vessel travels to the lower or middle Sepik. An overview of a six-day Sepik itinerary, departing from Madang in the late afternoon, is given here.

A Sepik itinerary

A visit to villages in the lower Sepik by speedboat, for example in Murik Lakes, may begin the cruise. The next morning *Discoverer* proceeds up river to Angoram, the Sepik administration centre. The town contains a market of impressive size with a range of distinctive artefacts for sale, and at least one crocodile farm. The Sepik region is justly regarded by collectors of 'primitive' art as among the richest in the world, although one's chances these days of buying anything of ancient significance are slim, since special approval is needed to take out of the country any artefact more than ten years old. In the afternoon a trip up the Keram River to Kambot is likely, to see the unique storyboards and *haus tambaran* (spirit house). The next stop, Kambaramba, is a water village, not so much on the river as **in** it. The stilts or piers which support many houses along the Sepik are at least three times higher here, and the elevation of the limited amount of soil above the water line must be measured in centimetres rather than metres. Children offer, for a small amount of money, to paddle visitors through the village in dugout canoes—a spine-numbing experience.

The ship continues up-river until nightfall, usually reaching the village of Tambanum for overnight anchorage. This is one of the largest villages on the Sepik and known—at least by some Western anthropologists—for its association with Margaret Mead at an earlier time. It is also a centre for craft, which not only is displayed extensively for tourist purchase but also can be seen in the process of manufacture by both men and women. The technique of face-painting has been developed to a remarkably high level here, and evidently appeals to a great number of visitors, who are also persuaded to purchase a carving of similar design. The effect on Europeans—admittedly odd, even comic—was satirised visually in O'Rourke's film.

A short distance away is Timbunke, adjacent to a large Roman Catholic mission. People here are often occupied in making sago, a staple of their diet derived from the centre of a type of palm. Women are traditionally forbidden access to the *haus tambaran* but a concession has been made to women tourists, providing they observe certain conditions. Inside *haus tambaran* the photography of sacred objects is generally prohibited.

The Chambri Lakes, seasonally rich in bird life, are approached via a long canal, necessitating the use of the speedboat. At the edge of the lake are the villages of Wombun, with its attractive *haus tambaran* and unique art form, and Aibom, famous for its open-fired pottery decorated with faces of striking profile.

The following morning Palembei village, once on the river but now a 25-minute walk from it, is reached through gardens of vegetable and fruit. At each end of a park-like ceremonial ground are *haus tambaran*, each containing statues, ceremonial lime containers, drums and masks. The women spread their colourful *bilum* (woven fibre bags) on the grass outside with selections of shell jewellery and other items. Yentchen village may also figure on the itinerary, as may nearby Korogo.

In the late afternoon the vessel arrives at Timbunke, one of the few reliable airstrips along the Sepik River, from where visitors depart by chartered flight to Mt Hagen or Madang, for connections to the capital, Port Moresby.

The variety of experiences within this relatively short time and distance astonishes most visitors, and quickly helps to dismiss the notion that all PNG, let alone all Sepik, art is similar. No two *haus tambaran* are alike, and art styles vary considerably from village to village. In addition to the abundance of artefacts for sale—one of the few sources of cash income in many villages—cultural performances are offered at some villages. The vessel's owners have attempted as far as possible to strike a balance between the 'attractions' of various villages and have had to take into account also the potential jealousy and rivalry between villages, so that some may not seem over-favoured, a difficult diplomatic situation that has proved the undoing of more than one commercial enterprise in the Pacific Islands.

One is likely to encounter Americans and Europeans more frequently than Australians as passengers on the Sepik cruise. This has partly to do with marketing and partly to do with long-held views among Australian travellers that PNG is both expensive and dangerous to travel in. There is some truth in both of these opinions. It is also the case that even an apparently remote area such as the Sepik suffers from the fallout caused by international crises or regional politics. In response to our inquiry in March 2003 about possible itinerary changes we received this message (personal communication, authors' emphasis):

We no longer go to Jayapura [in the Indonesian province of West Papua], so Cruise C & D are not presently undertaken. Also, the Louisiade

Archipelago [off the eastern tip of the PNG mainland] (Cruise F) was only listed once for this year and will be cancelled because there are not enough takers. But the Sepik and Trobriand Island cruises are still viable, *though the impending war has done horrible things to our bookings this year.*

Part 4

14

Romancing the sea: the imagery of cruising

Every luxury you can imagine. Service beyond your dreams.

<www.seabourn.com>

Although heaven on earth may not exist, discovering supreme happiness at sea is an entirely different matter.

(Silversea 1999)

You haven't lived until you've cruised.

(Slogan, Cruise Lines International Association)

You can't live in the past, but it's a glorious place to visit.

(Cunard 1999)

Travel advertising

More than any other consumer product—groceries, books, electronic appliances, motor cars, real estate—travel is driven by advertising. One cannot browse holiday destinations or vacation packages the way one can scrutinise the items on a supermarket shelf or inspect an issue of a magazine or a new book on the racks of a newsagency or book store. One cannot test-drive a resort the way one can a new vehicle, or enter into a travel product before buying it as one can a house or an apartment. Nor can one return the product for a refund if it does not meet expectations or fails to perform satisfactorily. The retailers of travel do not display goods on their shelves—they display advertising. The potential purchasers of a travel product are very rarely able to view the product itself before purchase; they have to rely almost entirely on promotional material. Perhaps for this reason, travel advertising, almost throughout the history of commercialised travel, has been arguably more elaborate and more expensively produced than most other kinds of promotional material. This is still the case. The reader who doubts this need only enter a typical travel agency to get an idea of the range and quality of the 'merchandise', and to become aware especially of the visual impact of cruise-related material. Not uncommonly, cruise brochures—sometimes referred to as catalogues—contain from 50 to 100 pages consisting of dazzling images of vessels and their interiors and the most striking features of their destinations. As early as 1930 Evelyn Waugh referred to the 'gay catalogues of the shipping companies'. 'Cruise lines spend a lot of money on brochures, their most important sales tool', writes Ethel Blum, author of *The total traveler by ship* (1993, p. 60) and veteran of more than 200 cruises. The production values are high and so is the cost of production. Magazines of similar page length, design technique and paper quality would retail to the consumer for up to $10 per copy: cruise catalogues are free.

Most holiday travel places us in a space/time dimension different from the one in which we normally exist. Cruising, especially ocean cruising, goes a step further by removing us from land entirely—except for brief, sometimes almost incidental, port visits—and placing us in a self-contained world from which space appears limitless and time seems of no consequence at all, ship's clocks and meal hours notwithstanding. 'The last thing you'll be aware of is travelling', says one cruise brochure (P&O 1993). This sense of unreality is heightened by the advertising claims made for cruising, which may seem endless but are actually dominated by a few frequently repeated concepts—romance, luxury, nostalgia and exotica. Almost from the beginning of cruising as a tourist experience, these concepts have been in the forefront of cruise imagery, both visual and verbal.

Promotion does not consist purely of advertising, the motives of which, for all the elaboration, are obvious enough. Less obvious, because they appear to record 'true' first-hand experiences, are the works by travel writers, these days an ever-proliferating breed. It is one of the many remarkable aspects of cruise history that travel writers, or writers writing about their travels, have been part of the business since the earliest times. The English novelist William Makepeace Thackeray was on one of the earliest P&O voyages to the eastern Mediterranean, at the company's invitation, and published the account of his travels in 1846. The American author Mark Twain wrote at length about both his experiences aboard ship and the many places he visited in two books: *Innocents abroad* (1869) and *Following the equator* (1897). The views of both Thackeray and Twain on pleasure travel by sea are still being quoted. The difference between promotional advertising copy and an apparently unsolicited endorsement by a well-known and respected writer is great.

Evelyn Waugh and Paul Theroux

Since Evelyn Waugh—also a 'literary traveller'—was one of the most widely read and frequently quoted writers of the 20th century, it is instructive to know something of what he wrote about cruising. His longest piece on the subject, a book entitled *Labels*, was the consequence of an invitation to take a Mediterranean cruise in 1929 on *Stella Polaris*. The 200-passenger, Norwegian-owned vessel exhibited, according to Waugh, 'an almost glacial cleanliness. I have never seen anything outside a hospital so much scrubbed and polished'. In addition to the cleanliness, a feature of Scandinavian ships often remarked on to this day, Waugh was clearly impressed by the efficiency of the officers and crew and displayed a novelist's interest in the other passengers. 'I soon found my fellow passengers and their behaviour in the different places we visited a far more absorbing study than the places themselves. One passenger type', he noted, 'which abounds on cruising ships is the middle-aged widow of comfortable means', whose children are 'safely stored away' in boarding schools and who is 'in control of more money' than she has been used to. Her eyes 'stray to the advertisements of shipping companies and find there just that assembly of phrases—half poetic, just perceptibly aphrodisiac—which can produce at will in the unsophisticated a state of mild unreality and glamour'. In these lines Waugh identified two features of cruising still strongly in evidence: the presence of the wealthy widow (or, increasingly these days, divorcee) and the nature of the promotional literature that guided her choice of travel.

He was equally perceptive about—but far more critical of—many of the ports of call, including the touts, pimps and hotel keepers he came across in them, and other cruise ships encountered in the course of his own voyage. In the harbour at Naples, there was a German-owned tourist ship, 'built on much the same lines as the *Stella*', the passengers on which 'were all middle-aged Germans, unbelievably ugly but dressed with courage and enterprise . . . Everyone on the *Stella* felt great contempt for this vulgar ship'. He could not be accused of having an Englishman's typical disdain for German things, since he was even more scathing of a well-known P&O ship, *Ranchi*, on which he spent a few days between his trips on *Stella Polaris*. On *Ranchi* he travelled from Port Said to Malta, in the company of mostly English passengers: 'Children were everywhere . . . the better sort lay and cried in perambulators; the worse ones fell all over the deck and were sick . . . There was an awful hour every evening at about six o'clock, when the band came down from the first-class deck to play Gilbert and Sullivan to us in the saloon'(Waugh 1951, pp. 19–45).

Waugh was one of modern English writing's best-known satirists and much of the content of *Labels* would probably have done little to encourage potential cruisers, as amusing as it is. The response of the shipping company that invited Waugh to cruise does not seem to have been recorded. But at about the same time, Waugh also published in the popular US magazine *Harper's Bazaar* a short piece entitled 'In defence of pleasure cruising', which omitted most of his critical observations about ports of call and concentrated almost entirely on cruising and passengers—widows of middle-age being treated a little more kindly this time. The advantages of cruising he outlined were hardly different from those that many articles on the subject continue to draw attention to more than 70 years later. They were the convenience of unpacking only once; not having one's passport examined every time one stepped ashore; the physical comfort and cleanliness of the vessel; and the 'one inclusive price'. In addition, he observed 'there is inevitably a great deal of falling in love on board ship . . . The boat deck during dances is a great centre of romance' (see the *Porthole* survey below under the heading 'Romance'). He concluded that 'one must make up one's mind that cruising is a pursuit entirely of its own kind. It is not a bogus kind of travelling, but an entirely new sport with its own aims and rules' (quoted in Prior 1993, pp. 112–17).

The American writer Paul Theroux, a stylistic descendant of Evelyn Waugh, is widely admired—though equally widely criticised—for his caustic style and his critical assessments of many travel experiences. Like Waugh, Theroux was also invited on a Mediterranean cruise. Unlike Waugh, he did not devote an entire book to the experience, merely 47 pages of a much longer work, *The Pillars of Hercules*, published in 1995. The ship was *Seabourn Spirit*, a modern equivalent of Waugh's *Stella Polaris*, with a relatively small number of very wealthy passengers, the great majority of them Americans. Although Theroux begins his account by being critical of his predecessor—Waugh's book, he writes, was 'full

Figure 14.1 'The boat deck is a great centre of romance'
(Courtesy Esther Corley)

"I believe this is our dance, Miss Harrington."

of snap judgements and obnoxious opinions that helped make his reputation' (p. 301)—the similarity between them is far greater than he realises
or admits. Theroux very quickly also makes fun of the passengers: their
names, their occupations or apparent wealth, and their eating habits.
Theroux's observation, 'Waugh knew better than most people that there
is a great deal of pleasure to be derived from a travel book in which the
traveller is having a very bad time . . .', might serve equally well as a
comment on most of his own works. On the subject of the 'free hospitality' offered travel writers by tourism organisations, he admits that 'my
writing made me seem as though I was continually biting the hand that
fed me, my ironizing was nailed as "grumpy" and I was seldom invited
back a second time' (p. 301).

Theroux—like Waugh, apparently—had never been on a cruise before,
and compared to many of his other travels (in which misfortune or, at least,
inconvenience seem to be regularly present) he seems to have enjoyed
the experience, succumbing to the comfort, ease and even the feeling of
detachment from hard reality that, for many, characterises cruising and

helps to distinguish it from other forms of travel. Observations on comfort and the high quality of the food figure strongly in Theroux's assessment, as they do in the promotional literature of cruising. Places on land appeared more acceptable seen from the ship: 'As a cruise passenger I saw the Mediterranean as much bluer, the coast much tidier, and from the deck of the *Seabourne* [sic] *Spirit* Nice had great charm . . . [It] was not the over-crowded seaside resort of retirees and dog merds that I had passed through on a jingling train so many months before' (p. 304). After two weeks on the vessel: 'The ship was now more than home—it had become the apotheosis of the Mediterranean' (p. 338). And when the cruise was at an end: 'Leaving the comfort of the *Seabourne Spirit* was . . . like a secular version of the expulsion from Paradise' (p. 346).

Those familiar with Theroux's work might be inclined to regard these statements as further examples of what he calls his 'ironizing'. However, allowing for the fact that *Seabourn Spirit* is an exceptional vessel (as was *Stella Polaris* in Evelyn Waugh's time), it is probably more accurate to acknowledge that even habitual 'ironists' can become captivated by the cruise experience, lapsing into language different only in degree from that used by the cruise marketers.

Authors of lesser professional standing than either Waugh or Theroux and amateurs whose cruise experience has so inspired them that they want to be considered part of cruising's 'literary circuit' may also be found on cruise ships giving lectures and signing their books. A return invitation to cruise is assured by openings such as the one used by Singaporean writer Catherine Lim in *Meet me on the QE2*: 'Somebody sent me a postcard of the *Queen Elizabeth 2*. I fell in love promptly, booked a cruise and fell into debt. But it was done. Such was the power of the ship. It is a power, I believe, well beyond any tourist brochure to capture'(p. 1).

The four fundamentals of cruise imagery: romance, luxury, exotica and nostalgia

Romance

Notions of romance, which imbued much of the early fictional literature of the sea, were rapidly reduced to clichés and incorporated into cruise promotion, in the process of which earlier connotations of the term, associating it with adventure and heroism, were replaced by those implying physical and emotional attraction. This tendency, evident as far back as the early 20th century, now leaps out from almost every cruise brochure or poster and is reflected even in the descriptions or actual names of the vessels. Princess Cruises established its reputation largely through the popular 1970s television series *The Love Boat*, a phrase which the company applied to all its ships for more than two decades, despite the fact that, increasingly, no aspect of the ship shown in the series resembled any in its fleet. The massive Carnival Corporation, with interests now in at least 13 well-known cruise brand names, takes an even more blunt approach to 'romance'. A number of ships of its own brand bear names such as *Fantasy*, *Sensation*, *Elation* and *Ecstasy*. Carnival quite literally likes to spell out the appeal of its cruises for people who might be in danger of missing the point. This is a far cry from the days when companies gave their ships names which emphasised their size (*Titanic*, *Majestic* and so on) or their regal aspect (Queens, Empresses, Princesses and so on).

In 1999 the US magazine *Porthole* conducted a poll in which cruisers were invited to nominate their favourite 'places for onboard intimacy'. Possibilities included 'by the pool', 'in a lifeboat' (cf. Evelyn Waugh, above), 'in the casino', 'in the gym' and 'in the galley'. The most popular location, 'in the cabin', suggested a fundamentally conservative attitude among most romantics, but a few voted for something more bizarre: 'the infirmary' [hospital] and the 'empty kids playroom' were two choices (<www.porthole.com>). It is worth noting also that the film *Titanic*, which depicts one of the greatest maritime disasters of the 20th century, is credited by industry sources with stimulating an increased interest in cruising, because for many film goers the love affair between the two principals was far more significant than the ship's fate. The irony in this hardly needs comment, but serves as another illustration of an apparently indestructible cruise myth. The perception that cruising = romance = sexual licence leads to regular excesses on 'schoolie' cruises, passengers on which are predominantly high school students in their late teens. A late 1999 example on P&O's *Fair Princess* was described as '11 days and 10 nights of testosterone and vomit' (Bearup 1999). Perhaps the company should not be too surprised at these developments. One finding of a 1999 *Fair Princess* passenger survey was that cruising was seen 'as sexier than other holiday experiences' (P&O 1999).

The contribution of *Fairstar* (predecessor to *Fair Princess* on the Pacific cruise circuit) to destination development in the Pacific is examined in Part 2 of this book. It should be noted here, however, that P&O acquired the formidable reputation of the vessel as a good-time ship along with the company's takeover of Sitmar in 1988. The sobriquet 'Fun Ship' used in *Fairstar*'s promotion hinted only vaguely at the reasons for its popularity. Among a considerable number of its passengers, notably high school leavers and football teams, it was also known as the 'fuck bucket', the 'shag boat' [cf. Princess Cruises' 'Love Boat'] and the 'pussy palace'. 'If you couldn't get a screw on that ship in the first couple of nights', one of the authors was told by a university student, 'you'd better give up trying' (personal communication). One of the ship's drinking places—called 'The Sharp End Bar' but generally known as the 'Animal Bar'—displayed a large whiteboard on which obscenities, many of them detailing recent or prospective sexual encounters, were scrawled daily. 'You could dance naked on the table if you wanted to', a former *Fairstar* social hostess informed us. As it shifts its public image upwards by several notches, P&O Australia is now said to regard its nine-year association with *Fairstar* with some embarrassment, even 'distaste' (Lloyd 2003, p. 94), as one might regard an elderly or deceased aunt found to have been a brothel keeper in her time. These cultural details, however, not entirely peculiar to *Fairstar* but still vital to that vessel's image, should not be overlooked in this survey of imagery.

In Doris Day's first film, *Romance on the High Seas*, the title of which could not be more explicit, the plot, which is built around a cruise from New York to Rio de Janeiro, begins with suspicions of philandering and continues with implications of adultery. It's all in good fun and the result of misunderstandings and mistaken identities, of course, but for the association between romance and cruising, already apparently inseparable, it provides an excellent illustration and might, with only slight adjustments to the script, have served as the pilot film for the much later *Love Boat* television series (1977–86). It is worth noting that the film was made in 1948, a time when the cruise business was doing its best to recover from the widespread destruction of World War II and had not yet begun to feel the threat of wide-bodied jet aircraft.

In *An Affair to Remember* (1957), the matter of illicit romance is treated more seriously. Deborah Kerr (the mistress of a tycoon) and Cary Grant (the fiancé [gigolo?] of a wealthy heiress) are both morally dubious characters over whom the cruise ship exerts some indefinable but obviously irresistible power, turning their temporary attraction into a profound—though ultimately tragic—attachment to each other. Again, the cruise ship is the catalyst.

Luxury

Luxury, well spent: life without boundaries.

(Silversea Cruises slogan, website Silversea.com)

Intimate ships, uncompromising luxury.

(Seabourn Cruise Line, The Yachts of Seabourn 2002)

The term 'luxury' is so freely applied that it has become almost inseparable from 'cruise' itself, turning up incongruously in reference to vessels with one- and two-star classifications, in which the facilities could more accurately be described as fundamental. Operators of higher-rated vessels are thus obliged to grope for even greater superlatives, resorting to 'ultimate luxury' or 'unsurpassed luxury'. Thus D. Pedelaborde, Silversea Cruises executive: 'Luxury has become the most universal language and imagery in the world and Silversea is committed to providing the ultimate ultra-luxury travel experience' (Pedelaborde 1997). It probably doesn't pay to examine this statement too closely—'ultimate, ultra-luxury'. Evidently, nothing in cruising succeeds quite like excess. One almost expects that a copyright on the term 'luxury' may be taken out by one of the cruise companies, giving exclusive right over its use. The notion of luxury at sea is something of a hangover from the 'Golden Age' of cruising or even earlier, when there was a world of difference separating first class from steerage—there was little luxury to be had in the latter. The final removal of class distinctions that took place with the revival of cruising in the 1970s helped to moderate some of the language used in the past, but the linguistic excesses have resurfaced as part of the reaction against too great a democratisation of the cruise experience.

In his 1991 book *BAD or the dumbing of America* Paul Fussell (1991, p. 94) discusses the use of the term 'luxury' as it is applied by US hotels, among most of which, according to Fussell, it seems to mean the turndown service:

> And there are further hotel words and ideas which serve as bait for the credulous and unsophisticated. Furnishings are **lush**, drinks **libations**, fare is **exotic** [and so, as we will see, is almost any port of call], service **gracious**, settings **elegant**. But lest the socially insecure suffer an attack of nerves when faced with all this unfamiliar **elegance**, one hotel specifies that its dining courtyard is 'elegantly casual'. . .

Fussell is here writing about hotels, but since hotel and resort concepts have become essential to the operation of most cruise ships also, what we might call 'the language of luxury' was brought in along with the management techniques. The following example from Silversea's 2002 brochure serves to both illustrate the excesses of Pedelaborde and reinforce the observations of Fussell: 'We've dedicated ourselves to an entirely new standard in cruising, the ultra-luxury class'.

Food is not merely food at Silversea, nor even fare, but 'inspired cuisine', and the atmosphere on board one of 'easygoing elegance without an ounce of pretension'. Do they mean **pretentiousness**? The accepted first-level meaning of **pretension** is 'an untruthful or dubious assertion'. But since Silversea's vessels qualify as 'small ships' and are so recognised in awards made by the magazine *Conde Nast Traveller*, another quality is required to help distinguish them: this is 'intimacy'. The ships, then, are like 'intimate and exclusive resorts' which feature 'intimate public rooms': 'Sailing on our intimate ships is like visiting a friend's home'. With friends who charge prices like that, one might note, you don't need very many enemies. As for eating, or rather 'inspired dining', why not enjoy 'an intimate evening in your suite'? Or, if you choose the restaurant, you won't be surprised to know that it is 'elegant, but not stuffy', and presumably lacking, therefore, in both pretension and pretentiousness. It hardly needs to be said that for its pre- or post-cruise accommodations Silversea offers a selection of 'more intimate hotels' (Silversea 2001, 2002).

Luxury, then, is associated with eating, not merely adequately, or even inspiringly, but often to excess. The publishers of the cruise magazine *Porthole* also publish a newsletter entitled *Cruiseline Cuisine*, featuring recipes drawn from the repertoire of outstanding chefs in the cruise business. Whether potential cruisers would be attracted to a particular ship primarily on the basis of a favourite recipe of its executive chef is doubtful, but the publication provides another illustration of the importance attached to food in the operation and reputation of cruise vessels.

Figure 14.2 The reception area ('Grand Piazza') of Star Cruises' *SuperStar Virgo*: Asian opulence (Courtesy Star Cruises)

Demonstrations of cooking appear regularly on ships' entertainment programs, conducted by the vessel's own chefs or by 'celebrity' chefs invited on the cruise to display their skills. They invariably attract large numbers of passengers eager to sample the results, even if they have only just eaten breakfast or lunch. Regardless of its star rating, the cruise ship that doesn't devote significant promotional space to the quality and quantity of its meals is unlikely to be given serious consideration by prospective passengers. This excerpt from a Carnival Cruises brochure (Carnival Cruise Lines 2000), though it may appear excessive to the person who has never cruised, is typical:

> On a Carnival Cruise holiday, every meal and snack is included. So, wherever you have breakfast, lunch or dinner, feel free to order just what you want. If you're hungry between meals, our wide choice of snacks includes ice cream, the pastry selection at tea time and the fresh-from-the-oven choices at the 24-hour pizzeria. If you're up late, don't miss the late-night buffet, an incredible selection of glorious food that's also a feast for your eyes. And, keep in mind, you can order complimentary stateroom service (light meals and snacks) any hour of the day or night.

It is probably perfectly appropriate to the 'Funship' character of many of Carnival's vessels that the above reads far more like 'pigging out' than the 'intimate' experience of eating offered by Silversea.

Changes in passenger eating habits and cruise ship eating patterns within the past decade have resulted in a gradual erosion of the almost institutionalised arrangements that characterised meal times for almost a century. This is evident in the removal of the once hallowed midnight buffet from the daily meal offerings of many vessels and the introduction of 'free-style dining' and healthy or special meals. Such innovations as kosher cruises are on offer. Having been rescued from impending oblivion by the South-East Asian company Star Cruises, the US-based Norwegian Cruise Line, in its search for a new promotional identity, stresses its devotion to 'free-style cruising'. This does not seem to mean much more than that passengers are no longer obliged to share their dining table with the same companions night after night. Clearly aware of the regional fondness for eating and frequent 'grazing' between larger meals, Star Cruises' own SuperStar ships offer a range of Asian restaurants as well as 24-hour casual dining.

The importance accorded to eating on cruise ships gave rise to a distinctive form of imagery—that which decorated ships' menus. For devoted cruisers, a ship's menu long ago acquired the status of a valuable, or at least collectible artefact, a souvenir that provided specific and often colourful detail of their cruise experience. The more important cruise companies commissioned artists to design distinctive menu covers that vied with cruise posters and other travel advertising as elevated forms of popular art. The work of US artists Frank MacIntosh and Eugene Savage for the San Francisco-based Matson Navigation Company made as great a contribution to the imagery of cruising and the Pacific Islands, particularly Hawai'i, as any other pictorial medium. In 1950 Savage's menu covers, first used by Matson in 1948, were awarded a Certificate of Excellence by the American Institute of Graphic Arts—the Institute's highest award. Their popularity with passengers and other collectors was so great that by 1952 more than 250 000 had been distributed. Even by that time, Hawaii's relentless nostalgia industry was already in full swing and its continuing profitability guarantees the survival of the work of MacIntosh and Savage in one form or another. Matson has sold reproduction rights to such companies as Liberty House, GTE Hawaiian Telephone Company, the Hawaii Prince Hotel, the Sheraton on Maui, and Land's End—the latter a firm that designs dishware (Hull 1999).

If eating practices on liners or cruise ships were hedonistic enough to give rise to a form of romantic imagery, then not infrequently excessive eating is associated with excessive indulgence in other activities, as this extract from the multiple-author novel *The Cruise* (Binchy et al. 1995, pp. 27–8) illustrates. The dialogue takes place between the characters Lisa and Jasmin: the latter having just won 'a bloody cruise in a soddin' raffle':

'Let's just start dieting right away so that we can have the biggest blowout of all time as soon as we step on board!'
'What else happens on cruises apart from food?'
'Oh, it's all boozing and sex, of course, everyone knows that. There'll be loads of furry chests on board, Lisa. It'll be a sex-buffet-de-lux, a banquet, a—'
'Wowee! I'm having an orgasm just thinking about it.'

It was a P&O cruise. Curiously, P&O allowed its name and the name of its then under-construction *Oriana* to be used as the setting for this 'novel of murder and romance', presumably on the assumption that almost any publicity is worthwhile. The company, however, insisted that the plot should not involve the hijacking or sinking of their ship and agreed only 'after much consideration' to a murder, perhaps mindful of what Agatha Christie had done for the Orient Express. They got three murders and some dope smuggling for good measure. The introduction notes that the book was written by 'a group of authors who had never been cruising!', although they evidently knew something of its mythology (Binchy et al. 1995, *passim*).

Figure 14.3 Matson's menu covers helped define the tourism imagery of the Pacific (Courtesy J. Hull, Matson Navigation Co.)

Exotica

Sail in splendour—beside sampans, junks, dhows and yachts—to the soaring skylines of Hong Kong and Singapore or the tranquil Edens of Bali and Phuket. Wander the souks, bazaars and markets where the warmth of the citizens charms you . . . Come face to face with Bedouins in the desert, talented Thai chefs and Borneo's endangered Orang Utans. Immerse yourself in the wisdom of Buddha as you explore countless temples in Myanmar. Explore Egypt's Valley of the Kings and Queens. Make the most of your time in exotic locales with Seabourn Journeys in India.

(<www.seabourn.com/destinations>)

The notion that a destination must necessarily be exotic to attract travellers is one of many assumptions built into tourism. It may be influenced by the ongoing, but increasingly artificial, distinction made between the 'traveller' and the 'tourist'. The privilege of being able to visit 'exotic' places, it suggests, is one reserved for the true 'traveller'. 'Why would ['elegant'] people travel to see the familiar?' is the implied question. The fact is, of course, that they do. Internal and domestic travel in almost any country attracts more people annually than foreign travel. In Australia, spending by domestic tourists is almost four times higher than spending by international visitors. The seaside resorts that came into being in Britain in the 19th century—from Brighton to Blackpool—owe their continuing existence to British travellers' fondness for the comfortably familiar, even if they have to decorate themselves with exotic flourishes from time to time. Torquay, for example, subject of merciless lampooning in the TV series *Fawlty Towers*, now refers to itself (together with its sister resorts of Paignton and Brixham) as 'The English Riviera', using Mediterranean-style imagery to reinforce the claim. In a novel inversion of the standard notion of what constitutes exotica, an award-winning advertisement shows a group of Arabs in a souk gazing longingly at a brightly coloured poster for the English Riviera, presumably envisaging an escape from their own colourless existence. Arab romantics notwithstanding, the people who keep Torquay successful are British; many of them long-term repeat visitors. As far as we are able to tell, no large influx of Arab visitors to the English Riviera resulted from the advertisement.

Nonetheless, the term 'exotic' has become a standard description in tourism and the phrase 'exotic destination' a cliché, ready to be applied to almost any place that appears even vaguely different. In this process of overuse, the word 'exotic' has all but lost its earlier meaning—foreign or alien—and taken on the less forceful meaning of 'more or less unusual'. It is now so firmly embedded in the vocabulary of travel and so frequently repeated that it has stopped serving any really useful purpose. This is of no particular concern to the publicists. Princess Cruises' *Exotic Adventures* brochure (Princess Cruises 1998) invites readers to 'Explore the Exotic World of Princess' and lists, among a number of 'exotic destinations', cruise ports in Canada and the United States, the very markets to whom the brochure is directed! 'Finding the exotic in your own backyard is easy', says the brochure. But to describe to North Americans such cities as Boston and New York as 'exotic' seems to be pushing the term to absurd limits.

If this example appears quaint, it is eclipsed in incongruity by the promotional material of Malaysia-based Star Cruises, which lists as 'exotic ports' 14 cruise destinations in South-East Asia, including in Malaysia and Singapore, from where the overwhelming majority of its passengers are drawn. The concept of the 'exotic', a Western construct in the first place to help position the East culturally in relation to the West, has been swallowed whole but only half-digested by destination marketers and is now regurgitated to describe the East to itself: 'aboard the *SuperStar Virgo* the most exotic parts of Asia come to you'. Ease of access to the exotic, as the Princess Cruises brochure also claims, is important (Asian Explorer Holidays 2000).

Star's Gulf of Siam cruises invite cruisers to: 'Explore the exotic pleasures of the Far East . . . You'll find destinations in Thailand and Vietnam full of mystique and charm, and you might lose yourself in the myriad of Oriental pleasures they have to offer'. This in an itinerary that includes Bangkok and Koh Samui and is marketed almost exclusively to Thais! (Star Cruises n.d., a). 'All the exoticism of the mysterious east is spectacularly revealed', announces a Star brochure aimed at the company's mainly Hong Kong market (Star Cruises n.d., b).

It may be necessary, of course, since both tourism and tourism promotion are fundamentally Western concepts, to spell out the exotic for people who for centuries have been the unwitting personification of it. Earlier cruise advertising—aimed exclusively at Europeans—tended to render it pictorially rather than verbally. Newsome's famous 1930 depiction of caparisoned Indian elephants for P&O's eastern services—an image employed also by the Thomas Cook organisation (Figure 14.4)—the Middle Eastern subjects by Greig which showed Arabs calmly watching the approach of a P&O vessel, or a simple street or even a desert landscape without a ship in view, very effectively conveyed the quality of The Other, without having to reinforce it with words. Greig's poster of a Strath class ship observed through an archway (Figure 14.5) manages to project an almost biblical quality—the three wise men of the East watching a new star appear out of the night. The accompanying text is minimal—'P&O Cruises'. However, occasionally there is a more specific message. A 1929 advertisement for P&O's 'East of Suez' services reads: 'Swift and sure, punctual in their arrival, these Liners are to Indians [and, they might have added, 'Arabs, Malays and Chinese'] symbolical of the might and splendour of the West' (quoted in Server 1996, p. 63).

Nostalgia (and patriotism)

For all the evocation of the exotic, however, there are times when a simple appeal to patriotic instincts works best. 'You're in good hands with our British officers', declares a picture caption in a P&O brochure. Patriotism may also underpin meal times and passenger activities: 'Do you favour a full English breakfast?' the same brochure asks, and later: 'To remind you that we're British, we offer bridge tournaments and, of course, traditional afternoon tea' (P&O 1993). As an indication that this was not mere short-lived whimsy on the part of the advertising copywriters, P&O was still vigorously reinforcing the patriotic theme in its 2000–01 season, promoting 'Classic British Cruising' and 'The Best of British Cruising' on its UK-based ships *Aurora* and *Oriana*. The former, it appears, 'ushered in a new millennium of cruising with P&O cruises. She was conceived, designed and built for British passengers' (P&O 2003, p. 50). Are other nationalities therefore excluded? This is left unsaid. Security and the comfort of the familiar are thus guaranteed. P&O (UK-based), which also operates Princess Cruises (US-based), prefers as a matter of policy to keep its British and American markets fairly distinct from each other, since the expectations of its passengers differ, depending on their national origins. Cunard, owned by the US Carnival Corporation but determinedly clinging to its UK clientele, counters with: 'You'll also appreciate the unique British ambience [of its 668-passenger *Caronia*], as you would expect of a ship which is British built, British registered and British officered' [but crewed in the main by Filipinos] (Cunard 2001, p. 4).

Related to the rather old-fashioned, but evidently successful, appeal to patriotism illustrated by these examples are the continual attempts by cruise marketers to evoke an earlier era, a misty time generally referred to as the 'golden age of travel', the supposed 'heyday' of cruising, the 1920s and 1930s. 'If the past is a foreign country', writes Lowenthal, 'nostalgia has made it the foreign country with the healthiest tourist trade of all' (Lowenthal 1985, p. 4). Elements of nostalgia as a marketing tool are better seen in cruising than in any other form of travel. We might note the repeated use of the term 'classic' by the now defunct Royal Viking Line (Royal Viking 1994); the use of colourful luggage labels that recall

Figure 14.4 Newsome's poster of caparisoned elephants. The image was also used by Thomas Cook (Courtesy P&O art collection)

Figure 14.5 Greig's famous poster evoked the exotic for P&O travellers (Courtesy P&O)

Figure 14.6 'Best of British' cruising. Cunarders enjoy the sea in a characteristically English manner—facing away from it (Source: Norman Douglas)

the 1920s and 1930s in P&O and Cunard brochures; the interior décor of the motor/sail cruise ship *Club Med II*; and posters and brochure covers which abandon photography in favour of a return to the art design of many decades ago, with full-frontal illustrations of the towering bow of *QE2* or some unnamed vessel, and which consciously resemble much earlier representations of ships such as *Normandie* or *Queen Mary* (Cunard 1999; Infinity Cruises 1993).

Just as there is comfort in knowing that your officers, food and diversions are all British, so there is evidently a feeling of security in travelling in a kind of time capsule in an era which unreliable memory assures us was much safer than the present. Passenger perceptions of security, after all, play a major part in the appeal of cruising. However, if nostalgic contrivance doesn't fully convince, then the long-term players in this very competitive game are anxious to assert their own historical significance. 'P&O, the company that invented cruising', reads that group's website. 'Cunard—advancing civilisation since 1840', says a newspaper advertisement for that cruise line (Cunard 2000). Although many cruise lines engage in pseudo-historical rhetoric from time to time, P&O and Cunard are masters of the 'Golden Age' marketing genre, both regularly contesting an imaginary 'Best of British' title. Cunard has clung determinedly to

Figure 14.7 A young boy's ambition (1958) (Courtesy P&O
Australia)

Figure 14.8 P&O revives a 1958 slogan, with artwork for the 21st century (Courtesy P&O Australia)

Figure 14.9 *Normandie* posters were much influenced by the
Art Deco style

Figure 14.10 Cunard's recent promotion for *QE2* recaptures the art style of an earlier time (Courtesy Cunard)

its British mystique and its nostalgic appeal, as this extract from its 2001 catalogue (Cunard 2000, p. 5) illustrates:

> Do you remember a time when the days passed joyously—even a bit lavishly—as you watched the world go by from the decks of a grand ocean liner? For anyone wishing to reclaim this vanishing lifestyle, there is only one clear choice in the world of travel. That choice is Cunard Line. Live your dream aboard the renowned flagship QUEEN ELIZABETH 2 and the classic CARONIA, two of the world's most distinctive liners . . . Within these bastions of civilisation, the legacy of Cunard White Star service blends perfectly with the best of modern luxuries and 21st-century British style.

When patriotism is combined with nostalgia, exotica and luxury (romance is implied), the marketers have a sure thing.

From about the 1960s onward the widespread use of colour photography in place of graphic art introduced a more realistic element into cruise and travel imagery generally that worked in a way against the romantic qualities which earlier art styles had helped to create or foster. The new (or, at least, more widely applied) visual technology was faster in capturing images and probably more economical in producing them in large quantities. But in the new era of cruising there was little to compare with the visual impact of the *Normandie* posters of Cassandre or other Art Deco stylists, or the imaginative use of location and design that characterised the work of artists such as Newsome and Greig for P&O, Walter Jardine for Burns Philp and Percy Trompf for Orient. A mere photograph of a ship did not convey the same excitement or glamour, despite the frequent use of soft or out-of-focus imagery, some of which looks merely like poor photography. Perhaps for this reason, brochures for P&O Australia's veteran *Fairstar* enhanced camera pictures of the vessel with leaping dolphins or outrigger canoes somewhat unconvincingly airbrushed in (see Figure 8.4). The practice appears to have ceased when *Fairstar* was retired.

But the legacy of earlier design forms persists where nostalgia remains a major marketing tool. The influence of the *Normandie* posters with their towering frontal view of the ships's bow suggesting power and authority can be seen in P&O's 1960s poster for *Canberra* —'Southampton to Southampton via The World'—and even more strongly in Cunard's 2001 series which place the still imposing *QE2* in a number of imaginative locations (figure 14.10), one of which all but replicates a *Normandie* poster (Figure 14.9).

Part 5

15

Cruise passenger behaviour

Why tourists do what they do has been the focus of a substantial amount of research in recent years. The underlying result of the majority of studies is that motivation determines not only if consumers will engage in a tourism activity but also when, where and what type of tourism experience they will seek (Pizam & Mansfield 1999). Maslow's 1943 hierarchy of needs has been the most widely used theory on which studies into tourist motivation have been based (Maslow 1943, cited in Hudson 1999). Hudson suggests its popularity is because of its simplicity, although there remains doubt about its true level of effectiveness. Studies by Plog (1974), Dann (1977), Crompton (1979), Mannel and Iso-Ahola (1987) and Krippendorf (1987) are where most tourist behaviour researchers start, and the resulting body of knowledge is far too wide to cover here. However, Hudson's (1999) review of these and more recent studies is useful. He summarises that consumer behaviour research in tourism has focused on motivations, typologies, destination choice and the decision process itself. It is generally assumed that once tourists have been classified and categorised in one or more of these areas, their actual behaviour on location is predetermined. Few studies have examined actual on-site behaviour. Six chapters in Pizam and Mansfield (1999) cover studies which conclude that while it might be possible to categorise tourists according to choice-of-holiday experience, another set of variables needs to be considered when examining what the same people actually do when they get to their holiday destination. The needs of the individual are paramount.

The method

The cruise ship environment offers an excellent opportunity to study tourist behaviour. The confines of a ship at sea makes it possible for continued, unobtrusive participant observation, and the data collected can be checked with information gathered from in-depth interviews with crew who are in positions of constant passenger contact. However, while Foster (1986) proposed that a typical cruise culture exists, and Morrison et al. (1996) profiled the typical cruise vacationer, we suggest that there is no common culture and that the cruise passenger profile is changing as fast as the industry itself.

This research examines the behaviour of passengers on three different ships on cruises with three different itineraries and describes the similarities and differences. Research techniques incorporated participant observation, structured interviews with ships' staff members and many informal conversations with passengers. Although participant observation may raise ethical issues about disclosure and privacy rights of respondents, the authors agree with Foster (1986) that the production of such research tools as tape recorders and structured questionnaires would introduce elements of constraint with fellow passengers that would be counterproductive. In the experience of the authors, they would be even more counterproductive if used with crew. Video and still camera records, however, were maintained because their use was not seen as atypical behaviour in the environment. Senior staff members were routinely informed of the purpose of interviews and conversations prior to their taking place. Other informants such as bar staff, waiters and room stewards were freely engaged in conversation in the same way as they might have been with regular passengers.

The ships

The three ships selected (*SuperStar Virgo*, *Crystal Symphony* and *QE2*) are all significantly different from each other in terms of size, age, quality, target market and passenger profile. Some details of their features and facilities will help to make the analysis of passenger behaviour more meaningful, as each ship offers a different product.

Superstar Virgo

SuperStar Virgo (henceforth *Virgo*) entered service in August 1999 as a sister ship to *SuperStar Leo*, which had appeared in 1998. Like the latter,

Virgo was 'built specifically for the Asian region, incorporating Asian tastes and influences aboard' (Star Cruises 2000). With a GRT of 76 800, a passenger capacity of 2000 and a crew capacity of 1000, it is the biggest as well as the newest of the three ships studied. Marketed as a 'sea resort', it is home-ported in Singapore and, depending on the dictates of the monsoon season, makes short cruises either through the Straits of Malacca or up the east coast of Malaysia. The arrival of the SuperStar ships marked a pinnacle of success for Star Cruises, the Malaysia-based company that has had a spectacular rise in the international cruise industry since it first appeared in 1993 with a single converted Scandinavian ferry dedicated to short gambling cruises out of Singapore. In 2003 the company became the third largest cruise company in the world.

Passenger facilities on *Virgo* include nine restaurants and cafés, an enormous outdoor swimming pool with four adjacent spa pools that only adults may use, a pool area, playground and video game arcade for children, a fitness centre, library, beauty salon, numerous bars including a karaoke lounge with 24-hour video, a duty-free shop and boutique, a magnificent show lounge seating more than 900 people and a film theatre. The largest public area on the ship is the 24-hour casino accommodating 1800 players. The entire environment is luxurious and extremely well-maintained while the service is excellent in all areas. Officers are mostly Scandinavian or Asian. The crew is generally described as 'international' and may include Americans, British and Australians (principally in the casino), but the majority are Asian. The passengers are overwhelmingly Singaporeans and Malaysians, although other Asian nationalities are increasingly represented as fly-cruise packages are becoming more widely accepted within Asian tourist cultures. The cruises are two- or three-night packages and, although there is evidence that the idea of a cruise for holiday purposes is becoming accepted, the motivation of most of the passengers is the access to full gaming facilities and the extraordinary dining options, the largest of which are included as part of the package price. Given the Asian fondness for gaming and grazing, *Virgo* is certainly meeting market needs.

Crystal Symphony

Crystal Symphony, with a GRT of 50 000, a passenger capacity of 1010 and 545 crew, entered service in May 1995 and is regarded as one of the new generation of floating resort hotels, with many features more common to land-based resorts than to ships. The vessel features a large hotel-style lobby with sweeping staircase, shopping arcade ('Avenue of the Stars'), superbly equipped business centre, specialty restaurants (with no surcharge) in addition to the main dining room, and spacious passenger accommodations. Many have private verandas. *Crystal Symphony* contains activity rooms for both young children and teenagers, but they are staffed only on certain sailings. The vessel's film theatre resembles a traditional cinema in appearance and its library is more capacious and much better equipped than many similar facilities at sea. The swimming pools are big enough to encourage serious lap-counters. The casino, operated by the Caesar's Palace organisation and named accordingly, is large and opulent and, in keeping with the traditions of Las Vegas, patrons receive free drinks at the casino's bar, one of eight bars on the ship. Slater and Basch (1996) give the Crystal ships (there are two of them and a third nearing completion) a six-star rating and add that 'the Crystal ships are for those who want—and are willing to pay for—the very best in a traditional big ship sailing experience' (p. 270). Officers are Norwegian and Japanese, while staff are 'international', although with a seemingly smaller number of Filipinos and Indonesians than encountered on the other vessels. Although built in Japan and owned by the Japanese NYK (Nippon Yusen Kaisha) Line, *Crystal Symphony* (together with its elder sister *Crystal Harmony*) is marketed chiefly in the United States and attracts an older and higher-income group.

Queen Elizabeth 2

Popularly called *QE2*, this ship is considered the grand old lady of the cruise business. Built as a two-class turbine steamer, her maiden voyage was in May 1969. *QE2* has a GRT of 70 327, a passenger capacity of 1777 and crew of 1015. In 1987 she was converted to diesel power; in 1994 the bathrooms were remodelled and public spaces relocated and reorganised; and in 1999 the ship received a cosmetic facelift throughout. But while these changes in many respects may have moved the ship into 21st-century cruising, *QE2* is the one ship afloat which retains a distinct two-class system. Passengers in the more expensive cabins, known as Grill Room class, have their own special dining rooms—there are three, of which the Queens Grill is the highest in quality—and exclusive-use lounges. Passengers in more moderate accommodation have their own dining rooms with their own ranking and use all other public spaces. 'As a "classless" cruise ship, the layout is rather disjointed', writes Douglas Ward (2000), 'but as a transatlantic liner, the layout is beautifully designed to keep you in your place'.

Service and food are excellent. Both the class system and the vessel's general appearance—a little dated with wood panelling and older-style fittings and layout—may be regarded as deliberate marketing tactics by Cunard. Fielding's guide rates the Grill Room experience five star and the rest four star. *QE2* has a casino, an excellent film and performance theatre, a show lounge, and the well-appointed Queens Lounge for dancing. The shopping arcade is comprehensive, although 'Harrods at Sea' is only a shadow of its London parent, and there are health and beauty facilities. Unlike many modern ships specifically designed for cruising in tropical climates on which swimming pools have become major features, *QE2* has one very small outdoor swimming pool and another below decks in the gym. However, also unlike many other ships, *QE2* has an exceptionally good library and bookshop. The vessel was, after all, designed to spend most of her time in colder, northern climates where indoor activities have priority. Elegance and a nostalgia for the days when passage on a large liner really did make getting somewhere half the fun are hallmarks of this Cunard product. The ship is a floating museum to Samuel Cunard and the great shipping company he founded in 1842, with prominently displayed collections of memorabilia. In keeping with *QE2*'s deliberate British ambience, many of the senior officers, including the captain and the cruise director, are British, although there are 50 nationalities among the crew.

The passengers

Tourists who choose to cruise are seeking experiences that are different from those who choose resorts, cities, land-based tours and theme parks. Although cruise operators have been claiming this all along according to their own observations and data, Moscardo et al. (1996) applied multi-dimensional scaling analysis to a Canadian leisure survey with over 12 000 responses, and concluded that cruise passengers chose the experience for the following reasons:

- sense of romance;
- good value for money;
- excellent dining;
- quality entertainment;
- access to water-based activities;
- variety of destinations;
- opportunity to visit international destinations in a controlled and organised way;
- safety.

It must be stated, however, that these are very Eurocentric results. As later discussion will show, the new Asian markets have quite different priorities. While several of these attributes can be identified with a number of other types of holiday, the last two are extremely significant in understanding the spectacular growth in demand for cruising. North

Americans (especially US citizens) comprise by far the largest market segment—approximately 65 per cent—and while they are frequent travellers, they are also nervous ones. In times of international crises such as the Gulf War in 1991, regional conflicts or terrorist activity, Americans fear being the target. This has intensified since the tragedy of 11 September 2001. They are not particularly adventurous in terms of culinary and cultural experiences, often preferring the opportunity to observe or sample cautiously without large-scale commitment. For these problems and perceptions of international travel the cruise ship seems to provide a solution. The self-contained environment is fully secured, with patrolling security staff, scanning machines for luggage and people, and extremely limited access via a single, constantly guarded gangway. While there may not be a **single** cruise culture in terms of passenger behaviour, there is increasingly a **corporate** cruise culture wherein the cocooned environment of the majority of ships is determinedly American. Passengers immediately feel a sense of familiar place when they embark.

Virgo presents an interesting environment in that the overall design and décor faithfully reflect the best traditions in British and American ships except in the predominant use of red, which is the colour of good luck and good fortune in Asian cultures. The authors were told that the company's founder, Tan Sri Lim Goh Tong, personally investigated the traditions of cruise ship design to ensure that his ships incorporated the best and most popular aspects of tradition.

On *Crystal Symphony* and *QE2* passengers are generally older, reflecting the availability of time and appropriate levels of disposable income necessary to participate on a world cruise or long segments thereof. On the cruises studied there were very nearly equal numbers of men and women; however, the gentleman hosts were still highly visible when the orchestras struck up every evening. Many of the passengers had travelled with *QE2* before—some many times. The evocative old world graciousness conveyed by the style of service, the staff uniforms and the feeling of travelling on a traditional ocean liner rather than a modern cruise ship are strong pull factors for many cruise aficionados. Cunard recognises the cultural differences between Americans and British passengers and heavily promotes the 'Britishness' of its ships.

It seems appropriate here to say something about the function of the gentleman host, a much-misunderstood addition to some cruise ships. The gentleman host (ambassador host on *Crystal Symphony*), subject of much innuendo and ineptly lampooned in the film *Out to Sea* (1997), is in the precise sense of the word a 'gigolo' (that is, a male dancing partner) and has a contractual obligation to remain essentially in that role. The defunct Royal Cruise Line is credited with having introduced the figure, acknowledging a fact long evident in cruising—that there are invariably numbers of unaccompanied women passengers. In previous times they were rescued from wallflower status on the dance floor by the ship's officers, an observable number of whom were far better mariners than dancers. The appearance of the gentleman host, whose ballroom skills must be demonstrated before he is accepted by recruiting agencies, relieved both officers and their dance partners of embarrassment. Hosts must be single, no younger than 45 years, though most appear to be somewhat older, and are expected to be good conversationalists also, although this is a secondary skill. Under threat of dismissal at the next port if they break the rules, they are not permitted to 'fraternise' or to enter a single woman's cabin. The innuendo, of course, persists.

Virgo passengers were predominantly male in the 20–50 age group, although compared to *QE2* and *Crystal Symphony* there was a surprising number of families on board. Parents took advantage of the childcare facilities and special services provided to free them to pursue their own interests. Very few people used any of the sports or pool facilities. Only the small handful of 'mad dogs and Englishmen' on board ventured out into the tropical noonday sun to lie around the pool deck. The majority of the passengers stayed within the air-conditioned luxury of the ship, dedicatedly attending to their own pastimes.

An unusual feature of the *QE2* passenger profile was the effect of people embarking for quite short segments. Thus between Hong Kong and Singapore there were a number of Asians and Australians. Between Mumbai and Cape Town there were significant numbers of Indian passengers, and between Mauritius and Durban and Durban and Cape Town several hundred local people were making the short journeys. The British contingent rose considerably from Cape Town to Southampton. The changing profile of the passengers made an interesting diversion for those experiencing the complete world cruise of three and a half months.

Crystal Symphony passengers are financially successful couples aged between 45 and 70 with a median age of 60. Young children are rarely seen, let alone heard. The host program ensures that a contingent of unattached women frequent the dance floors. Americans comprise over 90 per cent of passengers with the remainder from Canada, Japan, South America and Europe. Currently, more than 50 per cent are repeat Crystal clients and most of the others are experienced cruisers with other lines. The nature of many itineraries, where ports of call are kept to a minimum and days at sea maximised, is indicative of consumer preference, where it is the shipboard experience rather than the shore excursions which appeals more. Such terms as 'luxurious', 'soothing', 'choice' and 'celebrities' sprinkled throughout the line's promotional literature act like

Figure 15.1 An elephant greets *QE2* passengers at Cochin
(Source: Norman Douglas)

magnets to well-to-do people seeking the 'ultimate cruise experience'. The atmosphere on board resembles more that of an exclusive country club than a floating resort and the highly trained, impeccably presented staff provide discreet and quality service accordingly.

Passenger behaviour

Although the concept of a single cruise culture has been proposed (Foster 1986), the experience of these authors indicates that this is no more sound than the concept of a single tourist culture. There are necessarily basic experiences and activities common to all cruises which involve the participation of either all or the great majority of passengers—embarking, eating and disembarking are the most obvious ones. But there are also significant variations in the attitude and behaviour of passengers, not only between ships but also among passengers on the same vessel, and these may be attributable to age, and socioeconomic or cultural factors, which are by no means submerged within a common cruise culture.

Arrival and embarkation

Because of the scattered locations of the world's major cruise centres (e.g. Singapore, Hong Kong, Fort Lauderdale), a majority of passengers on *Crystal Symphony* and *QE2* cruises have already undertaken a journey—often over a long distance by plane—in order to reach the ship. A number of consequences follow from this: they are frequently tired by the time they embark and this promotes a feeling of disorientation common on entering the ship. Conversation for the first few days is likely to turn on such topics as the length of their journey to the ship, the discomfort experienced during the flight, the unfortunate fate of their luggage or their extraordinary feeling of relief at finding that it has actually arrived at the same time as they have. If conversations heard at random are any guide, an unreasonable number of passengers seem to experience the temporary loss of at least one piece of baggage, and a significant number appear disenchanted with the size or appointments of their cabins, no matter how luxurious these might be.

The first activity on any cruise likely to involve all passengers is the safety drill required by international maritime law, whereby within 24 hours of embarkation passengers are required to report to assigned muster stations with the life jackets provided in their cabins. Here they are instructed by members of the ship's company in the safety and emergency procedures. Remarkable as it may seem, some passengers choose not to attend these brief demonstrations (rarely lasting longer than 15–20 minutes), and others appear reluctant to take them seriously. Jokes about *Titanic* are whispered audibly during such demonstrations and the phrase 'abandon ship', which occurs during the instructions, provokes a good deal of uneasy laughter. Cunard actually has a passenger checklist for each muster station while the others claim to have ways of knowing whether passengers attend or not.

The food

Since the great majority of cruises depart from their port of embarkation in the late afternoon or early evening, the next large-scale activity engaging the participation of passengers is their first meal—dinner. It is fair to say that on a cruise ship food probably becomes a far more significant part of one's daily routine than it might otherwise be. This aspect is not only displayed in the promotional literature but acknowledged at considerable length in a number of guides to cruising and cruise ships. Under the section 'Cruise cuisine', Berlitz devotes eight and a half pages to the various aspects of shipboard meals (Ward 1994). Fielding's guide offers seven pages, which include 'Tips on reading a shipboard menu' and a discussion of ship sanitation inspections—usually involving correct food storage (Slater & Basch 1996). Since all meals on board are invariably included in the price, passengers are inclined to take full advantage of them. Indeed, Fielding includes advice on 'How to avoid pigging out at sea'.

The amount of food has become a standard quip in the repertoire of cruise directors and guest comedians, besides being a regular topic of conversation among passengers. It is possible on many ships to begin eating at about 6 am and continue almost unchecked until past midnight. Twenty-four-hour room service is increasingly available. If the quality of food varies considerably from one cruise ship to another, the enthusiasm for eating displayed by most passengers does not. Absences from table are a sound indication not that the absentees are being sensibly cautious about the extent of their food intake but that they are seasick and unable to eat at all.

Meals taken in the ship's dining room, however, also offer interpersonal experiences that can be regarded as essential to the cruise. At the first meal passengers may meet fellow travellers for the first time, perhaps establishing a friendship that will last for the duration of the voyage or a lifetime, or they may request a change of table altogether. Passengers will also meet their waiter and the waiter's assistant for the first time (this may be the first formal encounter with any members of the ship's company), thereby establishing another sort of relationship, one in which the waiter's performance is likely to be strongly motivated by the anticipation of reward—a tip—at the end of the cruise. The cruise ships that discourage tipping or build it into the overall cost are few indeed. Far more frequently passengers are instructed both verbally and in writing not only how they should go about it but also how much they should tip. Cunard advises passengers that a daily amount determined by the cabin category is charged to their shipboard account and duly distributed to the appropriate cabin steward, waiters and so on. Conversely, Star advises passengers that tipping is neither expected nor necessary.

Within the British orientation of the *QE2* dining rooms theme nights are much more restrained than on most American-owned ships. Even the ubiquitous baked-Alaska parade is more controlled in precision and execution. The multinational profile of the passengers is a distinctive dif-

Figure 15.2 Day in the lIfe of a cruise passenger
(Courtesy Esther Corley)

ference between *QE2* and the other ships in this study. It is especially reflected in the food served in the Lido buffet, making this casual form of dining an interesting option for all. While the same basic menu appears in all *QE2* restaurants, the Grill classes have a much wider à la carte choice to distinguish them. The dining experiences on *Crystal Symphony* were also superb, with specially designed tableware a feature. *Virgo* offered three inclusive restaurants and six other specialist restaurants with a moderate charge. Chinese, Indian, Italian, Japanese and fine dining options were all popular, even though the inclusive restaurants were exceptionally good and very spacious. A commendable feature of *Virgo* dining was the freestyle form. There were no allocated tables and waiters even in the inclusive restaurants. Free-style dining is increasingly demanded by experienced cruise passengers who want to escape the obligations imposed by the more traditional table allocation system.

Passenger activities

Once the ship is under way, an extensive range of activities are offered to passengers throughout the day and night, and these may be categorised as organised and unorganised. Organised activities are those requiring direction from, or interaction with, at least one member of the cruise staff, for example supervised deck-game competitions, aerobics, dance instruction and lectures (Table 16.1). Unorganised activities are those requiring no direction from, or interaction with, a member of the cruise staff, for example sunning, reading, promenading and unsupervised deck games (Table 16.2). With the exception of those generally small vessels which emphasise the expeditionary aspects of cruising, the range of organised activities on those days that the vessel is at sea is great enough to keep passengers involved for almost all their waking hours. A smaller choice is offered on days when the ship is in port, to cater for those passengers who choose to stay on board. These activities and other relevant daily information are listed in the ship's newspaper, compiled by the cruise director and/or his/her team and usually delivered to passenger cabins on the previous evening. Passengers consult it keenly throughout the day. On *Virgo* a daily newspaper announced many of the usual daily activities but, perhaps reflecting cultural differences, there was not a craft class or bridge game to be seen. The vessel, however, boasts a 52-seat mahjong room. The established international favourites (horseracing, bingo, cooking demonstrations and exercise classes) were also present.

The levels of participation recorded in Tables 15.1 and 15.2 are based—following discussions with appropriate members of the respective cruise staffs—on an assessment of participation considered representative of the activity. Thus, while 24 passengers might represent a medium level of participation in aerobics, craft or bridge, that figure would represent a very low level of participation in bingo or show attendance. Conversely, a representative bingo or show audience—perhaps 200 to 300—would be unthinkable for an activity such as craft. Sporting participation is determined by the space allocated for these activities.

A number of inferences may be drawn from Tables 15.1 and 15.2. Traditional cruise pursuits, such as deck games (e.g. shuffleboard, deck quoits), once the highlight of daytime activities, have declined in

Table 15.1 Selected organised activities: level of passenger participation

	Aerobics	Bingo	Lectures*	Craft classes	Bridge	Evening shows
SuperStar Virgo	M	H	N/A	N/A	N/A	H
Crystal Symphony	M	H	M	L	H	H
QE2	L	L	M	L	L	H

* other than port briefings
H = high level of participation
M = medium level of participation
L = low level of participation
N/A = absent or not applicable

Table 15.2 Selected unorganised activities: level of passenger participation

	Sunbathing	Deck games	Shopping on board	Cinema attendance	Casino play
SuperStar Virgo	L	L	H	L	H
Crystal Symphony	L	L	L	L	M
QE2	M	H	L	M	L

H = high level of participation
M = medium level of participation
L = low level of participation

popularity, a development which may be related to changes in ship design and consequent limitations of open deck space. On *QE2*, however, participation in these was quite high, which may be further reflection of the strong British presence on board. Cinema attendance appears to have suffered on all ships, even though the facilities are usually excellent and the films screened are in the main first-run films. All cabins have television these days. Craft classes seem to attract very few and yet no ship sails without either specialist craft instructors or cruise staff with some skills in this area. Observations about shopping, evidently as much a recreational pursuit on a cruise ship as on a land-based vacation, are qualified here by the fact that *Crystal Symphony* and *QE2* had, in addition to a multipurpose shop, several other outlets specialising in such items as resort wear, glass, porcelain and jewellery. Paintings and art prints were also available for sale on *Crystal Symphony*, displayed gallery-style in a wide passageway rather than in a shop. Compared with the multipurpose shop, these specialty outlets did not appear to be particularly busy, perhaps reflecting their price structure. *QE2* had a shop in which nothing was over US$10, featuring watches, scarves and costume jewellery at prices comparable with hard bargaining prospects in some of the Asian ports. For passengers who don't like that sort of experience, it was a clever alternative provided by the company.

Gambling

From regular observations of the casinos on both *QE2* and *Crystal Symphony*, it would be easy to form the opinion that—with the exception of blackjack—table gambling at sea was not very popular, since there was very little consumer involvement in roulette or craps. Casino staff confirmed this view for these particular segments, but added that in the Caribbean and trans-Atlantic crossings casino use was high. The Indian passengers who appeared on *QE2* between Mumbai and Cape Town were enthusiastic clients of the casino, but otherwise there was little action overall apart from some slot-machine use. Bridge, under the supervision of instructors, is popular with dedicated players of the game. *Crystal Symphony*'s bridge lounge was regularly full of enthusiastic players, while on *QE2* there were morning and afternoon sessions in both introductory and advanced techniques. Bingo—played at least once a day on sea days on most cruise ships—presented some interesting observations. On *Crystal Symphony* bingo far outstripped any other activity in popularity. Nothing else was allowed to clash with the timetabling of bingo. It was quite the reverse on *QE2*. In the course of a month, the game never attracted more than two dozen people at any daily session. On *Virgo* the casino—The Oasis Club—with eight table games and 150 slot machines, was busy day and night. When bingo and horseracing gambling were added to the mix, the rationale of the cruise was clear. Security on board was very high at all times. Six hundred cameras and numerous guards watched every avenue. At embarkation a considerable number of passengers arrived with just a briefcase or a very small overnight bag. Unlike on the other ships, making a fashion statement was obviously not a priority.

Attendance at lectures varies considerably according to the topic, the time of day and the skills of the lecturer. *Virgo* does not appear to employ lecturers. *Crystal Symphony* and *QE2* may have six or more lecturers per cruise, including specialists whose subjects might range from drama criticism to finance and investment to regional history and culture, and celebrity guests whose subjects are their own experiences or those of their celebrity friends. Lecturers may have to compete with half a dozen other organised activities as well as the traditional passenger pastime of lying on a deckchair in the sun.

Evening entertainment

The formal entertainment on vessels catering to the US market is determinedly American, with many guest performers recognised by passengers for their appearances on American television. The stage show presentations are often based on famous Broadway shows. *Crystal Symphony* had its own specialist entertainment troupe whose members doubled as assistants for the cruise director. Evening performances could be either a stage show or a cabaret-style performance with a magician, comedian or singer. The principal entertainers on *QE2* are predominantly British celebrities who work very hard to carry their international audience along with them. On the cruise segment in this study 38 per cent of passengers were British, 21 per cent American, nine per cent Australian, nine per cent German and the rest from some 25 other countries. Classical concerts performed by professors from London's Royal Academy of Music and professional light opera groups are daily highlights on a *QE2* world cruise segment.

The passenger talent show was popular on *Crystal Symphony* and *QE2*. This has its origin in the early days of ship travel when passengers had to make their own fun on board. The warbling singers, the stumbling bards, the leaden piano renditions and the little skits are all cheerfully enjoyed by fellow passengers, who are relieved they did not volunteer their own abilities. Occasionally a real 'talent' appears and receives compliments for the remainder of the cruise. The other common and well-established activity is the passenger fancy dress. This is usually a late-night affair with a good deal of improvisation evident in the costumes, although real enthusiasts and regular cruisers pack a prepared costume for the event. *QE2* formalised the otherwise informal affair by having several themed balls. These were embraced enthusiastically by many passengers who dressed elaborately and complemented the themed decorations in the Queens Room. So far these remain Western entertainments. There were no comparable events on *Virgo*. The most popular night-time activities by any measure are the cabaret-style or production shows that are now a well-publicised feature of many cruise ships. There are sound reasons for their popularity. For many passengers they represent an essential aspect of an evening out—'dinner and a show' at no extra charge; their quality is generally highly professional; and, importantly, they have no, or very little, competition from any other activity during their time of presentation. Shows on all three ships are presented in lounges designed essentially for their staging and typically attract capacity attendance—that is, several hundreds. *QE2* occasionally featured a production in the afternoon and a cabaret performance in the evening. A special feature was the additional late-evening classical performances, which were extremely well attended. On *Virgo* a very skilful cabaret-style show was presented by artists from Eastern Europe and Central Asia. More distinctively, the entertainment also included a midnight 'Las Vegas style topless revue'. This featured a number of strikingly tall, mostly blonde Russian chorus girls who made up in body dimensions what they lacked in grace, for which an entry fee was charged. It is fair to say that on all three ships consumer satisfaction with the shows was at a very high level.

Ports of call

The itinerary of a cruise is one of the most significant reasons for its success, although it is by no means the sole or even the major determinant. There are some cruise locations that perennially appeal to a greater number of people than others, and many of these are evidently happy enough to have cruised the same area and seen more or less the same ports

Figure 15.3 'There aren't enough men on board so I bought him. Any objections?' (Courtesy Esther Corley)

"There aren't enough men on board so I bought him. Any objections?"

several times. The Caribbean attracts by far the greatest number of passengers in any given year, to the extent that many of the larger vessels going into service will be permanently positioned in that region. However, in the early 21st century there is barely a major waterway in the world to which a cruise ship of some kind has not been, and as the Caribbean becomes more congested, other regions are almost certain to experience an increase in cruise traffic as itinerary planners look for more options.

Itineraries travelled for this study

- *SuperStar Virgo:* Singapore, Phuket (Thailand), Langkawi (Malaysia), Singapore, Port Klang (Malaysia), Singapore.
- *Crystal Symphony:* Apia (Western Samoa), Savusavu (Fiji), Port Vila (Vanuatu), Sydney.
- *QE2:* Hong Kong, Bangkok (Laem Chabang, Thailand), Singapore, Cochin and Mumbai (India), Port Victoria (Seychelles), Port Louis (Mauritius), Durban and Cape Town (South Africa).

The itineraries studied here attract far fewer cruise passengers overall than the Caribbean or the Mediterranean; indeed, they are still regarded as novelties by the Americans who comprise the majority of passengers on *Crystal Symphony*. Because of the nature of the round-the-world voyage of which this itinerary was just a part, *QE2* passengers had a variety of experiences and perceptions, whether as regular voyagers or regional residents. *Virgo*'s predominantly Asian passengers went shopping and during the Phuket call, from 6 pm to 3 am, cabaret shows and dinner packages were popular.

On port days, passengers may generally choose between participating in organised shore excursions, going ashore independently or remaining on the ship, an option not infrequently accepted by the elderly or disabled, especially if the prospects ashore appear daunting as a result of weather conditions or sociopolitical and cultural factors. In Bali and the Andaman Islands, for example, we have observed American passengers step tentatively ashore, only to return to the ship on the same tender because they felt threatened by vendors or were otherwise discomfited. It is not uncommon for some passengers to proceed no further than the wharf, especially if souvenir stalls are accessible there. Places such as Mumbai provoke either intense aversion or enthusiasm. It is apparently impossible to be half-hearted about such a port of call. The cultural practices, the overwhelming crowds, the completely alien way of life and traditions of India are too confronting for many Westerners, no matter how much advance information the cruise company tries to provide passengers. Sometimes it is simply impossible to meet passenger expectations.

Conclusion

More than any other kind of tourism experience, cruising offers traditional activities (deck games, bridge, passenger talent concerts) alongside modern diversions (discos, lessons in computer awareness, health and beauty spas). The element of tradition is strongly maintained in promotional material, which frequently suffuses verbal descriptions of modern facilities with nostalgic images, a technique that evidently appeals to many consumers. Even the Asian company Star Cruises promotes cruise tradition in both design and activities, despite the fact the Asian market is very young and inexperienced with this form of tourism. Cruise ships now offer far more choices than ever, which reflects both the challenges in keeping consumers occupied and the growing competition within the industry. In any meaningful discussion of whether a common cruise culture exists, a variety of factors must be considered. These include the size and physical aspects of the cruise vessel, the amenities it provides, the cultural backgrounds of the passengers it attracts, the activities it features and the nature of the cruise itinerary.

The concept of a typical cruise society or cruise culture is not borne out by this research. While there are some similarities in cruise consumer experiences and behaviour, there are also a significant number of differences that outweigh the similarities. Even the experience of a shared environment (the ship) is strongly qualified by the attitudes and expectations that consumers carry on board as part of their baggage. These reflect the consumers' national, cultural and socioeconomic backgrounds and their age levels, factors which will not only influence the type of ship chosen but also influence their behaviour and their response to certain conditions and activities on the ship itself. The only significant factor shared by *Virgo* passengers, *QE2* passengers and *Crystal Symphony* passengers is that they all chose to cruise.

Part 6

The extent of the contribution made by the cruise business to the economy of a nation, region or port is a matter of considerable significance. It is also in some respects contentious. The industry itself, ever seeking to enhance its importance, is keen to stress the benefits derived from its presence, if not to exaggerate them too greatly. Bald figures are sometimes provided by companies, ports or national authorities without any real explanation of how these are arrived at. 'Cruise ships currently inject as much as A$31 million into the Victorian economy annually', says the Minister for Transport, Victoria, Australia (Batchelor 2003). On a far more extensive level, the economic benefits of the US cruise business to the national economy are said to have amounted to US$20 billion in 2001, despite the setbacks caused by the attacks on New York on 11 September. Direct spending of cruise lines and passengers on US goods and services amounted to US$11 billion, more than half the total figure. Passenger spending contributed US$1.85 billion to this (ICCL 2002b). Even allowing for occasional exaggeration, the economic contribution made by cruising is obviously considerable, although it is not always as persuasive an argument for its presence as the cruise companies would want, as the following example illustrates.

In late 2002 residents of the small island of Moloka'i in the Hawaiian group opposed the intended visits of cruise ships of both Princess Cruises and Holland America when serious doubts were expressed about the actual benefits of the visits and their consequences to the island's lifestyle. The Moloka'i Visitors Association estimated that 60 per cent of the Holland America ship's passengers and 40 per cent of the crew (1018 people in total) would inject US$74 283 into the island's economy on their visit. Including indirect benefits, the total economic impact of one cruise ship visit could amount to US$130 000. Sandy Beddow, executive director of the Moloka'i Visitors Association, called the estimate 'conservative', although in overall terms what the additional business would mean was unclear, because there are apparently no estimates of the actual size of Moloka'i's economy or the value of goods and services produced by its 7300 residents. The uncertainty, however, was sufficient to prevent the ships' visits—at least for one season. Communities in Alaska, Mexico, Panama and elsewhere are said to be grappling with similar issues (Hao 2003). This, of course, is yet another instance of a perennial issue within tourism: the debate between economic benefits and social costs.

Chapters 16 and 17 approach the matter of the economic contribution made by cruise ships from different angles. Dwyer and Forsyth, who have written extensively on this subject, propose a framework which would serve a number of purposes, including distinguishing between the impacts made at various administrative levels and being used as a device for forecasting those impacts. Because of the comprehensive nature of the framework, a number of variables are included that are simply absent or not applicable at many smaller ports. They refer, for example to 'passenger-related expenditure', a category that includes spending by **the company** on passenger-related needs, such as food and drink. But in many ports, especially small island ports, vessels do not take on provisions for a number of reasons, including the possibly risky nature of these or the inadequacy of their supply. On the many occasions like these, **direct** spending by passengers on goods and services becomes a major contribution to the economy of the port or, if the country is small (as are many Pacific Islands), to the nation. Chapter 17 considers this input more closely, using as a case study a single cruise on P&O Australia's *Pacific Sky*. This also introduces a number of other factors influencing passenger spending in ports of call, including weather, the nature of the port itself and certain cultural perceptions, which may help to explain **why** passengers spend, as well as how much. It also considers the sorts of items on which passengers—and, to a limited extent, crew—spend money. To small-scale entrepreneurs, such as those found in many cruise ports, this is significant.

16

A framework for assessing the economic impacts of cruise tourism

Larry Dwyer and Peter Forsyth

Cruise tourism is one of the major growth areas of international tourism. Several nations have been developing strategies to enable the country as a whole, and particular regions, to enjoy the economic and social benefits of a strong, efficient and viable cruise-shipping industry. Policy making to achieve the economic aims depends on a clear understanding of the economic impacts of cruise tourism on both home ports and transit ports of call.

This chapter has three major objectives:

1. It develops a framework for assessing the economic impacts of cruise tourism for a nation as a whole and for smaller regions within it (e.g. states, counties or provinces).

2. It provides a case study, showing how this framework can be used as a basis for estimating the relevant economic impacts, nationally and regionally.

3. It identifies and discusses some policy implications of the analysis.

The framework

Some preliminary research on development of a suitable economic assessment framework has been undertaken by Dwyer and Forsyth (1996, 1998). An assessment framework must be comprehensive enough to be able to:

- include all of the various expenditure items associated with cruise tourism that have economic impacts;
- distinguish national, state and regional impacts of cruise tourism;
- account for different types of cruises with different implications for expenditure by passengers, operators and crew;
- account for different types of economic impacts depending on the different ports of call associated with different cruise types;
- serve as a device for forecasting the economic impacts of cruise tourism under different assumptions of demand, supply and policy contexts.

Development of a framework to assess the economic impacts of cruise tourism requires six major steps to be undertaken. While Australian examples are used to illustrate many of the issues that are addressed in the discussion below, the framework is of generic import, applicable to any economy. Issues that must be addressed include the scope of analysis, expenditure categories, injected expenditure, government taxes and charges, direct leakages, the application of multipliers, and estimation of economic impacts. An additional step, going beyond economic impact analysis, involves the estimation of net benefits.

Scope of analysis

The first step is to determine the scope of the analysis—that is, the area that is the scope of the economic impact study. For cruise tourism this can be national, state or regional. Thus, the expenditure associated with cruise tourism can be studied for its impact on the national economy, a state economy, a regional economy or even a particular port. While passengers spend money aboard ship, it is only expenditure which is injected into an economy that has economic impacts on a destination. The wider the scope of analysis (that is, the larger the geographic area of interest), the greater will be the injected expenditure.

The scope of analysis can also relate to whether a port is taken to be a home port, a transit port or both. Cruise ship visitors disembarking at a transit port may purchase shopping items, local sightseeing tours, souvenirs, meals and drinks, and so on. Where a port is a home port, there will be additional cruise-related expenditures associated with pre- and post-cruise touring, land-based accommodation and other expenses, and business expenses of the cruise-shipping company.

Expenditure categories

The second step in estimating the economic impacts is to classify the types of expenditure associated with cruise tourism. In a report prepared for the New Zealand Tourism Board and Cruise New Zealand (McDermott Fairgray 2001), direct expenditure is divided into four major categories:

* passenger-related expenditure;
* crew-related expenditure;
* vessel-related expenditure;
* supporting expenditure.

Given its importance to economic impact estimation, the components of expenditure associated with cruise tourism deserve careful attention.

Passenger-related expenditure

Passenger-related expenditure includes that incurred as part of the cruise (port visit expenditure) and also that which is associated with making the cruise (incurred both before and after the voyage itself). Expenditures undertaken by passengers while aboard the ship do not *per se* have economic effects on the ports visited and are thus irrelevant to economic impact estimation. On the other hand, those expenditures made by the cruise ship operators in ports of call in the purchase of goods and services on behalf of passengers are relevant because they inject money into a destination. Relevant expenditure items include:

* retail spending during stopover;
* pre- and post-cruise expenditure;
* land-based excursions;
* provedoring (food and alcohol);
* local transportation;
* incidental expenses;
* departure tax.

Many cities operate as both a transit and a base port. Thus, passenger-related expenditure in these cities includes that incurred as part of the cruise (port visit expenditure) and also that which is incurred both before and after some cruises.

The category 'pre- and post-cruise expenditure' needs clarification. This refers to expenditure within a region by passengers who board or leave a ship in that region. Some add-on expenditure is essential for the cruise: for example, accommodation, food and beverage expenses, local transport and, possibly, excursions in port before the cruise begins or following disembarkation. In a sense, this expenditure can be regarded as being 'generated' by the cruise, as it is unlikely to have been made, at least to the same extent, if the cruise had not taken place.

It is likely that, for many passengers, pre- and post-cruise expenditure will be associated with regions in a country other than the port region. Thus, there may also be internal travel within the wider destination. In Australia this is mainly by air, though not exclusively. In this case, domestically owned airlines will obtain a share of international air fares paid by people joining cruises. Most of this expenditure will be effectively dispersed throughout the economy. Only a small proportion of it, associated with servicing flights, will be spent at the regional level: a port may have flights in and out, and some expenditure will be incurred in supporting these. Quantifying the expenditure flows to a port region from airlines carrying cruise tourists is a formidable task. Such cruise-related expenditure is best subsumed under the category 'Supporting expenditure' (see below).

Cruise passengers also make direct expenditures on items such as excursions, attractions and shopping while their ship is in port. They then incur incidental expenses associated with visits to a doctor, foreign exchange facility and so on. The cruise operator will purchase food and beverage items to provide to passengers while the cruise is in progress. While, strictly, such provedoring expenditure is not directly attributable to the passengers, it is on behalf of the passengers that such expenditures are made. It is for this reason that we include 'provedoring' under passenger-related expenditure.

Passengers pay various taxes while purchasing goods and services. Some Australian examples may be helpful. A goods and services tax (GST) component (10 per cent) is included in most expenditures. Additional taxes might include a departure tax of A$30 (US$18) for those who depart Australia from Cairns airport; a noise tax imposed on those who fly to Sydney; and a passenger movement charge (departure tax) of A$38 (US$22.80) imposed by Australian Customs on all passengers departing Australia. Passengers transiting Australia are exempt if their stay terminates within 48 hours of arrival. In application, any cruise ship that has more than a single port of call in Australia is charged A$38.00 (US$22.80) for each passenger on board, as all passengers are deemed as having entered and departed the country.

The taxes collected above are not earmarked for return to the regional economy, and thus represent leakages from total passenger expenditure. The extent to which taxes are returned wholly or in part to a regional economy will differ according to context.

Crew-related expenditure

Expenditure by crew members can cover all of the categories of passenger expenditure:

- retail spending;
- pre- and post-cruise accommodation;
- land-based excursions;
- local transportation;
- incidental expenses.

Expenditure injections into an area by crew members can represent an important additional source of cruise-related expenditure relevant to economic impact evaluation.

Vessel-related expenditure

Vessel-related expenditure covers the following types of items:

- port agency fees;
- storage;
- port charges including terminal charges;
- water;
- pilotage;
- berthage, baggage handling and stevedoring;
- fuel bunkering;
- marine engineering;
- dry-dock charges;
- waste disposal;
- towage.

Cruise operators make a range of expenditures. They pay charges associated with the use of the port. There are charges levied by the port authority, and these will include charges for the terminal used and pilotage charges. In Australia both port pilotage and pilotage on the Great Barrier Reef are compulsory. Towage charges for the use of tugs are paid to private operators for services provided, as are stevedoring charges. Baggage handling and stevedoring will occur in a base port.

Even when the expenditure items can clearly be identified, it is often very difficult to distinguish local from external effects. Port charges, towage and stevedoring will be mainly for services that are supplied in the region and thus the expenditure will be incurred within the region. While some fuel may be produced within a region, most of it will not be. Where a vessel is refuelled in port, there will be some local component due to the services in actually supplying fuel but most of the revenue will go to outside suppliers. Where the vessel is provided with stores and so on, there will be both local and national expenditure. Services purchased (e.g. waste disposal, water, electricity) come mainly from the region.

Apart from these expenditures, the operator will make expenditures on ship maintenance. Ship maintenance, including marine engineering and dry-dock charges, is likely to be undertaken by regionally based firms.

Supporting expenditure

Supporting expenditure includes such items as:

- direct payments by owners into a home or transit port including office expenses, wages, and injected funds to support passengers and crew; shipping agent commissions and so on;
- marketing expenses (these are likely to have regional and national components).

The very presence of a cruise line office in a port implies injections of expenditure into the area for the above-mentioned items. While often difficult to estimate with precision, particularly as regards the allocation of such expenditures locally and elsewhere, they are inevitably related to cruise ship operations and have economic impacts on destinations.

Injected expenditure

The third step is to estimate the injection of expenditure associated with each of the different categories. This is not a straightforward task, as relevant data are often either poor or non-existent. Surveys of passenger expenditure may be unreliable. Typically, the analyst must make judgements regarding some of the monetary amounts that comprise total direct cruise-related expenditure. This exercise is important to our understanding of the framework's operational validity in a regional context. Limitations of existing data must be explicitly acknowledged in order to determine what other information may be required for a viable and comprehensive economic impact analysis.

Government taxes and charges

The fourth step is to estimate the taxes and charges component of gross tourism expenditure, as some amounts are not retained in the local area but go to the federal and state governments. This enables estimation of gross expenditure associated with cruise tourism to an area, net of taxes and government charges.

Most taxes, however, are likely to mainly go outside the region. In Australia, most of the taxes will be collected by the Commonwealth and, to a lesser extent, the state government. Some examples of taxes payable in Australia, specifically in Far North Queensland, are as follows:

- Australian Maritime Safety Authority (AMSA) Marine Navigation and Oil Pollution Levy;

- Queensland Transport—State Conservancy;

- Australian Taxation Office—Freight Tax;

- Great Barrier Reef Marine Park Authority (GBRMPA)—Environmental Management Charge;

- Reef Pilotage.

Other taxes may be levied on cruise operators. These will usually include income taxes; some operators will be exempt, due to the operations of tax agreements and the nature of their cruises. There may be customs duties payable, and departure taxes will be levied. Where the charges are for navigational facilities, and these are in the region, expenditure will come back to the region. There may be a flow back of some taxes—for example departure taxes, which are charged for services performed. In general, however, amounts paid in taxes will flow outside the port area, the region and possibly the state, and will not have any economic impacts.

Direct leakages

The fifth step is to estimate the amount of direct expenditure that 'leaks out' of a local area to pay for goods and services 'imported' into the area from outside. The goods and services purchased by passengers, crew, vessels and support come partly from within and partly from outside the region. Where they come from within the region, local production is stimulated. This in turn results in more purchases of goods and services, again from within and outside the region. When local production is stimulated, directly and indirectly, there is increased demand for factors of production. These may come from increased local supply (e.g. people working longer hours or from people previously unemployed), from factors previously employed elsewhere in the local economy, or from factors from elsewhere in the national economy.

Many products purchased by the cruise ship visitors are sourced from outside the regional economy. That is to say, they are 'imported' from outside the area and must be paid for in money that represents a 'leakage' from the money injected into the local economy through cruise-related expenditure. For example, passengers may purchase liquor that is directly imported: apart from the productive services in importing and selling this, this purchase gives rise to a leakage into imports. Similarly, fuel purchased by a cruise ship may be refined outside a local area. These leakages reduce the multiplier impact on income and employment in a region. Such expenditure has little economic impact on the regional economy.

The economic impacts of cruise shipping will depend on the extent to which the items purchased are sourced locally (Dwyer & Forsyth 1994). To determine impacts on activity, it is necessary to subtract direct leakages from the gross expenditure to determine 'net' direct expenditure.

Application of multipliers

The sixth step is to apply multipliers to estimate the contribution of cruise tourism to gross regional product and employment. Cruise tourism expenditure has direct, indirect and induced effects on the economy and regions within. The direct effect is on suppliers who sell goods and services directly to tourists or cruise operators. Tourist expenditure is received as revenue by food and beverage suppliers, fuel suppliers, hotels, restaurants, tour and transport companies, shops and entertainment venues. In the process of satisfying tourist demand, value added accrues to the employees as wages, to the owners as profits, or to the government as tax revenue (thus constituting a source of development financing). Indirect effects result from 'flow-ons' when direct suppliers purchase inputs from other firms which in turn purchase inputs from other firms and so on. The induced effects arise when the recipients of the direct and indirect expenditure—firm owners, managers and their employees—spend their increased income, which in turn sets off a process of successive rounds of purchases by supplying industries and further induced consumption.

These effects are often analysed using multipliers derived from input–output models (Mescon & Vosikis 1985; de la Vina & Ford 2000). However, an expanding tourism industry tends to 'crowd out' other sectors of economic activity, reducing the demand for traditional export and import competing industries. For example, the indirect increase in expenditure from cruise-related demand for goods and services gives rise to additional demands for factors: to the extent that these were previously unemployed, there is no reduction in activity elsewhere. However, there will be a reduction in activity in other industries which lose factors to the expanding industries. Further, there will be industries which contract because they lose factors directly to the expanding region. Finally, there will be effects on activity in the national economy due to macroeconomic effects. An increase in spending by foreign visitors on cruises will lead to an increase in foreign exchange. This leads to an increase in demand for the home currency and, consequently, an increase in its price. This in turn will lead to other export and import competing industries being less competitive and thus contracting.

The extent of these 'crowding out' effects depends, in turn, on the workings of labour markets, changes in prices and the real exchange rate, and the fiscal policy context. It is argued that these mechanisms can only properly be taken into account using Computable General Equilibrium (CGE) models rather than input–output modelling (Dwyer et al. 2000). The impacts on state or national economies, when estimated using CGE models, will normally be considerably smaller than when using alternative techniques, such as input–output models, because of the recognition of these offsetting effects. It is also important to recognise that the economic impact on a region may be much larger than that on the state or nation, because at least some of the increased economic activity in a region will be at the expense of activity elsewhere, and because some of the resources drawn into the region will not be able to be used for production elsewhere.

Economic impacts

The result of following the above steps is to arrive at estimates of the economic impacts of cruise tourism. The economic impacts can be estimated for a single port visit by a particular ship or for many ships in aggregate. The economic impacts relate to changes in such variables as gross domestic product (national), gross regional product (local) and employment generation. The estimated economic impacts will vary, of course, depending on the scope of analysis. For example, regional impacts are generally smaller than national impacts, given the aforementioned expenditure 'leakages' associated with cruising. As the above discussion indicates, however, gains in gross product and employment to the host region may be offset by reduced economic activity in other regions.

Net benefits

An additional step, beyond economic impact analysis, is to estimate the real costs and benefits associated with cruise tourism. Unfortunately, the distinction between 'impacts' and 'benefits' is often not clearly understood in the economics of tourism literature. 'Impacts' on economic activity are measured by changes in gross domestic product or similar measures, in contrast with 'net benefits', which are a measure of the gain in economic activity less the cost needed to enable this extra activity. The measured impacts on economic activity of most changes, such as increases in tourism expenditure, are normally very much greater than the net benefits they generate for the community (or, in other words, the measure of the extent to which they make the community better off). There are several sources of costs and benefits, including externalities, unemployed resources, taxes and subsidies, monopoly practices and terms of trade effects (Dwyer & Forsyth 1994, 1998). A recent study of the hidden costs of cruise shipping indicates that the impact of ship emissions into the environment, the social impact of the cruise industry on local communities and the working conditions on ships all need to be taken into account in a comprehensive cost–benefit study of this tourism market (Klein 2003).

An assessment framework

Based on the discussion above, we now present a framework that indicates the key variables involved in assessing the economic significance of cruise tourism to a region, state or nation. The framework is displayed in Table 16.1.

Operational validity of framework

The framework indicates the key variables involved in assessing the economic significance of cruise tourism to a region, state or an entire nation, and is capable of accommodating any number of additional expenditure-related variables. While it appears to capture the main variables, others can be added as required. The basic framework was developed for the Australian Government Cruise Shipping Strategy (Department of Tourism 1995; Dwyer & Forsyth 1996), and employed to undertake case studies for Tourism Queensland (Tourism Queensland 2002). It has also been used to estimate the economic impact of cruise tourism on the port of Cairns (Dwyer, Douglas & Livaic 2003).

One difficulty in applying the assessment framework is that, in many cases, there is very little empirical information available on which to estimate the economic impacts of cruise tourism on both transit and home ports. Cruises differ considerably among themselves and there is no 'typical' cruise. Such data that do exist are in a form that does not easily translate into the framework as exhibited in Table 16.1. Thus the following results must be regarded as tentative and be treated with caution.

Table 16.1   Framework for assessing economic impacts of cruise shipping

Expenditure source	Expenditure per port call (net of taxes)	Taxes and charges paid to governments	Direct leakages from region	Expenditure retained in region	Expenditure retained within state (after deduction of additional leakages)	Expenditure retained within Australia (after deduction of additional leakages)
1. Passenger-related expenditure						
Retail spending during stopover						
Pre/post-cruise expenditure						
Land-based excursions						
Incidentals including local transport						
Provedoring (food and alcohol)						
Departure tax						
2. Crew-related expenditure						
Retail spending						
Pre/post-cruise expenditure						
Land-based excursions						
Incidentals including local transport						
3. Vessel-related expenditure						
Passenger embarkation charges						
Fuel costs (bunkering)						
Port dues						
Port agency fees						
Additional agency fees						
Pilotage						
Water						
Garbage						
Berthage						
Stevedoring						
Towage						
Miscellaneous expenses						
Dry-dock charges						
Government taxes and charges						
4. Supporting expenditure						
Direct payments by ship owners into region						
Total direct expenditure						
Value-added multiplier						
Total value added						
Employment (FTEs)						

In the first study using this type of framework, Dwyer and Forsyth (1996) provide estimates of expenditure within Australia for two types of cruises—a coastal cruise and a foreign cruise. The coastal cruise was a six-day cruise in Australian waters with a Sydney–Brisbane–Townsville–Cairns itinerary. The costs associated with the Sydney and Cairns visits are averaged over two cruises, since these are turnaround ports. Thus this cruise is taken as a three-visit cruise, with two visits to stopover ports and one to a home port. Assuming all passengers are foreigners, the coastal cruise is estimated to inject A$755 867 (US$453 520) of foreign exchange into Australia per cruise (1994 dollars). Passenger and crew expenditure injection is approximately A$239 000 (US$143 400). The bulk of ship operating costs is for provedoring (A$76 240, US$45 744), followed by port charges, fuel and taxes. Taking all expenditure into account the average expenditure within Australia generated by the cruise is A$825 (US$495) per passenger.

With respect to the international cruise, only expenditure in the home port (Sydney) is relevant to assessing its economic impact on Australia. The international cruise is estimated to inject only A$367 000 (US$220 200) expenditure per visit. Passenger and crew expenditure injection is approximately A$172 000 (US$103 200), while ship operating costs total approximately A$195 000 (US$117 000). Assuming that all passengers on the international cruise are foreigners the average foreign exchange injection into Australia is A$401 (US$240.60) per passenger per cruise. This is less than half of the corresponding figure for coastal cruising.

For each type of cruise tourism passenger, however, the average expenditure per day exceeds the estimated A$79 (US$47.40) per day for 'all' visitors to Australia at the time, and the figure of A$95 (US$57) per day for 'holiday' visitors (Bureau of Tourism Research 1995). Compared with other international visitors to Australia, it was concluded that cruise tourism results in substantially greater direct expenditure per visitor day than for the average tourist to Australia. Additional economic impacts would result from expenditure of cruise passengers who combine their cruise with other tourism in Australia. To the extent that such 'add-on' expenditure would not have occurred without the cruise, it may be considered as cruise-associated expenditure.

The next study to employ the framework was undertaken in association with the development of the Queensland Cruise Shipping Plan. The objective was to estimate the total expenditure associated with cruise shipping to the state of Queensland. It was estimated that 75 port visits occur each year for ports located on the mainland and that, on average, the total passenger- and vessel-related expenditure is A$88 666 (US$53 200) per port visit. Additionally, 34 port visits take place in the Whitsundays and small anchorages at A$28 616 (US$17 170) per port visit. Total estimated current annual revenue in Queensland from cruise shipping is estimated to be A$14.2 (US$8.52) million (Tourism Queensland 2002). The potential additional expenditure following expansion of the industry is estimated to be A$66 (US$39.6) million, making for a total expenditure into the state of A$80.2 (US$48.12) million per year.

The operational validity of this framework was also tested in a case study of the expenditure associated with cruise tourism to the port of Cairns. The case study indicated that a representative mid-sized ship X, with 1050 passengers and 500 crew, would inject around A$245 000 (US$147 000) into the Cairns economy per transit visit. If ship X were an average or representative ship, the annual gross expenditure injection into Cairns from cruise ships would be around A$30 425 000 (US$18 255 000). More accurate estimates will be contingent on the provision of better data.

Given the paucity of reliable data, each of the above findings must be treated with caution. In each of the main categories of cruise-related expenditure—passenger, crew, vessel and support—there are significant limitations in the available data. In some cases data are missing entirely. In other cases the estimates of expenditure are not based on appropriate survey or other assessment techniques. More precise and accurate data are needed if the model is to be used to generate credible results. Because of the importance of passenger expenditure in determining the overall economic impacts of cruise tourism to a destination, it is essential that more accurate data be obtained regarding this.

Conclusion

The type of framework outlined above, both as a theoretical construct and when it is applied to actual data, is of value in considering policy, planning and development of this special-interest tourism market. Knowledge of regional impacts can be valuable in planning infrastructure, for example. If a region is to determine the appropriate amount of resources to allocate to the development or support of this sector, such as expenditure on upgrading existing facilities or investing in new, purpose-built infrastructure or in marketing/promotion activity, accurate information is needed on the expenditure associated with cruise shipping as an input into the estimation of the net benefits from this activity. When decisions are made to commit resources to promote tourism, it is necessary to compare these to the net benefits from such tourism, rather than the much larger, overall expenditure impacts. It is also possible to examine the advantages and disadvantages, from a regional and national viewpoint, of measures designed to encourage cruise tourism, such as reductions in fuel taxes levied on operators. It is further necessary to take into account any effects on domestic-based cruise passengers, who may be encouraged to switch to home-based cruises if they become more price competitive, or who might be inclined to switch to overseas trips if the local product becomes too popular and expensive. These types of issues are expected to be at the forefront of further study of the economic significance of cruise tourism.

17

Cruise ship passenger spending: a South Pacific case study

With such illustrious bodies as the CLIA claiming future spectacular growth in the cruise sector and predicting revenue generation of US$85 billion, it is important for ports of call to be able to determine how much income they can expect from a six- to eight-hour visit. There are clearly costs as well as benefits of being a cruise ship port and unless the benefits can outweigh the costs (Dwyer & Forsyth 1996), small island ports may well decide to resist a company's requests to host their ships. Dwyer, Douglas and Livaic (2003) state it is difficult to measure the economic impact of a cruise ship's visit. Variables to consider include whether it is a port of embarkation and/or disembarkation or a port of call, as well as the range of facilities and infrastructure available for both ship operations and passenger needs. The differences in the port's role are highlighted by Dwyer (1999). In his study of two ports in Queensland, Australia, he looked at both scenarios. His first estimate of US$64 800 expenditure in Cairns was based on the visit of a ship in transit. The second estimate, US$408 000, was based on a ship using the port as a home port. *The Victorian Cruise Shipping Strategy 1998–2000* claims that a transit visit to Melbourne can inject up to US$600 000 into the local economy (Cruising Victoria 1998), while a recent New Zealand study found that an average economic injection into a port was US$64 200 (McDermott Fairgray 2001). The R&R (rest and recreation) visits of military ships also provide opportunities for a whole range of facilities and services. In a five-day visit to Townsville, Australia, a US navy vessel contributed US$5.4 million to the regional economy in both direct and indirect spending (AEC Group Ltd 2001).

Dwyer, Douglas and Livaic (2003), by refining the framework developed earlier by Dwyer and Forsyth (1996), designed a user-friendly computer program to contribute to the forecasting of the economic significance of cruise tourism to ports. Despite the best efforts of all these researchers, however, the fact remains that it is difficult to get accurate and reliable data for expenditure studies.

For the purposes of this work, a regional study relating to a cruise ship's economic contribution to the South Pacific Islands seemed appropriate. With the exception of a survey dealing with various aspects of cruise ship visits to Port Vila, Vanuatu, conducted by the Tourism Council of the South Pacific (TCSP 1991), little else of this nature appears to have been done on this port, which receives up to 32 visits a year. Port Vila is the most frequently visited port in the South Pacific Islands and therefore reliable data are essential for sustainable planning and management.

The cruise and the questionnaire

In 2002, after considerable negotiation, P&O Cruises Australia gave the authors permission to survey the passengers on a cruise on *Pacific Sky* from Sydney into the South Pacific. *Pacific Sky* was brought into service for the Islands in 2000, following the unsatisfactory performance of its predecessor, *Fair Princess*. The vessel was transferred from Princess Cruises based in Los Angeles, under whose flag it served as *Sky Princess*; before that it had been one of the fleet of Sitmar International and was known as *Fairsky*. The Sitmar connection is a historically interesting one because the ship that introduced thousands of Australians to cruising throughout the 1970s and 1980s was another Sitmar ship, *Fairstar. Pacific Sky* was constructed in 1984 and was the last large steam turbine passenger vessel built (Slater & Basch 1996, p. 567) and unquestionably superior in technical and design features to *Fair Princess*. In its present manifestation it can accommodate 1550 passengers, and it carries some 500 crew.

Cruise P221 sailed from Sydney and called at Port Vila in Vanuatu, and three ports in New Caledonia—Lifou, Isle of Pines and Noumea. Noumea and Port Vila have been ports of call for passenger-carrying ships for over a century. Isle of Pines has been an occasional call for many years, while Lifou has only recently been added to cruise itineraries, having been pioneered by P&O. The study sought to measure how much a cruise ship visit contributed to a range of Pacific Island ports and on what items passengers spent their money. Initially, it was planned to include crew expenditure, but with the multinational composition of the crew the company stated a ship's officer would have to explain the questionnaire and its purpose to all crew members and it would have to be translated into at least two other common crew languages (in this case Indonesian and Tagalog). Thus the company was reluctant to interrupt a busy officer's schedule, and the authors did not have the financial resources to fund the translations necessary. An assessment of crew spending based on personal observation and communication, therefore, was made.

The questionnaires were distributed by the hotel department to each adult passenger (over the age of 15 years) at the beginning of the cruise and a reminder notice was placed in each cabin just prior to the last port of call. The cruise was operating at capacity. In total 1248 questionnaires were delivered, with a 32.6 per cent (407) successful return rate after editing. As expected in a self-administered sample, respondents were not precisely representative of passengers on the cruise. Men were slightly underrepresented in the sample, particularly in the 15–24 and 25–34 age groups, while women in the 45–54 age group were overrepresented in the sample. This corresponds with a trend generally observed in self-administered surveys. There is a response bias towards

Figure 17.1 *Pacific Sky's* itinerary, Cruise P221

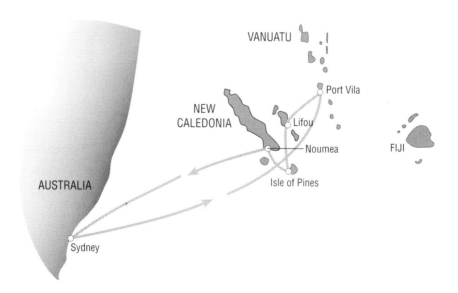

social groups more willing to complete surveys or more comfortable completing written questionnaires. The net effect of this response bias is uncertain, although it has implications for the extent to which the data can be generalised. Men reported higher spending overall and there were indications in the data that respondents in couples and small groups may have had difficulty isolating their individual expenditures. The response gender balance of male 40 per cent and female 60 per cent compares with the overall profiles of the passengers, where 44 per cent were male and 56 per cent were female. Respondents were slightly older on average than the cruise passengers as a whole. A group size of three to six people (50 per cent) was the most common configuration, followed by pairs at 33 per cent. A total of 74 per cent of respondents nominated incomes of less than US$36 000. (See Table 17.1.) This is in keeping with P&O Australia's acknowledgement of their main market profile. Although the company has made several attempts to shift its product appeal to a more up-market passenger, the 'fun ship' reputation inherited with the purchase of *Fairstar* from Sitmar in 1988 has been a difficult image to change. Ultimately, the company admits, paying passengers are valuable no matter what socioeconomic group they come

Table 17.1   Profile of cruise passengers on P221

P221 10 nights Sydney/Port Vila/Lifou/Isle of Pines/Noumea/Sydney		%
Gender	Male	40
	Female	60
Age	15–44 yrs	44
	45–75+ yrs	56
Group size	3–6 people	50
	couple	33
	alone	3
	>7	13
Income range	<US$12 000	18
	US$12 000–US$20 900	26
	US$21 000–US$35 900	30
	US$36 000–US$53 900	10
	>US$54 000	8
Occupation	Professional	27
	Home duties	12
	Self-employed	12
	Clerical	11
	Tradesperson	7
	Retired	10

from, and its passenger base has been a consistently loyal one, generating solid repeat business.

What passengers buy and why

Currency amounts were converted to US dollars for the study. Although a degree of error is obviously possible in this exercise, the authors consider the data to be reasonably accurate. (See Table 17.2.)

A cruise package includes all meals and entertainment on board. This obviously affects expenditure in some areas in particular: having paid for all meals, many Australians, the majority of passengers on this cruise apart from some New Zealanders, are not inclined to buy food ashore. The survey also inquired about pre- and post-cruise expenditure in Sydney. Some 28 per cent of passengers who responded spent time in Sydney before and after the cruise. The questionnaire distinguished between those who lived within the greater Sydney area and those who had to travel to join the ship. The average length of stay pre-cruise was 1.92 days, while the post-cruise stay was 3.05 days. This is a valuable, underestimated and underexploited market for service providers in the Sydney area.

On any cruise a variety of factors can influence port expenditure. Thus while the discussion is related to this case study, the comments can be considered in other ports of a similar nature throughout the world.

The ports

Sydney has a particular role as the port of embarkation and disembarkation. Although the ship's proven market resides within easy driving distance of the port area, a considerable number of passengers must travel

Table 17.2 Average passenger expenditure (all figures rounded up to nearest US$)

	Food and beverage	*Pacific Sky* tours	Activities purchased in port	Transport	Shopping in Sydney	Souvenirs	Duty-free cosmetics, perfumes, alcohol, electrical goods	Total spent in port
Sydney (pre-& post-cruise)	24	N/A	8	6	31	N/A	N/A	69
Port Vila	9	11	4	6	N/A	29	42	101
Noumea	5	20	3	5	N/A	13	5	51
Lifou	1	3	1	1	N/A	N/A	N/A	7
Isle of Pines	1	N/A	1	1	N/A	1	N/A	4

from further afield. Some of these will fly in from elsewhere in Australia and, to a lesser extent, from New Zealand. Others come by coach or drive themselves. As indicated earlier, the post-cruise stay is the longest, and visiting friends and relatives and/or holiday are given as the main reasons for staying on. While P&O offers package deals for pre- and post-cruise accommodation and so on, many people choose to make their own arrangements because of familiarity with Sydney. Ports of embarkation and disembarkation which have a large fly-cruise market based in other countries will have higher passenger expenditure in areas such as accommodation. Therefore, the nature of the port and the passenger-generating regions will considerably influence pre- and post-cruise expenditure patterns.

Port Vila and Noumea are large towns with all necessary infrastructure. They have substantial European communities and long historical exposure to tourists and cruise ships. The ship is docked, making disembarking easy. Taxis and buses are readily available. Isle of Pines and Lifou are very small, isolated, island locations where a lazy day on a South Pacific beach is the main activity, perhaps supplemented by a brief drive around the area or a ride in a canoe. Local villagers set up small handicraft stalls along the beach and some try stalls to entice the visitors to attempt local foods. Others sell canoe rides or local taxi trips. However, in such locations the cruise ship takes ashore food and drinks, setting up a big barbeque lunch. This, of course, is included in the cruise package and so most people prefer to eat this way. Drinks are simply signed to their shipboard accounts. Consequently, very little direct cash input to the community occurs through food and beverage sales.

The weather

From Sydney to the first port of call—either Port Vila or Noumea—is a sailing time of two and three days respectively. The seas often have long running swells and many passengers spend their first cruise days feeling decidedly unwell. Many people report feeling seasick as soon as the ship leaves the dock, even though it is a protected and usually calm passage down to Sydney Heads from Darling Harbour, the home base of *Pacific Sky*. Because of this they may not have eaten very much during the first couple of days, and so the opportunity to go ashore and eat a meal that has the chance of staying where it is supposed to stay is an appealing one. Both Port Vila and Noumea offer a range of interesting restaurants and unfamiliar beers and wines which tourists like to try. By the time the ship sails for the next port most passengers have acquired their sea legs and have relaxed into holiday mode.

The weather also strongly influences spending patterns in each port.

Wet weather in Port Vila and Noumea means that more people spend time and money in shops, bars and restaurants. Wet weather in island ports, such as Lifou, where the ship must lie at anchor and tenders run a shuttle service, means that the majority of tourists may choose not to go ashore at all, remaining in the familiar comfort of the ship. Fine weather in Port Vila and Noumea sees passengers passing more of their time on the beaches and engaging in water sports and outdoor activities. They may purchase tours or transport ashore if they have not already done so on board. Fine weather at island ports means that local entrepreneurs will make some money. Thus weather, often fickle in the South Pacific, can have a major impact on spending patterns.

The shopping

Shopping is an essential part of the holiday experience. Cruise ship boutique stocks are based on the sorts of items they know tourists are likely to buy in the forthcoming ports. Indeed, there appears to be more and more second-guessing of passenger needs on cruise ships than ever before. *Pacific Sky* carries a very large range of duty-free perfumes and cosmetics. One may also obtain duty-free alcohol on the ship, although it is placed in bond until disembarkation. However, the business communities of Noumea and Port Vila are also long familiar with, and well-tuned to, tourists' needs. Passengers generally rush to go ashore at these ports, sweeping down the gangway on an average of 30 times a year. They have either had previous successful shopping experiences or have been told about other people's purchases. They are keen to shop.

Port Vila generally enjoys a more profitable visit than Noumea, as prices are more reasonable and the shopping area is more compact, manageable and accessible. Cosmetics and perfumes are the most purchased items followed by duty-free alcohol and electrical goods. There may also be cultural factors involved. Australians have long regarded the colonial French as being 'arrogant' and uncooperative, in addition to the demonstrably greater expense of most goods and services in Noumea, while the people of Vanuatu are regarded as among the greatest assets to the country's tourism, and their generally retiring manner is seen as an encouragement to spend.

T-shirts and sarongs, *sulus* or *pareus* (1.8 metres of vividly patterned cotton material) are the most popular souvenirs, followed by local craft items (necklaces and brown dolls in indigenous costume), incidental souvenir items (postcards, fridge magnets, beer holders and so on), fancy dress for 'Island Night' on the ship (grass or raffia skirts, coconut-shell bras, and woven or shell leis) and local wood carvings. These satisfy the need for exotic artefacts to show friends, to give as gifts or to keep as

Figure 17.2 Small traders in Port Vila do regular business with
Pacific Sky passengers (Source: Norman Douglas)

mementos of the cruise. There is strong personally obtained evidence that cruise ship passengers in this context are not particularly interested in authenticity in handicrafts. For example, while hundreds of 'grass' skirts are sold on every cruise visit to Port Vila—many by indigenous entrepreneurs on the wharf—passengers prefer the cheaper, single-colour, artificial raffia variety to the pandanus-leaf, multicoloured skirts actually worn by ni-Vanuatu village women. The raffia items are bought for fancy dress, not as artefacts for display. Pacific Islanders generally have long learnt to make their handicraft items 'packable and portable'. Handicraft stalls on cruise ship day remain among the few areas where local people get direct access to the cash expenditure by tourists. This is vitally important on the isolated islands as it may well be the only source of revenue for an entire village.

Although French is spoken in Vanuatu, English is more widely used. In New Caledonia French is the main language and English is secondary, making shopping a more challenging activity. Although the vatu is the currency of Vanuatu and the French Pacific franc is the currency of New Caledonia, much trade is done in Australian dollars and so the potential for confusion in dealing with unfamiliar currencies is minimal. Mistakes, however, do occasionally happen for both parties in a transaction that tries to convert a price or offer into something each understands.

In Sydney shopping money is directed towards items to be taken on the cruise or on items not readily available in the location in which the passenger lives. New clothes and cameras go on board; newer clothes, Sydney souvenirs, shoes and jewellery go home. *Pacific Sky*'s berth is conveniently located close to both a large, tourist-oriented shopping complex—Darling Harbour—and the central business district, so shopping opportunities are very accessible. This is not always the situation with wharf areas, often a considerable distance from such services and facilities.

Tours and other activities

Cruise ships work in close association with a designated operator based within each port of call to provide a range of experiences tailored to accommodate the few hours of a ship's visit. The logistics of a successful operation are daunting, particularly in less developed areas. Transport infrastructure varies widely in quality and quantity. Commitment by entertainment and other service providers can fluctuate for a variety of reasons. Weather is unpredictable. Passengers are encouraged to purchase tours several days before reaching port. This is necessary for catering to specific numbers. Thus the ship, the inbound operator and any subcontractors must make their profits. So while the tours are expensive, convenience in an unfamiliar environment is a strong motivation for passengers to make these arrangements. Repeat cruisers are familiar with the ports and opportunities and therefore usually prefer to make their own arrangements as soon as they go ashore, as do experienced tourists who are more quickly comfortable in a new location. These people must take responsibility for ensuring that they are back on the ship before the appointed sailing time. A ship will delay its departure time if necessary for groups on shore excursions but not for individual latecomers, who must meet their own costs to rejoin the ship in the next port. This happens occasionally.

Conclusion

It is useful to examine a single port in more detail. *Pacific Sky* called at Port Vila 32 times in 2002. Occupancy is consistently very high, according to P&O, hence the results of this study give a good indication of how much each visit contributes to the national economy. Table 17.2 shows that average passenger spending was US$101. A Tourism Council of the South Pacific study in 1991 found that cruise passengers spent on average US$94. Thus if the average expenditure (US$101) is multiplied by the average number of adults (1248) on a cruise, then *Pacific Sky* passengers contribute approximately US$126 000 per visit and US$4.03 million per annum to Port Vila's economy. To this must be added the actual expenditure of the company (see Table 17.3).

Finally, expenditure by crew needs to be considered. The problems of surveying the crew in this study were outlined earlier. But crew members do spend money. Although most have only a few hours ashore, they hire taxis, travel on buses, go to restaurants and bars and purchase activities if time permits. They also spend a significant amount of money in two other areas. Despite the widespread use of mobile phones, many crew members still make long international calls to home through the local telephone exchange. The second area of expenditure is in personal supplies. Crew purchase drinks and foodstuffs, toiletries, pharmaceuticals and so on. It is extremely difficult to put a precise figure on this category, but a conservative estimate might be US$30 per day. If two-thirds of the 500 crew per voyage go ashore, then crew expenditure might be US$10 000 in a day in Port Vila. Thus a fortnightly visit by *Pacific Sky* may be said to inject US$152 500 into Port Vila's economy. Annually this amounts to US$4.84 million.

Because of the considerable differences between the national economies, currency values and marketable tourism products in each Pacific Island country, it would be inadvisable to draw too many generalised inferences from this study. However, as this cruise represents a typical program on the part of not only P&O, which introduced the new vessel *Pacific Princess* to the same circuit in 2002, but also almost every other cruise line that has offered a Pacific itinerary in recent years, it may provide some valuable insight into how much and on what items cruise passengers spend their money.

Table 17.3   Port Vila average call company expense estimate for *Pacific Sky* (US$)

Port agency fees	$1 110	Port charges incl. terminal and towage	$10 050
Water	$300	Pilotage	$960
Berthage	$570	Fuel bunkering	n/a
Waste disposal	$1 020	Providoring	n/a
Security	$210	Customs	$1 500
Agency expenses	$300	Miscellaneous	$480

TOTAL economic input per visit (estimate)   US$16 500

Source: P&O Australia.

Conclusion

Cruising has for decades been arguably the most dynamic sector of tourism. Whatever else the cruise experience may be, it is not static. A number of factors had a marked effect on cruising in the first part of 2003 (when this book was being completed), some that could hardly have been foreseen a year earlier. These included the US-led war with Iraq and the uncertainty leading up to it; the outbreak of Severe Acute Respiratory Syndrome (SARS) in China and its spread; and the heightened fear of terrorist activity, including the possibility of terrorist acts directed against cruise ships.

The World, which began this book, intending to live up to its name with its inaugural round-the-world voyage, was forced to cancel its planned South-East Asian itinerary because of the spread of SARS and to return to 'safe' Australia and then the United States, pending further deployment. SARS-related information and guidelines appeared on the websites of some cruise lines and on the website of the International Council of Cruise Lines, an association representing 15 of the leading US-based cruise companies. The guidelines, based on information provided by the World Health Organization and other health authorities, sought to allay the fears of prospective cruisers by stressing the measures taken to 'protect ships' passengers, crew and ports of call alike' (ICCL 2003).

Indirect consequences sometimes took a curious turn. One response of Malaysia-based Star Cruises (not a member of ICCL) to the SARS outbreak and the possibly calamitous effect of this on its Asian markets was to redeploy two SuperStar vessels, *Virgo* and *Leo*, from their bases in Singapore and Hong Kong respectively to temporary programs in Australia and the South Pacific, regions in which they had not offered programs previously. Their presence in Australia drew an immediate reaction from the executive director of the Australian Casino Association, who called for a ban on 'gambling on short term trips to nowhere that are promoted by cruise lines' or, at the very least, an application of the same taxation rate as that paid by Australian land-based casinos (Australian Casino

Association press release, 23 April 2003). The call appeared to ignore the fact that all ships' casinos are obliged to remain closed until the vessels are outside Australian territorial waters, in order to comply with long-standing customs regulations, and that P&O Australia's Sydney-based *Pacific Sky* (albeit with a casino of more modest size) also offered the occasional 'cruise to nowhere'. Star's reputation as an operator of 'floating casinos' had evidently preceded the appearance of its vessels. The response is significant, however, because it provides an illustration of a growing tendency for shore-based operators of recreational facilities to regard cruise ships—with their remarkable variety of leisure and entertainment options—as a threat.

Heightened fears of potential terrorism since the 11 September 2001 attacks on the United States and the bombing of tourists in Bali on 12 October 2002 led to a number of responses. Security measures, which had for some time excluded unauthorised visitors, such as family and friends, from cruise ships—thereby bringing to an end a longstanding tradition—were heightened, and explanations of them appeared on cruise line websites. 'Homeland Cruising' programs, described as 'America hugging' by an industry figure (personal communication), were quickly introduced or extended by a number of US-based lines, particularly Norwegian Cruise Line, which also announced a 'Project America' program that included US-registered and '100 per cent US crewed' vessels (NCL 2003). Vessels at sea and heading for Bali at the time of the bombing were diverted to Broome, Australia, and future calls at Bali put on hold. The possibility of terrorist attacks on cruise vessels, seemingly extremely vulnerable targets, was discussed in some detail in the media, particularly after a French oil tanker had been rammed in Yemen by a speedboat laden with explosives. 'The most feared scenario', according to one report, was that something similar would happen to a cruise ship containing two thousand or more people. Organisations ranging from the National Geographic to the US Coast Guard entered into the discussion. The appearance of the Norwalk virus (with symptoms that included vomiting and diarrhoea) among a number of US cruise passengers was feared by some to be a form of biological terrorism. The possibility of an aerial attack on a cruise ship by a suicide pilot was also considered (Loy 2002; Feltner 2002). Not surprisingly, cruise industry figures responded to these speculations by stressing the increased security measures being applied. Coincidentally, the arrest of Palestinian Abu Abbas, chief organiser of the 1985 hijacking of *Achille Lauro* (to date the only attack of political terrorism on a cruise ship in peace time), occurred in Iraq, as an incidental outcome of the war in that country.

Uncertainty over the effects of the war in Iraq led to a decline in cruise bookings before the conflict began, even to some extent in politically 'safe' regions such as the Caribbean, which became even more heavily populated with cruise ships than hitherto, as vessels were temporarily repositioned from the Mediterranean and elsewhere. This trend was met by offers of refunds of up to 90 per cent on cruises booked and paid for, and discounts on subsequent cruises, by Carnival and other lines. 'Deep' discounting, as it is known in the trade, was widespread and even deeper. The phenomenon had long been observable in cruising, with '2 for 1' offers and '50 per cent off for second passenger' deals, but was never as obvious as it became in early 2003. The decline in revenues encouraged Carnival to slow down the pace of delivery of new vessels on order.

At the same time as the difficulties of early 2003 were reducing the geographical scope of itineraries, P&O's advance programs for 2004 promoted world voyages that included a transit of the Suez Canal and ports of call in Egypt, avoided by cruise companies during 2003 and at other recent times.

Future trends

Forecasts of any kind are risky, particularly in an area that has proved to be as fickle and vulnerable as tourism. With an appropriate measure of caution, however, it is possible to make some predictions about what will happen in the cruise world if the challenges discussed above are overcome or prove to be less significant than they first appeared. If observable trends persist, future directions are likely to be determined by at least some of the following developments.

The family cruise market will grow, providing further illustration of the concept of the cruise ship as total resort. Cruise lines are said to be 'stocking their ships with family friendly amenities'. This has been spearheaded by Carnival Cruise Lines, which alone expected 'to host a record 400 000 children in 2003, a fourfold increase over eight years ago' (*Porthole Cruise News*, 25 April 2003, <www.porthole.com>), but has been taken up by other, seemingly less likely, contenders such as Crystal Cruises. Throughout the 1990s, when it was consolidating its reputation, Crystal tended to discourage young children as passengers, because their presence conflicted with its promotional image. However, in 2003 it was soliciting their presence with 'Junior Activities Programs for our younger Crystal cruisers aged three to 17' and offering such enticements to the family market as free travel for children 12 years and under on its Alaskan runs (<www.port hole.com>). 'Child free' cruising had acquired a different meaning.

The European market will mature and grow. Baby boomers throughout the world are increasingly discerning and demanding in their travel needs. This will be accompanied by a decline in the average age of

European passengers, with a consequent increase in demand for a variety of shorter cruises—that is, of less than seven days.

The size of cruise ships will continue to increase. Cunard's US$800 million *Queen Mary 2* (due to join the fleet in early 2004) was given advance promotion as 'the world's longest, tallest, largest, greatest, widest, highest, sleekest, grandest, most expensive . . . taller than the Statue of Liberty, longer than four New York city blocks . . .' (Cunard 2003). *QM2* is at least a tangible vessel, for all the hype surrounding it. Still on the drawing board in 2003, but possibly ready to be 'navigating the world's oceans by early 2005' was *Freedom Ship*, not, as one might suppose from its name, a more advanced form of refugee transport, but 'a vessel four times longer than the *Queen Mary* . . . a mobile modern city featuring luxurious living, an extensive duty-free international shopping mall, and a full 1.7 million square foot [158 000 square metre] floor space for various companies to showcase their products' (<www.freedomship.com/overview.php>). '*Freedom Ship*', the description continues, 'would not be a cruise ship', and so probably does not deserve any further mention here.

The size of the new vessels will restrict their movements as they become too big to negotiate the Panama Canal and will thus reduce their repositioning options. For example, repositioning from the Caribbean to the Mediterranean could be possible, but not from the Caribbean to the Alaskan region. Restrictions in access to necessary facilities for many of these will mean fewer destination choices for itinerary planners. Smaller and more manoeuvrable ships, however, offering necessarily more expensive cruises, will continue to provide an up-market alternative.

Both prospective and past cruise passengers will continue to be attracted by the predictable, but extraordinarily persuasive, imagery employed in cruising. Robert Dickinson, president of Carnival Cruise Lines, has doubted that the sort of imagery used in cruise promotion (including that of Carnival itself) represented what the 'average vacationer' was looking for. 'Most past cruisers, with their first hand experience, can penetrate the hype and fanciful advertising', he wrote. 'They know what liberties are being taken' (Dickinson & Vladimir 1997, p. 151). If they do, one can only assume that they thrive on exaggeration and that the hype itself becomes a sought-after part of the experience, since there has been little, if any, marked change in the themes of cruise imagery within the past few decades. Indeed, as we have noted, the past is often revived or at least referred to.

The amount of finance required for investment in port infrastructure to handle the size of the ships and the transit of large volumes of passengers will be very high and not profitable in the short term. Private enterprise has had to become involved in providing necessary infrastructure. Star

Cruises' construction of dedicated cruise terminals in South-East Asia, Carnival's investment in the Port of Miami, and the Disney Cruise Line's terminal in Port Canaveral (said to be the first terminal built at this port to a cruise line's specifications, at a cost of US$27 million) are examples of this.

The move towards oligopoly in the business will contribute to the disappearance of the medium-sized independent shipping company in the three-to-four-star rating categories. Only the specialised operators with their own niche market and those with strong economic backing will survive. In the midst of the downturn from the threat of terrorism, the uncertain outcome of the war in Iraq and the possibility of SARS spreading, the Carnival corporation emerged as not merely 'world's leading cruise lines' (one of its many brands) but with the potential to become the 'world's **only** cruise line'. Who would next be 'merged'—Star, Royal Caribbean, Crystal? Industry sources, having been taken by surprise at the relative ease with which Carnival absorbed P&O Princess, were cautiously tipping one . . . or the other.

Ships offering a complete holiday experience will continue to grow in popularity. The great variety of activities they can provide makes them highly competitive with land-based resorts. Cruise ships, as responses to the challenges named above have shown, are movable feasts: given the importance placed on food in cruising, this is an apt image. It is at once a strength and a weakness that the resort, even the lifestyle, to refer to the kind of concept that began this book, can be flexible enough to change location so readily. This is not an option available to land-based resorts, which, when their markets are threatened by epidemics or terrorism, simply have to stay put and tough it out. The weakness is that if this sort of thing continues, potential cruisers may well lose faith in the promotional promises. If one books an expensive cruise in order to experience the exotic locations one reads about in the catalogue, will one be satisfied with a sudden change of itinerary that frustrates those aims? But with more and more novelties available on board, the concept of the ship itself as resort and ports of call as temporary diversions—even as mere window dressing—has been reinforced. 'Just sit there', reads one advertisement, 'we'll change the scenery'. The ports of call, once a major reason to take a cruise, may become mere backdrops, like a series of stage sets: the real cruise experience will be the ship itself. Many cruise companies offer theme cruises to satisfy a remarkable number of special interests, from wine tasting to line dancing. Literary cruises and music cruises, such as those offered on QE2's trans-Atlantic runs, guarantee passengers a cultural experience as well. One thing is certain: cruise ships can no longer be regarded simply—or even mainly—as a 'transportation system'.

Abbreviations used

AMSA	Australian Marine Safety Authority
BISN	British India Steam Navigation
BP	Burns Philp & Co. Ltd.
CDC	Centre for Disease Control and Prevention
CEO	Chief Executive Officer
CGE	Computable General Equilibrium
CLIA	Cruise Lines International Association
CRS	Computer Reservation System
EHO	Environmental Heath Officers
FOC	Flag of convenience
GBRMPA	Great Barrier Reef Marine Park Authority
GPS	Global Positioning System
GRT	Gross registered tons
GST	Goods and services tax
ICCL	International Council of Cruise Lines
IMO	International Maritime Organisation
ITWF	International Transport Workers' Federation
NCL	Norwegian Cruise Line
NYK	Nippon Yusen Kaisha
P&O	Peninsular and Oriental Steam Navigation Company
PNG	Papua New Guinea
POEA	Philippine Overseas Employment Agency
PSC	Port State Control
SAFENVSHIP	SAF for safety, ENV for environment
SARS	Severe Acute Respiratory Syndrome
SOLAS	Safety of Life at Sea
TCSP	Tourism Council of the South Pacific
UNEP	United Nations Environment Program
USS	Union Steam Ship Co. (of New Zealand)
VSP	Vessel Sanitation Program

References

AEC Group Ltd 2000, *Economic impact assessment of a US navy ship visit on the Townsville regional economy*, Townsville Enterprise Ltd and Townsville Port Authority, Townsville.

Allen, F. L. 1952, *Only yesterday: an informal history of the nineteen-twenties*, Bantam Books, New York.

Asian Explorer Holidays 2000, *Star Cruises, 2001–2002 itineraries*.

Batchelor 2003, Minister for Transport, Victoria, press release, 19 February 2003, <www.dpc.vic.gov.au/domino/Web_Notes/newmedia.nsf>

Bearup, G. 1999, 'Terror on the good ship schoolie', *Sydney Morning Herald*, 8 December, p. 3.

Binchy, M. et al. 1995, *The Cruise*, HarperCollins, Sydney.

Blum, E. 1993, *The total traveler by ship*, Graphic Arts Center Publishing, Portland, OR.

Brendon, P. 1991, *Thomas Cook: 150 years of popular tourism*, Secker & Warburg, London.

Brewer, N. H. 1982, *A century of style: great ships of the Union Line, 1875–1976*, A. H. & A. W. Reed, Wellington.

Broeze, F. 1998, *Island nation: a history of Australians and the sea*, Allen & Unwin, Sydney.

Buckley, K. & Klugman, K. 1981, *The history of Burns Philp: the Australian company in the South Pacific*, Burns Philp, Sydney.

Bureau of Tourism Research 1995, *International visitor survey 1995*, Bureau of Tourism Research, Canberra.

Burns, Philp & Co Ltd. 1933, *The BP Magazine*, vol. 1, no. 4.

Burns, Philp & Co Ltd. 1928, *The BP Magazine*, vol. 1, no. 1.

Burns, Philp & Co. Ltd. 1921, *Picturesque Travel* (unnumbered), Burns Philp, Sydney.

Burns, Philp & Co. Ltd. 1911, *Picturesque Travel*, no. 2, Burns Philp, Sydney.

Butler, R. W. 1980, 'The concept of a tourist area cycle of evolution: implications for management of resources', *Canadian Geographer*, vol. 24, no. 1, pp. 5–12.

Carbonara, G. V. 1997, Futuristic cruise liners, Seatrade Asia Pacific Cruise Convention, Singapore, 4–7 December 1996.

Carnival Cruise Lines 2000, *Carnival: your kind of fun 2001–2002*.

Carnival Cruise Lines 1999, *Carnival: your kind of fun 2000–2001 cruises*.

Cartwright, R. & Baird, C. 1999, *The development and growth of the cruise industry*, Butterworth-Heinemann, Oxford.

CLIA 2002a, *The cruise industry: an overview*, Spring, Cruise Lines International Association.

CLIA 1994, *The cruise industry: an overview*, Cruise Lines International Association, July.

Crompton, J. L. 1979, 'Why people go on pleasure vacation', *Annals of Tourism Research*, vol. 6, no. 4, pp. 404–24.

Cruise Industry News Quarterly, Fall 2002.

Cruising Victoria 1999, *The Victorian Cruise Shipping Strategy 1998–2000*, Department of Infrastructure, Melbourne.

Cunard 2003, *Introducing Queen Mary: the greatest ocean liner of our time*, Cunard.

Cunard 2001, *Caronia: leisurely round trip cruises from Southampton, May–December 2002*.

Cunard 2000, *Grand ocean liners of the 21st century*.

Cunard 1999, Advertisement, *Conde Nast Traveler, September.*

Dann, G. 1977, 'Anomie, ego-enhancement and tourism', *Annals of Tourism Research*, vol. 4, pp. 184–94.

De la Vina, L. & Ford, J. 2000, 'Economic impact of proposed cruiseship business', *Annals of Tourism Research*, vol. 27.

Department of Tourism 1995, *National Cruise Shipping Strategy*, Commonwealth Department of Tourism, Canberra.

Dickinson, R.H. 1995, ' "Fun Ship" marketing philosophy', *FIU Hospitality Review*, Spring.

Dickinson, R. H. & Vladimir, A. 1997, *Selling the sea: an inside look at the cruise industry*, John Wiley & Sons, New York.

Douglas, N. 1996, *They came for savages: 100 years of tourism in Melanesia*, Southern Cross University Press, Lismore.

Douglas, N. 1995, 'Live volcano adds zest to river cruise', *Pacific Magazine*, March–April, pp. 59–61.

Douglas, N. & Douglas, N. 2001, 'The short, unhappy life of an Australia-based cruise line', *Pacific Tourism Review*, vol. 5, no. 3/4, pp. 131–42.

Douglas, N. & Douglas, N. 2000, Internet tourism site review: cruising, *International Journal of Tourism Research*, 2, pp. 301–2.

Douglas, N., Douglas, N. & Derrett, R. (eds) 2001, *Special interest tourism: context and cases*, John Wiley & Sons, Brisbane.

Dwyer, L. 1999, *The impact of cruise tourism on the economics of Townsville and Queensland*, Tourism Queensland, May.

Dwyer, L. & Forsyth, P. 1998, 'Economic significance of cruise tourism', *Annals of Tourism Research*, vol. 25, no. 2, pp. 393–415.

Dwyer, L. & Forsyth, P. 1996, 'Economic impacts of cruise tourism in Australia', *Journal of Tourism Studies*, vol. 7, no. 2, pp. 36–45.

Dwyer, L. & Forsyth, P. 1994, 'Foreign tourism investment: motivation and impact', *Annals of Tourism Research*, vol. 21, no. 3, pp. 512–37.

Dwyer, L., Douglas, N. & Livaic, Z. 2003, *Measuring the economic impacts of a cruise ship visit*, CAUTHE Conference, Coffs Harbour, 5–8 February.

Dwyer, L., Forsyth, P., Madden, J. & Spurr, R. 2000, 'Economic impact of inbound tourism under different assumptions about the macroeconomy', *Current Issues in Tourism*, vol. 3, no. 4, pp. 325–63.

Feltner, M. 2002, *Cruise industry fighting terror, virus outbreaks*, <news.nationalgeo graphic.com/news/2002/12/1211_021211_travcruise>

Fitchett, T. K. 1977, *The great liners*, Rigby, Adelaide.

Foster, G. M. 1986, 'South Seas cruise: a case study of a short-lived society', *Annals of Tourism Research*, vol. 13, pp. 215–38.

French, N. 1995, *Ormonde to Oriana: Orient Line to Australia and beyond: a purser remembers*, Navigator Books, Ringwood, Hampshire.

Fussell, P. 1991, *BAD or the dumbing of America*, Simon & Schuster, New York.

Goldsack, R. 1995, *A silver jubilee: Captain Cook Cruises*, Fendwave, Sydney.

Hao, S. 2003, 'Moloka'i debates cost of tourism in wake of cruise-ship plans', *Honolulu Advertiser*, 27 February.

Howarth, D. & Howarth, S. 1994, *The story of P&O: the Peninsular and Oriental Steam Navigation Company*, rev. edn, Weidenfield & Nicolson, London.

Hudson, S. 1999, 'Consumer behaviour related to tourism', in A. Pizam & Y. Mansfield (eds), *Consumer behaviour in travel and tourism*, Haworth Hospitality Press, New York.

Hull, J. 1999, 'Matson menu covers that became Hawaiian classics', *Matsonnewsletter*, June.

ICCL 2003, *Cruise industry adopts aggressive new guidelines to prevent SARS and reduce risk*, International Council of Cruise Lines, 28 April, <www.iccl.org/press room/advisory042803.cfm>

ICCL 2002b, *The cruise industry: a partner in North America's economic growth*, International Council of Cruise Lines, Arlington, Virginia.

Infinity Cruises 1993, *The cruise book*, Infinity Cruises, Sydney.

Kelly, I. & Nankervis, T. 2001, *Visitor destinations*, John Wiley & Sons, Brisbane.

Klein, R. 2003, *Cruising-out of control: the cruise industry, the environment, workers and the maritimes*, Canadian Centre for Policy Alternatives, Halifax, Nova Scotia.

Krippendorf, J. 1987, *The Holidaymakers*, Heinemann, London.

Landon, M. 1997, *The cruise ships crews: the real truth about cruise ship jobs*, Mark Landon, London.

Lawton, L. J. & Butler, R. W. 1987, 'Cruise ship industry patterns in the Caribbean 1880–1986', *Tourism Management*, December.

Lim, C. 1993, *Meet me on the QE2*, Horizon Books, Singapore.

Lindblad, L-E. (with Fuller, J. G.) 1983, *Passport to anywhere: the story of Lars-Eric Lindblad*, Times Books, New York.

Lloyd, S. 2003, 'P&O cruises upmarket', *Business Review Weekly*, 20 March, p. 94.

Loftie, W. J. (ed.) 1901, *Orient Line guide: chapters for travellers by sea and by land*, 6th edn, Sampson, Low, Marston & Company, London.

Lowenthal, D. 1985, *The past is a foreign country*, Cambridge University Press, Cambridge.

Loy, J. M. 2002, *Seaports, cruise ships vulnerable to terrorism*, <www.politicsol.com/guest-commentaries/2002-07-28.html>

Mannel, R. C. & Iso-Ahola, S. E. 1987, 'Psychological nature of leisure and tourism experience', *Annals of Tourism Research*, vol. 19, no. 3, pp. 399–419.

Maris Freighter Cruises 2001, 'Happy Sailings in 2002', *Freighter Cruises Magazine* (Holiday Issue), December.

Maxtone-Graham, J. 2000, *Liners to the sun*, Sheridan House, New York.

McCart, N. 1987, *Passenger ships of the Orient Line*, Patrick Stephens, Wellingborough.

McCauley, R. 1997, *The liners*, Boxtree, London.

McDermott Fairgray 2001, *The economic impacts of cruise ship visits: 2000/01 season*, New Zealand Tourism Board and Cruise New Zealand, July.

McLauchlan, G. (ed.) 1987, *The line that dared: a history of the Union Steam Ship Company*, Four Star Books, Mission Bay.

McLean, G. 1990, *The southern octopus: the rise of a shipping empire*, New Zealand Ship and Marine Society & Wellington Harbour Board Maritime Museum, Wellington.

Mescon, T. & Vosikis, G. 1985, 'The economic impact of tourism at the Port of Miami', *Annals of Tourism Research*, vol. 12, pp. 515–28.

Morrison, A., Yang, C., O'Leary, J. T. & Nadkarni, N. 1996, 'Comparative profiles of travellers on cruises and land-based resort vacations', *Journal of Tourism Studies*, vol. 7, no. 2, pp. 15–27.

Moscardo, G., Morrison, A. S. M., Cai, L., Nadkarni, N. & O'Leary, J. T. 1996, 'Tourist perspectives on cruising: multidimensional scaling analyses of cruising and other holiday types', *Journal of Tourism Research*, vol. 7, no. 2, pp. 54–63.

National Centre for Environmental Health, <www.2.cdc.gov/nceh/vsp/vspmain.asp>

NCL 2003, *Project America: NCL launches US flag brand*, <www.ncl.com/fleet/15/pj_amer1.htm>

Orenstein, C. 1997, 'Fantasy island: Royal Caribbean parcels off a piece of Haiti', *The Progressive*, vol. 61, no. 8, pp. 28–31.

Orient Line 1943, *Orient Line: Australian annals*, Orient Line, Sydney.

Pedelaborde, D. 1997, 'Anatomy of a global cruise industry: ultra-luxury cruising for the "been there, done that" crowd', *Seatrade Pacific Cruise Convention Conference Papers*, 3–5 November.

Peisley, T. 2000, 'Cruising in crisis', *Travel and tourism analyst*, no. 5.

P&O 2003, *P&O Cruises 2003*, 3rd edn, The Peninsular and Oriental Steam Navigation Co., Southampton.

P&O 2002, *P&O Cruises South Pacific: January 2003–January 2004*, The Peninsular and Oriental Steam Navigation Co., Sydney.

P&O 2000, *South Pacific cruises: February 2001–February 2002*, October.

P&O 1999, Fair Princess facts (www.fairprincess.com.au).

P&O 1993, P&O *World Voyages*, P&O Holidays, Sydney.

P&O c.1967, *Asian crew, an officer's guide*, The Peninsular and Oriental Steam Navigation Co., Southampton.

P&O 1952, *Regulations*, The Peninsular and Oriental Steam Navigation Co., Southampton.

P&O 1934, *The BP Magazine: Australia's Finest Quarterly*, vol. vi, no. 2.

P&O Cruises, 2002, *Think of it as a floating seaside resort: January 2003–January 2004*, P&O Cruises, Sydney.

P&O Princess Cruises 2003a, *Peter Ratcliffe interview*, press release, 17 March (copy in authors' possession).

P&O Princess Cruises 2003b, press release, 17 March.

P&O Princess Cruises 2003c, press release, 16 April.

Pizam, A. & Mansfield, Y. (eds) 1999, *Consumer behaviour in travel and tourism*, Haworth Hospitality Press, New York.

Plog, S. C. 1974, 'Why destination areas rise and fall in popularity', *Cornell Hotel and Restaurant Administration Quarterly*, vol. 14, no. 4, pp. 55–8, 13–16 November.

Plowman, P. 1992, *From immigrant ships to luxury liners*, University of New South Wales Press, Sydney.

Prager, J. H. 1997, 'For cruise workers life is no "Love Boat"', *The Wall Street Journal*, CCXXX no. 3, July.

Prior, R. 1993, *Ocean liners, the golden years: a pictorial anthology*, Tiger Books International, London.

Rabson, S. & O'Donoghue, K. 1988, *P&O: a fleet history*, World Ship Society, Kendal.

Residensea Ltd 2002, *The World of Residensea* (media package), Residensea Ltd, Miami, FL.

Ritzer, G. 1998, '"McDisneyization" and "Post-Tourism": complementary perspectives on contemporary tourism', in G. Ritzer (ed.), *The McDonaldization thesis: exploration and extensions*, Sage, London, pp. 135–50.

Rooney, K. (ed.) 1999, *Encarta World English Dictionary*, Pan Macmillan Australia, Sydney.

Royal Viking Line 1994, *Royal Viking Cruise Atlas*, Royal Viking Line, Coral Gables, Florida.

Server, L. 1996, *The golden age of ocean liners*, Todtri Productions, New York.

Silversea 2002, *September 2002 – January 2003*, March.

Silversea 2001, *The Journal*, June.

Silversea 1999, *Cruises Mediterranean and Northern Europe: 1999 Cruise Collection*.

Slater, S. & Basch, H. 1996, *Fielding's worldwide cruises, 1997*, Fielding Worldwide, Redondo Beach, CA.

Star Cruises 2000, *Corporate profile*, Star Cruises.

Star Cruises 1999, *Star Cruises: The leading cruise line in Asia-Pacific*, Star Cruises.

Star Cruises, n.d., a, *Star Aquarius Gulf of Siam Cruises, October 2000 – March 2001*.

Star Cruises n.d., b, *SuperStar Leo: Hong Kong South China Sea Cruises, October 2000 – March 2001*.

US Department of Transportation, c. 2000, *The changing face of transportation*, US Department of Transportation, Bureau of Statistics, Washington, DC.

Stindt, F. A. 1991, *Matson's century of ships*, 2nd edn, privately published, Modesto.

Stonehouse, B. 1997, Sustainable tourism: Country Report 2, Antarctica, *People & the Planet*, vol. 6, no. 4.

Swinglehurst, E. 1982, *Cook's Tours: the story of popular travel*, Blandford Press, Poole.

TCSP 1992, *Vanuatu cruise visitor survey 1991*, Tourism Council of the South Pacific, Suva.

Thackeray, W. M. 1991, *Notes of a journey from Cornhill to Grand Cairo*, Cockbird Press, Heathfield (original edition 1845).

Theroux, P. 1995, *The Pillars of Hercules,* Hamish Hamilton, London.

Tourism Queensland 2002, *Queensland Cruise Shipping Plan*, Queensland Government State Development.

Treacy, J. (ed.) 2002, 'Cruise safety practices exceed standards', *World Wide Cruising News & Pictorial*, issue 18, Winter, Brisbane.

Turner, L. & Ash, J. 1975, *The golden hordes: international tourism and the pleasure periphery*, Constable, London.

Ward, D. 2000, *Berlitz complete guide to cruising and cruise ships 2001*, Berlitz Publishing, Princeton, NJ.

Ward, D. 1998, *Berlitz guide to cruising and cruise ships—1999,* Berlitz Publishing, Princeton, NJ and London.

Ward, D. 1994, *Berlitz complete guide to cruising and cruise ships*, Berlitz Publishing, New York.

Ward, D. 1992, *Berlitz complete guide to cruising and cruise ships*, Berlitz Publishing, Oxford.

Waters, M. 1995, *Globalization,* Routledge, London.

Waples, J. 2002a, 'P&O wants £500 m deposit from Carnival', *Sunday Times*, 13 January.

Waples, J. 2002b, 'Carnival accused of spoiling cruise deals', *Sunday Times*, 20 January.

Waugh, E. 1951, *When the going was good*, Penguin Books, London.

Wazir, B. & Mathiason, N. 2002, 'Cruise liner crews slave below decks: passengers enjoy luxury on the high seas, but a new study reveals the misery of those who serve them', *Guardian Observer*, 8 September <www.observer.co.uk/uk_news/story/0,6903, 788047,00.html>

Wood, R. E. 2000, 'Caribbean cruise tourism: globalization at sea', *Annals of Tourism Research*, vol. 27, no. 2, pp. 345–70.

Young, G. 1986, *Slow boats home*, Random House, New York.

Young, G. 1981, *Slow boats to China*, HarperCollins, New York.

Websites

<www.ananova.com/business/story/sm>
<www.bluelagooncruises.com>
<www.captaincook.com.au>
<www.cruises.about.com/cs/cruisejobs>
<www.cruisewest.com>
<www.cruising.org/press/overview/ind.>
<www.eastafrican.com> 19 February 2003
<www.freightercruises.com>
<www.freighter–travel.com>
<www.freighter–world.com>
<www.genting.com.my>
<www.lindblad.com>
<www.meltours.com/mts_discoverer>
<www.poprincesscruises.com/mainsite/press>
<www.portcanaveral.org/floridafun/cruise.htm>
<www.smallships.com>
<www.starcruises.com>
<www.waronwant.org/?lid=2860>

Glossary

Not all these terms are peculiar to cruise ships, nor are they all used in this book; but for the student or general reader some knowledge of them is essential to an understanding of the subject.

Aft: towards or at the rear of a vessel or aircraft.
Amidships: the middle of a ship.
Astern: behind a ship.
Beam: the maximum width of a vessel.
Berth: i. a structure for mooring a ship. ii. a bed on a ship.
Bow: the most forward part of a ship.
Bridge: the navigational centre located in the forward part of the ship.
Bulkhead: a wall separating a ship's compartments.
Bunkering: refuelling the ship.
Cabin: the basic accommodation on a passenger or cruise ship. Many earlier examples were extremely basic, containing sleeping facilities only.
Cabin class: on three-class vessels the intermediate class between first and tourist.
Cabotage: the reservation of coastal trades to national flag shipping. For years the practice was held to be a major impediment to the growth of the Australian cruise business. Its removal in late 1997 has not resulted in any perceptible difference in this growth. A similar regulation in the United States is referred to as the Jones Act.
Chart: nautical map used to navigate a ship.
Companionway: a stairway between decks on a ship.
Course: the point of the compass or direction towards which a ship is sailing.
Cruise: voyage on a ship undertaken wholly for reasons of leisure and recreation.
Cruise director: individual responsible for the organisation and

presentation of public activities and entertainment on a cruise ship. This person has senior officer status.

Cruise to nowhere: a cruise, usually of very short duration, that does not call at any ports.

Disembark (US Debark): to leave a ship.

Draft: the depth from the keel to the water line when a ship is in the water.

Dry-docking: the withdrawal of a ship from service in order to survey and overhaul all the underwater parts. Passenger vessels must be dry-docked every two years. Major repairs and maintenance items are usually programmed to coincide with dry-docking to minimise the time the vessel is out of service.

Embark: to go aboard a ship.

Escort: usually a middle-aged man, engaged on some cruise ships to be mainly a dancing partner to single woman (see also **host**). Because of other connotations of the term 'escort', the term host or **gentleman host** is now preferred.

Flagstaff: a pole at the stern of the ship where the flag of the ship's country is flown.

Fly-cruise: packaged holiday whereby passengers fly to a port of embarkation to join a ship (usually in a foreign country), take a cruise and then fly home from another port.

Food and beverage (F&B) manager: person responsible for operations in all food and beverage outlets on the vessel.

Fore and aft: running in the direction of the keel, from the bow to the stern.

Forward: towards or at the front of a vessel or aircraft (pronounced 'forrid').

Freighter: a ship or aircraft, the primary purpose of which is the carriage of freight (cargo). Freighter cruises, however, have become an increasingly popular form of specialist travel.

Funnel: the smokestack of a ship.

Galley: once a large ship often propelled by oars (hence, 'galley-slave'), now used to refer to the kitchen on various forms of transport including ships, aircraft and trains.

Gentleman host: a single man of mature years (usually 45 or over), engaged by the cruise company primarily to be a dance partner for single women. Sometimes called an 'ambassador host' (see also **escort**).

Gross registered tons (GRT): a measurement of a ship's cubic capacity rather than its weight. The GRT is calculated at $100 \text{ ft}^3 = 1$ ton.

High seas: the entire ocean beyond the territorial limits not under the jurisdiction of any country.

Home port: the port where a ship is said to be based (sometimes called the 'hub').

Host (or **Gentleman host**): see **escort**.

Hotel manager: the person in charge of all the passenger operations on a ship.

Hull: the framework of a ship.

Keel: lowest longitudinal centre line of the ship: the first piece of metal placed on blocks when a new vessel is being built.

Knot: one nautical mile per hour. A nautical mile equals approximately 1852 metres (6080 feet), compared with a land mile, which measures 1609 metres (5280 feet).

Latitude: distance north or south of the equator.

Leeward: the direction away from the wind.

Liner: a term applicable to all passenger ships, but most often applied to larger and grander vessels. It is also applicable to passenger aircraft, but now is only rarely used in this context.

Line voyage: a voyage undertaken essentially as a means of getting from point A to point B, rather than a pleasure cruise. The term was more frequently used by earlier passenger shipping than by cruise shipping, although it is still used for promotional purposes from time to time.

Mooring: securing a ship in a particular place by means of chains and/or ropes fastened either to the shore or to anchors.

Onboard: a neologism, apparently introduced by the passenger/cruise ship industry, which, at least in the promotional literature, appears to have replaced two previous prepositional phrases, 'aboard' and 'on board'. These are preferred in this book.

Owner's suite: a term generally used to refer to the best passenger accommodation on a cruise ship. A ship's owner rarely travels on the vessel. In any event, cruise ships are generally owned by corporations.

Passageway: a corridor or hallway in a ship.

Pilot: person licensed to navigate ships into or out of harbour or through difficult waters and to advise the captain on handling the ship during these times.

Port: i. left side of a ship looking forward (red light). ii. an opening in the side of a ship. iii. a harbour where ships arrive and depart.

Port of call: port where a ship calls in for a few hours or sometimes overnight while on a cruise itinerary.

Port of embarkation/disembarkation: port where passengers join/leave a cruise.

Provedoring: the supply of fresh, chilled and refrigerated food as well as dry stores and liquor for consumption by passengers and crew.

Purser: person in charge of passenger administration on a ship.

Safety drill: requirement of international maritime law that all people embarking on a ship must have instruction in emergency procedures within 24 hours of arrival on board.

Screw: ship's propeller.

Shore (tour) escort: an individual, usually a member of the regular crew of a cruise ship or an entertainer from the ship, who accompanies a tour group in a port of call in the interests of additional passenger safety and as the representative of the ship.

Shore excursion: organised activity in a port of call. Passengers book participation in excursions prior to arrival in the port of call. Costs are charged to passenger account.

Social hostess: person working with the cruise director who facilitates daily activities and organises social events on behalf of the captain and senior staff when necessary.

Starboard: the right side of a ship as one looks forward towards a ship's bow (green light).

Stateroom: larger and more luxuriously furnished accommodation than that found in a **cabin** (see above). The term is used more often in the United States than elsewhere, sometimes as a synonym for cabin.

Steerage: in earlier times the cheapest accommodation on a passenger ship, near the steering gear, hence the name. As cruising developed, the term was replaced by **tourist class**.

Stern: the aft end of the ship.

Stevedoring: the process of loading and unloading the ship. Stevedores also handle baggage for cruise vessels.

Tender: a small boat—on cruise ships usually a launch, used to transport passengers between the ship and land if the ship cannot come alongside a dock area.

Tour desk: location on the ship where passengers book shore excursions.

Tourist class: term used in the days before one-class ships became popular, to indicate a cheaper passage than first class.

Weigh anchor: to raise the anchor.

Windward: towards the wind.

Index

Achille Lauro 30, 222
activities 31, 45–6, 72, 188
add-on price formula 16
adventure cruises 127–32
advertising 127, 151–3, 174, *see also*
  brochures, imagery, Internet,
  posters
  appealing to women 7–8
  between the wars 70, 71, 75, 174
  'British' appeal 97, 166, 169
  nostalgia 70, 71, 166, 169, 174
  TV commercials 11
Africa 97, 129
Aggie Grey's Hotel, Samoa 118
Aida 11, 13
Air New Zealand 129
Airtours 11
Alaska 79, 86–8, 131, 223, 224
  impact of cruises 196
Alexandria 63, 94
all-inclusive price formula 16
Amazon, river cruises 142
ambassador host, *see* gentleman host
  182
Amedee 90
An Affair to Remember 158
Andaman Islands 193
Anderson, Arthur 62–3, 93
Anna C 11
Antarctic 127, 129–30
Antwerp 135–7
Apia 193
Arison, Ted 14, 81
Art Deco 71, 169, 172–3, 174
Asia, destination 97, 135
Asia, south 90
Asia–Pacific 86–7, 91–2, 111, *see also*
  Pacific
  market 5, 15, 16
Athena 111, *see also Star Aquarius*

Atlantic City 48
Atlantic crossing services 66–7, 73, 78,
  95
Atlantic islands 66
atriums 7, 23
Auckland 138
Aurora 80, 82, 166
Australasia 68
Australia 77
  and New Zealand 5, 16, 137–8
  destination 70, 75, 86–7, 102–3
  market 79–80
  outbound 74–5, 78–9
Australian Casino Association 221
Australian Government Cruise Shipping
  Strategy 206
Australian Maritime Safety Authority
  203
Australian–Oriental Line 123
Azores 96

baby boomers, market 5, 6, 223
Bahamas 14, 92, 95, 97
balconies 13, 19
Bali 193, 222
Bangkok 193
bar staff 40, 178
Barbados 98
Barter, Lady Janet 144
Barter, Sir Peter 143–4
beach calls 105
Beddow, Sandy 196
Beirut 94
Berengaria 67
Bermuda 95, 97
bingo 132, 188, 190
Blue Lagoon 119
Blue Lagoon Cruises 117, 118–21, 122,
  125–6
Blue Riband 66–7

Bombay   38, 68, 88, *see also* Mumbai
booze cruises   48, 66, 97–8
Bounty   137
Bremen   67
bridge, card game   45, 46, 188, 190, 194
Britain, *see* United Kingdom
British colonial   97, 98
British Columbia   117
British India Steam Navigation Co
    (BISN)   38, 74, 133
British Medical Journal   47, 94
British style, *see* Cunard, nostalgia,
    Queen Elizabeth 2
Broadway shows   47, 191
brochures   71, 122, 152, 156, 165, *see
    also* advertising, imagery
    nostalgia   98, 166–74
Bruce's Shipyard   ix
buffet dining   12, 45, 46, 47, 165, 187
Bulolo   102
Burns Philp & Co.   74, 75, 77, 79,
    99–102
    advertising   100, 174
    semi-cargo ships   133
business centre   179
Butler, Richard   99

cabin steward   138
cabins, all outside   12–13
Cadiz   94
Cairns   117, 124, 206, 209
Cairo   94
Caledonian Star   131, *see also
    Endeavour*
Cameron Highlands, Malaysia   110
Canada   77
Canadian Pacific   72
Canberra   12, 79, 103, 174
Cancun   98
Cannibal Tours   144, 146
capacity of ships   9–11
Cape Town   89, 183, 193
captain   9, 27–9, 32, 90, 91
    nationalities   26–7
Captain Cook   123
Captain Cook Cruises   117, 118,
    122–5
Captain Cook II   123
cargo ship travel, *see* freighter travel
    107
Caribbean   13, 14, 66, 81, 87, 88–9
    resort areas   19, 92
    decline   86, 98–9, 223
    destination, history   64–5, 79, 95–9
Carnival Conquest   116
Carnival Corporation   11, 12–13, 56,
    113, 166, 225
    acquisitions   11, 82–4, 225

Carnival Cruise Lines   11, 81–4, 111,
    114
    advertising and promotion   19, 97,
        157, 161, 223, 224
    Fantasy Class ships   50
    'ship as destination'   85, 95
    ships   116
Caronia   77, 82, 166, 174
casinos   23, 32, 47–50, 114–15, 221–2
    Crystal Symphony   180, 190
    Genting Bhd casino   109, 110
    QE2   180, 190
    SuperStar Virgo   48, 179, 190
Cassandre, A.M   174
Castaway   121
Castaway Cay   20, 92
catalogues, *see* advertising, brochures
Celebrity Cruises 13
Central America   131
Ceylon (Sri Lanka)   70
Champagne Bay, Vanuatu   105
Chandris Group   13, 77, 79
chartering vessels   15, 70, 112, 129, 131
chief engineer   27, 29, 31–2
chief purser   27, 29, 32
Chinese   48, 110
Christie, Agatha   162
cinemas   23, 30, 180
Circle Line   123
City of Sydney   123
civil unrest   90, 147–8
classes of travel   67, 180, 187
    first class   67, 75, 95, 159
    second class   67
    steerage/tourist/third cabin   67, 71,
        159
classical concerts   191, 192
classless cruising   81, 180
Club Med II   169
coastal cruise   208
Cochin   193
Colombo   38, 90
colonial cultures   98
Computer Reservation System (CRS)   16
computer facilities   46–7, 194
Congo, river cruises   142
consolidation   80–1
Constantinople (Istanbul)   94
container ships   134
Cook, Thomas   61
corporate cruise culture   182
cost per day   7
Costa Crociere   11
Costa Cruise Lines   11, 82
craft classes   188, 189
crew
    contact with passengers   20, 39, 43,
        120

expenditure   207, 208, 220
work conditions   20, 36, 38, 39, 52,
    56
nationalities   25, 38–9, 53, 140, 166
crew-to-passenger ratio   114
Crimean War   94
Crown Jewel, see also SuperStar Gemini
Crown Monarch   40–1
cruise destinations today   86–8
cruise director   27–8, 30, 32, 188
Cruise Line Resources Pty Ltd   43
Cruise Lines International Association
    (CLIA)   4, 5–7, 8, 16, 86, 211
Cruise P221   212–19
Cruise Ship Forum   52
Cruise West   117, 118
CruiseMatch 2000, CRS   16
cruises to nowhere   16, 48, 114, 115,
    221–2
Crystal Cruises   9–11, 14, 87, 109, 116,
    223
    gambling   50, 180, 190
Crystal Harmony   180
Crystal Symphony   88, 180, 187, 190
    dining and entertainment   179, 187,
        191
    passenger facilities   179–80, 189–90
    passenger study   178, 179–80,
        182–5, 187, 189–91, 193–4
    passengers, profile   182, 183
CTC Cruise Line   80
Cuba, US blockade   98
Cunard, Samuel   181
Cunard Line   11, 12, 64, 66–7, 82, 111,
    185
    'Britishness' and nostalgia   166, 169,
        174, 182
    casinos   180, 190
    developments   40–1, 77–8, 80, 87
    promotion   77–8, 88, 118
Curaçao   98
Currie, Sir William   77
cyclones   79, 126, 137, 138

Day, Doris   158
Daydream II   123, *see also Captain Cook*
deck games   23, 30, 72, 188, 189, 194
    deck quoits   46, 188
    shuffleboard   46, 188
dedicated cruise terminals   224–5
deep discounting   223
democratisation of cruising   77, 93
Department of Labour and Employment
    42
departure tax   199, 200, 203, 207
design and comfort between wars   95
destinations   85, 86–7, 87–8
    determinants   88–92

company owned   92, 99
    development   74, 85–105
    history   92–105
    limited by size of ships   19
    rise and fall in popularity   92
Dickinson, Robert H.   81, 85, 224
dietary considerations   22, 56–8, 161
dining, *see also* grazing
    freestyle   14, 22, 50, 161, 188
    more choice   22, 179
dining room staff, nationalities   37
dining rooms and restaurants   22, 46,
    179, 186–7
disco   22, 194
Disney Cruise Line   15, 19, 92, 225
distribution channels   16–17
    call centres   16
    Computer Reservation System (CRS)
        16
    travel agents   16
Dominican Republic   98
Dravuni   103
dress code for guests   22, 46, 47
dress codes for crew   35
Dunk Island   124
Durban   183, 193

East Africa   129
East Asia
    short cruises   13, 15
    market   5
economic impacts of cruise tourism
    framework for assessing   197–210
economies of scale   18
Ecstasy   157
effluent discharge   51
Egypt   30, 70
Elation   157
emergency drills   29, 52, 53
emergency equipment   52
employment on cruise ships, *see also*
    working conditions
    illegal agents   39
    Internet employment sites   37, 41, 44
    organisations   44
    recruiting agencies   41, 42
    strong growth   43
Empress of Britain   72
Empress of Canada   81, *see also Mardi*
    Gras
enclave style of development   19, 20
Endeavour   131
engine room employees   36, 37
ensuite bathrooms   7
entertainment   30, 31, 32, 143, 191–2
    director   29, 30
    lounges and venues, location   23
    staff   32, 191

entrepreneurs, local 196, 217
environmental disasters caused by ships
 34
environmental protection 52
ethnic division of employment 37
Europa 112, *see also MegaStar Aries*
Europe, destination 67, 86–7, 130
 market 4–5, 15, 86, 223
 outbound 67, 73, 77, 102–3
European Commission, Brussels 82
European Union 35
expedition cruises, *see* adventure cruises
expenditure
 add-on 208
 crew 195–6, 201, 204–5
 direct 195–6, 199–202, 204, 212,
 208
 indirect 204, 212
 injected 201, 202, 208
 passengers 195–6, 199, 202, 204–5,
 211–20, *see also* passenger
 spending, case study
 pre- and post-cruise 199, 200, 201,
 215
 vessel-related 201–2, 208

Faeroe Islands 62
Fair Princess 55, 157, 212
Fairsky 212, *see also Sky Princess,*
 Pacific Sky
Fairstar 52, 99, 103, 105, 174
 Fun Ship 103, 157–8, 214
 purchase from Sitmar by P&O 81,
 103–5, 212, 214
family cruise market 223
Fantasy Class ships 50
fantasyscape 19
Far East, destination 68–70, 78–9, 86–7
ferries (river cruises) 142
Fiji 20, 75, 105, 122, 124–5
 Blue Lagoon Cruises 117–21
Fiji Airways 119
Fiji Marine College 121
Fiji National Training Council 121
fire fighting training for crew 29
fire safety drills 52
first aid training 29
First Choice 13
flags of convenience (FOCs) 34–5, 36,
 81–2
floating casinos 222
floating hotels 18, 67, 142, 179
floating resorts 13, 24, 32, 72, 99
Florida 55, 95
fly-cruise packages 13, 79, 80, 179
 long flights a deterrent 86, 91–2
food 54, 56, 57, 160–1, 185–8, 225
 storage 53, 186

food and beverage management 29, 32
France, destination 94
 market 5
Freedom Ship 224
Freeport 95–6
freighter cruises 107, 133–41
 first-hand experiences 135–40
French colonial 98
French Line (Companie Générale
 Transatlantique) 71
French Polynesia 75
French Riviera 95
Fun Ships, Carnival 11, 81, 85, 161
Fun Ship, *Fairstar* 103, 157–8, 214
Fussell, Paul 159
future growth 211
future trends 223–5

Galapagos Islands 131
gambling at sea 14, 16, 47–50, 179, 190
 Star Cruises 26–7, 111, 114
gambling, Havana 97–8
Gatty, Harold 118–19
Genting Berhad 15, 48, 110–11
Genting Highlands casino 48, 109, 110
gentleman hosts 182, 182–3
geographical spread of cruising 64–6
German market 5
Gibraltar 94
Global Position System Navigator (GPS)
 136–7
globalisation 34
Golden Age 66–73, 159, 166, 169, 174
golf 20, 46
goods and services tax 200
Goroka 143
Grand Pacific hotel 102
Grand Princess 9, 116
Grant, Cary 158
gratuities 30, 39–41, 186
grazing 14, 23, 50, 161, 179
Great Barrier Reef 117, 124, 201, 203
great depression 68, 75
Greece, destination 94
Greek shipping postwar 77
Greenland 131
Greig, artist 165, 168, 174
gross domestic product 205, 206
gross regional product 204, 205
gross tourism expenditure 203
growth of cruise tourism since 1980 4
Gulf of Siam cruises 165
Gulf States 90
Gulf War 1991 90, 182
gyms 46, 55

Haiti 20
halal food 22

Hamburg–Amerika   66, 67, 68, 97
Hanseatic Cruises   15
haus tambaran   146, 147
Havana   97–8
Hawaii   75–6, 86–7
    imagery   162–3
Haworth, Trevor, Captain   122–4
health and safety   51–7
    training programs   54
health care   30, 55
Herbertshoe (Kokopo)   100
Himalaya   103
history of cruising   61–84, 93
Ho Chi Minh City (Saigon)   38, 127
Holland, Braydon   113
Holland America Line   11, 12, 195–6
homeland cruising programs   222
Hong Kong   88, 89, 183, 193, 221
Honolulu   89, 102
hospital facilities   55
hosts and hostesses   32
hotel manager   27, 29, 30, 32
hotel operations   25, 32–3
Hudson Bay   131
Hunt, Captain Steve   105
Hyatt hotel group   13

ice skating   7
Iceland   62
imagery   68–73, 151–74, 224
    exotica   70, 96, 152, 164–6, 225
    luxury   152, 158–63
    nostalgia   152, 166–74
    Pacific Islands   74, 75, 99, 103–4,
        162–3
    romance   152, 155, 156–8
Imperator   67
Inchcape, Lord (James Mackay)   71–2,
    74
inclusive price   154
India, destination   68–70, 78–9, 193–4
    emigration postwar   77
Indian Ocean, destinations   86
Indonesia   90, 131
International Council of Cruise Lines
    221
International Date Line   92, 138
International Labour Organisation   35
international maritime law   185
International Maritime Organisation
    (IMO)   52
international regulations   51, 52
International Transport Workers
    Federation (ITWU)   35, 36
Internet   7, 16, 37, 44, 47, 99
Inyeug (Mystery Island)   90, 105
Island Princess   46
island-hopping   97

Isle of Pines   212, 216
Israel and Palestine   90, 94
Istanbul, *see* Constantinople   94
Italia Line   67, 72, 95
Italian shipping, postwar   77
Italy, destination   70, 94
itinerary planning   17, 89, 90
Izmir (Smyrna)   94

Jaffa (Tel Aviv-Yafo)   94
Japan   15, 68, 115
    market   5
Jardine, Walter   174
Jerusalem   94
jet aircraft   78–9

Kalypso, see also Star Pisces   111
Kastaway Island   99
Kerr, Deborah   158
Kioa   105, 125–6
Kloster, Knut U.   xi, 14, 81
Klosters Rederi   80
Kokopo (Herbertshoe)   100
kosher food   22
    cruises   161
Krakatau, Indonesia   131
Kuala Lumpur   110

Labadee   20
labour laws   34, 35
Lady Hawkesbury   124
Laem Chabang   115
Lamen Bay   105
Landskrona   ix
Langkawi   193
Las Vegas style   23, 48, 180, 192
Lauro line   77, 80
    ships   30, 222
layout of ship   20–4
leakages   200–1, 203–4, 205
Lebanon   90, 94
lectures   23, 46, 73, 156, 188, 190
    specialist   7, 32, 45–6, 132
length of stay
    post-cruise   215, 216
    pre-cruise   215
lengths of cruises   15–16, 114
Levant (eastern Mediterranean)   94
libraries   23, 46, 134, 144, 179, 180;
    180–1
Lido   72, 95
life jackets   185
lifeboat drill for passengers   53
Lifelong New Englanders   131
Lifou   105, 212–13, 216–17
Lim, Catherine   156
Lindblad, Lars-Eric   128–30
Lindblad, Sven-Olof   130–1

Lindblad Expeditions   128–32
Lindblad Explorer   129
Lindblad Travel   130
  Special Expeditions   130
Lisbon   94
literary travellers   153
Lizard Island   124
local people   101, 145
  impact on lifestyle   102, 195–6, 206
  limited contact with   19, 20
Lord Howe Island   100
Los Angeles   81, 89, 88
Love Boat   118
Loyalty Group   105
Lurline   75
Lusitania   64, 66, 67
luxury   6, 7, 14, 15, 75, 80, *see also*
  imagery

MacIntosh, Frank   162
Mackay, James (Lord Inchcape)   74
Madeira   96
mail ships   63
Majestic   157
Makira   100
Malakula   100
Malaysia   82, 90, 179
Malolo   75
Malta   94
Mamanuca Islands   117, 120, 125
Manila   38
Mardi Gras   11, 81
Mariposa   75, 76
market segments   5
Martinique   98
mass tourism, beginnings   62
Matson Navigation Co.   75–6, 102–3,
  162, 163
Mauretania   12, 67
Mauritius   183, 193
McDisneyization   19
medical staff   30–32
  doctor   29, 31, 55, 134
medical/health food requirements   56–7
Mediterranean, destination   9, 13, 86–7,
  93–95
  eastern   63, 90, 94
  pre World War II   66, 89, 93–5,
    153–6
  repositioning of cruise ships   223,
    224
mega-ships   9, 112
MegaStar Aries   111, 112
MegaStar Taurus   111
Mekong, river cruises   142
Melanesia   100, 101
Melanesian (MTS) Discoverer   143,
  144–6

Melanesian Foundation   143
Melanesian Tourist Services   143–8
Melbourne   62, 138
menus   56, 161–3, 186
  style   71, 162–3
merchant ships   35
Messageries Maritimes   101
Mexican Riviera   12
Mexico   12, 98, 117, 196
Miami   11–15, 50, 95, 225
Micronesia   125–6
migration, postwar   77
military ships   212
Millar, Captain Claude   119
miniature golf   13
Mississippi, river cruises   142
Moloka'i   195–6
Moloka'i Visitors Association   196
Monaco   94
monsoons   90, 179
Monterey   75, 76
Montreal   135–7
Mooltan   102
motivation of tourists   177
Mumbai   50, 183, 193, *see also* Bombay
Murray River   122
  paddle-steamers   124
Murray, Sir Hubert   102
Muslim dietary requirements   56–7
Mystery Island (Inyeug)   90, 105
Mystic Passage   88
Mystique Princess   120, 125, 126
mythology, promotional   117–18

Nadi International Airport   20
Nanuya Lailai   120
Nappa, Luigi   103, 105
Nassau   95
Netherlands America Steamship
  Company   12
Netherlands colonial   98
New Britain   100
New Caledonia   49, 74, 90, 105, 212,
  218
New Hebrides   100, *see also* Vanuatu
New Hebrides Condominium   102
New York   123, 158
  September 11   30, 51, 90, 182, 195,
    222
New Zealand   74, 77
  destination   70, 75–6, 86–7, 102–3,
    137–8
New Zealand Civil Aviation Authorities
  119
Newsome, artist   165, 167, 174
Nice   156
nightclub/disco   22, 47
Nile, river cruises   142

Nippon Yusen Kaisha (NYK)   14, 109,
    180
Norfolk Island   74, 100, 100–1
Normandie   xi, 71, 169, 174
North Africa, destination   94
North America   64, 90
    eastern coast   131
    market   4, 16, 80, 181–2
    outbound   73, 89
North Sea   137
Northern Europeans, to French Riviera
    95
northern hemisphere destinations   88
Norway   64, 131
Norwegian American Cruises   80
Norwegian Capricorn Line   55, 114,
    122
Norwegian Caribbean Lines   80,
    81
Norwegian Cruise Line (NCL)   14, 22,
    40, 50, 55, 92
    acquisition by Star Cruises   40, 50,
    82, 113–15, 161
    cruises   115, 222
Norwegian Star   54–5, 114
nostalgia   3, 152, 166–74, 181, 194, *see
    also QE2*
    feeling of security   169, 170
    Hawaii   162–3
Noumea   89, 91, 96, 101, 105
    Cruise P221   212–17
    French culture   102
Norwalk virus   222

O'Rourke, Dennis   144, 146
Ocean Village   11, 13
Oceana   80, 82, 166
Oceanic Steamship Co.   75
officers   183
    nationalities   25, 26–7, 38, 179, 180,
    181
oil crisis, 1973   78
oligopoly   225
one-class cruises   14
opulence, in 1930s   68, 71–2
Oriana   79, 82, 103, 162, 166
Orient Line   70–1, 74, 77, 115
    acquired by Star   113
    advertising   65, 96, 174
    subsidiary of NCL   14, 114
Orient, the   68, 74–5, 78–9
    Oriental, added to PSNC   63
Oronsay   74
Oslo   80
Ostend   137
Out to Sea   182
Ovalau, Fiji   125
owner's suite   24, 134

P&O   11, 12–13, 99, 162
    advertising   70, 72, 99, 118, 165–71,
    174
    between wars   71–2, 100–2
    British ambience, nostalgia   12,
    166–9
    early history   62, 63–4, 74, 93, 94, 99
    India and Far East   12, 68–70, 79
    late 20th–early 21st century   78–81,
    86, 92, 223
    monopoly in South Pacific   111, 114
    officers and staff   27, 37, 38
    postwar to 1970s   77, 78–80, 102–3
    Strath class liners   73, 74, 102, 116,
    165–166
    takeovers   38, 74, 81, 102, 103, 133
    Thackeray   63, 94, 153
P&O and Orient   78–80
P&O Cruises Australia   11, 13, 157–8,
    212–20
    domination of Pacific   5, 16, 114
    in Pacific   12, 81, 86, 91, 99, 101–5
South Pacific case study, *Pacific Sky*
    212–20
P&O Princess Cruises   4, 9, 11–13
    takeover by Carnival   11–13, 74,
    82–4, 113, 225
Pacific   19, 73–6, 135, 137–8 *see also*
    Asia–Pacific, P&O, South Pacific
    Pacific Ocean swells   90
Pacific Princess   12, 220
Pacific Sky   21, 22–3, 31, 57, 82, 99, *see
    also Fairsky, Sky Princess*
    passenger study   212–20
Pacific Princess   12, 220
packages   14, 16, 215, 216, *see also*
    fly-cruise packages
paddle-steamer   122
Pago Pago   76
Panama   35, 196
Panama Canal, destination   97
    ships too big   9, 18, 224, *see also*
    post-Panama
Pan-American Airways   78
Papua   102
Papua and New Guinea   100, 101, 129
Papua New Guinea   91
    river cruises   143
passenger spending
    case study   211–20
    on cruise   7
passenger-to-staff ratio   25
passengers
    activities   188–90, 190
    behaviour   153–4, 161, 162, 177–94
    nationalities   179
    profiles   5, 6, 181–4, 183
Pedelaborde, D.   159

Peninsular and Oriental Steam Navigation Company (P&O)   62, 91
Peninsular Steam Navigation Company   63
Philippine Overseas Employment Administration (POEA)   41–2
Philippines economy, remittance monies   41–2
Phuket   193
Pitcairn Island   137
Plantation Island   20
pleasure cruises   68, 95
Polaris   131
Port Canaveral, Florida   95–6, 225
port experience   8, 19–20, 95, 193
port infrastructure for larger ships   224
Port Klang   114, 193
Port Louis   193
Port Moresby   55, 91, 99, 100, 101, 147
Port Said to Malta   154
Port State Control (PSC)   35
Port Victoria, Seychelles   193
Port Vila   105, 193, 212
    impact of spending on economy   216–17, 218, 219–20
    pre World War II   100, 101, 102
ports
    for bunkering   89
    for provedoring   89, 208
    home   198–9, 206
    in passenger study   215–16
    of disembarkation   89, 211, 215
    of embarkation   89, 211, 215
    transit   198, 206
ports of call   7
    activities   105, 192, 216
    discomforts   153, 193–4
    economic impact of visits   211–12, 216
    incidental to cruise   81, 95, 152, 183, 225, see also ship as destination
Portugal   63, 94
POSH, term   68
post-Panama ships   18, 19, 32
posters, see also advertising, imagery
    between the wars   70, 71, 172, 174
    nostalgia   171, 173
    P&O   70, 167–8, 170–1, 174
    pre World War I   65, 96–7
    postwar   171, 173, 174
Princess Cruises   11, 49–50, 74, 81, 92, 195–6
    in Pacific   80
    Love Boat   157
    promotional images   80, 118, 165
Princess Patricia   12
Prinzessin Victoria Luise   97
Project America program   222

promotional
    language   100, 127, 142
    material, see advertising
    mythology   117–18
provedoring   55–7, 199, 200, 208
proximity of market to destination   92
Puerto Plata   98
purser's office
    location & style   23–4
    staff nationalities   32
Pyongtaek   115

Qantas   124, 125, 129
Quebec Line   64
Queen Elizabeth 2 (QE2)   12, 26, 56–7, 82, 135, 180
    cruises   89, 225
    old-world British style   18, 24, 180, 181, 182, 186
    passenger facilities   50, 55, 180–1, 189–92
    passenger study   178, 180–1, 182–7, 189–92, 193–4
    promotion   88, 156, 174
Queen Mary   12, 71, 169, 224
Queen Mary 2 (QM2)   12, 82, 224
Queensland   208–9
Queensland, North   124
Queensland Cruise Shipping Plan   208
Queensland Star   137

Rabaul   101
Rabi   125–6
Radisson Hotel Group   15
Radisson Seven Seas Cruises   15
Rajputana   68
Ranchi   68, 154
Ratcliffe, Peter   83
Rawalpindi   68
reef cruisers   124–5
Reef Endeavour   124, 125, 126
Reef Escape   124–5
Regal Princess   88
Renaissance Cruises   131–2
Rio de Janeiro   158
river cruises   107, 142–8
    passenger facilities   142–3
rock walls   7
romance   107, 162, 181
    advertising imagery   152, 156–8
Romance on the High Seas   158
room service   22, 186
room stewards   39, 178
Rotuma   105
round the world cruising   56, 135, 138–40, 193, 221
    in southern hemisphere summer   86, 88

round trip   61
Royal Caribbean Cruises   xi, 4, 9, 13,
   111
Royal Caribbean International   13, 16,
   82–3
   privately owned destinations   20, 92
Royal Cruise Line   182–3
Royal Olympia Cruises   15
Royal Viking Line   xi, 14, 80, 166

SAFENVSHIP project   51
safety   27, 29, 51–7, 90, 181
   drills   29–30, 52, 185
   safety centre   52–3
Safety of Life at Sea (SOLAS)   52–3
safety regulations, avoidance   34
Saigon River   46, 127
Saigon, *see* Ho Chi Minh City
Samarai   101
Samoa   75, 103, 118
   American Samoa   76
   Western Samoa   193
San Francisco   75
sanitation   53–5
Santa Anna   100
Santa Cruz group   100
SARS   13, 221, 225
Savage, Eugene   162
Savannah   137–8
Savusavu   193
Scandinavia   66
schoolie cruises   157
Sea Bird   131
Sea Lion   131
Sea of Cortez   117, 131
Sea Voyager   131
Seabourn Cruises   11, 82, 116, 164
Seabourn Spirit   154, 156
seasonal variations   88
seasons   79, 88, 90, 102–3
security   29, 30, 48, 190, 182, 222
   staff, nationalities   48
semi-cargo ships   133
semi-passenger ships, *see* semi-cargo
   ships   133
Sensation   157
Sepik Explorer   143
Sepik River cruise   143, 144–8
Sepik Spirit   143
Serenity   9–11
Seven Seas Cruises   15
Seward, Alaska   88
Seychelles   129
Shetland Islands   62, 129
ship as destination   19, 85, 95, 99, *see
   also* ports of call incidental
   as resort   77, 179, 223, 225
ship operations   25–32

shopping
   duty-free   105, 179, 217
   on board   24, 181, 189–90, 217,
      224
   on shore   103, 217–19
   souvenirs   193, 217–18
shore activities, *see* ports of call
shore excursions   46, 91, 102, 193,
      219
   adventure cruising   132
   managers   91
   planners   32
show lounges   181
shows   47
Silversea Cruises   9, 116, 159–60, 161
Singapore   50, 89, 110, 183, 185
   Genting Bhd, home port   48, 179,
      221
Sitmar International   77, 81, 103, 212
six-star status   14
size of ships   9, 224
Sky Princess   212, *see also Pacific Sky*
slot machines   49, 50
small ship cruising   7, 5, 116–26, 127,
      224
   Silversea   9, 159–60
smoke-free environments   55
   ships   11
Smyrna (Izmir)   94
Solomon Islands   91, 100, 101, 102
South Africa, postwar immigration   77
South America   91
South Korea   115
South Pacific   40–1, 72, 86, 89, 96,
      99–105 *see also* Asia–Pacific,
      P&O, Pacific
   company-owned resorts   92
   gambling   49, 50
   passenger spending study   212–19
   ports of call   89, 91, 101–2
   SARS crisis   13–14, 221
   seasonal popularity   77, 79–80, 88,
      90, 103
   Sepik River cruises   143–9
   small shipping initiatives   118–21,
      125–6
   South Seas myth   75, 100
South-East Asia   19, 40–1, 86–7, 88,
      90–1
   postwar emigration   77
   Star Cruises   13, 48, 224–5
Spain, destination   63, 94
Spanish colonial   98
spas   23, 54, 55, 179, 194
special class   67
Special Expeditions   130–1
special interest cruises   .80, 225
Spirit of Oceanus   117, 126

Sri Lanka   70, 90
St Maarten   98
stabilisers   90, 141
staff, nationalities   120
staff captain   27, 29, 30
stage, dedicated, first   11
standards of safety and environmental
      protection   52
Star Aquarius   111
Star Pisces   111
Star Cruises   4, 13–14, 108, 109–15,
      186
   decor   23–4, 182
   gambling   15–16, 26, 48, 112–13,
      179, 190
   hierarchies   25–7
   initiatives   86, 221–2, 224–5
   Star Cruises, passengers   5, 9,
      15–16, 38
   promoting tradition   194
   promotion   165
   takeovers   40, 50, 82, 113–14, 161
star rating   56
stateroom service   161
steam engine   61
steam turbine engine   66
Stella Polaris   153–4
Sterling, Lord   82
Stevenson, Robert Louis   100
Straits of Malacca   179
Strath class liners   73, 74, 102, 116,
      165–6
Strathaird   102
Stratheden   73
Strathnaver   74
style, between the wars   68–73
Suez Canal   79, 138
sundeck   20, 24
Suntan Cruises   72
superships   103
SuperStar class   111–12, 161, 179
SuperStar Gemini   111, 115
SuperStar Leo   112, 178, 221
SuperStar Virgo   26, 111–12, 178–9,
      182, 221
   activities and entertainment   188,
      191–2
   casino   48, 179, 190, 115
   passenger facilities   179, 183, 187–8
   passenger study   178–9, 182, 183,
      187–9, 190–3
supply   55–7
Suva   101, 102, 105, 118
Swan Hellenic   11, 13
swimming pools   23, 95, 133, 134, 180,
      183
   indoor   68, 69, 71, 139, 181
   outdoor   72, 95, 179, 181

Swire Corporation   80
Sydney   80
   Sydney, outbound   77, 96, 212–19
   port   89, 102, 118, 212, 219
Sydney Harbour   79–80, 122, 123

Tahiti   76, 103, 139, 140
Taiping   123
Taiwan   115
Talco Tours   143
talent show   191, 194
Tan Sri Lim Goh Tong   48, 110, 182
Tanna Island   100
Taveuni   125–6
Tel Aviv-Yafo (Jaffa)   94
Tenerife   96
tennis   20, 46
Tennyson   100
Territory Airlines   143
terrorism   51, 182, 222, 225
Thackeray, William Makepeace   63, 94,
      153
Thailand   115
The Love Boat   12, 81, 157, 158
The World   ix–xii, 221
theatres   11, 47, 180, 186
themed cruises   19, 80, 225
Theroux, Paul   154–6
Thomas Cook organisation   62, 70, 93,
      165
three-mile limit   49
Thursday Island   99
timetables introduced   63
tipping, *see* gratuities
Titanic   64, 67, 185
Titanic, film   157
Tofua   102
Tonga   103
Tourism Council of the South Pacific
      212, 219
tourism life-cycle model   99
Tourism Queensland   206
tours   219
town calls   105
Townsville   212
Trafalgar House   80
travel agencies   16, 135
travel writers   94, 135, 152–3
Trobriand Islands   144, 146
Trompf, Percy   174
tropical island, privately owned   99
Tulagi   100, 101, 102
Tunku Abdul Rahman   110
Turaga Levu   119
turbine steamer   180
Turkey   94
Turtle Island   20, 118
Twain, Mark   153

Ugi   100
ultra-luxury   159
Ulu Kali   110
Union Steamship Company   74, 75, 77
   early initiatives   74, 77, 99, 101
   passenger services abandoned   74,
      79, 102
United Fruit Co   64
United Kingdom   13, 35, 68
   market   4, 12, 89
   outbound   68, 73, 77, 88
United Nations   37
United States   78
United States   35, 55, 49, 79
   Centers for Disease Control and
      Prevention (CDC)   53
   Coast Guard   52, 222
   Department of Transportation   34–5
   Federal Trade Commission   82
   fly-cruise packages   92
   in Pacific   80, 88, 92, 122
   market   4, 5, 86, 91, 191
   National Center for Environmental
      Health   52, 53
   outbound   67, 72, 102–3, 127, 139
   prohibition   44, 66, 97–8
   Vessel Sanitation Program   52, 53–5

Vanua Levu, Fiji   125
Vanuatu   90, 101, 102, 105, 217–18, *see
   also* New Hebrides
Vectis   64–6
vegetarian food   22, 56–7
Veitch, Colin   50
verandas, private   24, 180
veterinary skills, required in doctor   55
Viceroy of India   68, 69
Victoria Luise   97
Vietnam   38, 46, 127
visitors, unauthorised   30, 222
volleyball   46

waiter   178, 186
waiter 39, 40, 178, 186

waiter's assistant   186
Walu Bay, Suva
war in Iraq   221, 222–3, 225
War on Want   35
water quality   53, 54
waterfall, Kastaway Island   99
waterfalls   7, 23
Waugh, Evelyn   152, 153–4
Waya Lailai   119
weather
   cyclones   79, 126, 137–8, 141
   influence on spending patterns, 193,
      196, 216–17, 219
   monsoons   90, 179
   ocean swells   90
   Roaring Forties   19
weekend cruise   95–6
West, Charles (Chuck or Mr Alaska)
      118
West Indies   64, 65
Whitsundays   208
Willcox, Brodie McGhie   62, 63
Windstar Cruises   11, 82
winter excursions   64
Withers, Trevor   118–19, 122, 123
working conditions   35, 36, 42, 206, *see
   also* crew, employment
   contract   36–7
   ship training simulator   114
   training, in-house   120–1
   wages   39, 40
world cruises, determinants   89
World Health Organization   221
World War I   66, 67, 77, 94, 97
World War II   73, 76–7, 94, 102,
      158
World's Greatest Cruise Lines   82

Yangtze River Cruises   142
Yasawa Island   117, 119, 120,
      125
Yasawa-I-Rara   105
Young, Phil   103, 105
Yule Island, Papua   100